The Stone Guide to
Dog Grooming for All Breeds

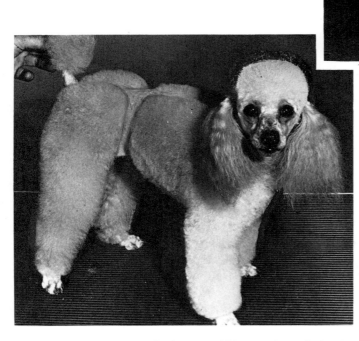

The Poodle, because of his grooming and trimming needs made dog owners everywhere more conscious of the beauty and cleanliness requirements of all dogs. Because of the Poodle's great popularity and the appeal of such trims as the Sporting (top), Bikini (center) and Dutch (bottom) an entire new concept in canine beauty culture developed. The clips shown here are all modelled by the same dog, a further tribute to the breed's adaptibility.

The Stone Guide to DOG GROOMING For ALL BREEDS

By Ben and Pearl Stone
Of the International School of Animal Arts

Drawings by Judith J. Tillinger

1984

First Edition—Third Printing

HOWELL BOOK HOUSE

230 Park Avenue   New York, N.Y. 10169

636.1

S

Library of Congress Cataloging in Publication Data

Stone, Ben.
  The Stone guide to dog grooming for all breeds.

  1. Dogs—Grooming. I. Stone, Pearl. II. Title.
SF427.5.S765   636.7'0833   81-7089
ISBN 0-87605-403-3   AACR2

*To the Professional Groomer
who has turned a labor of love
into a rewarding career.*

Contents

Part III—The Shorthaired Breeds

Part IV—The Smoothhaired Breeds

Part V

Part VI

Acknowledgements

WE WISH IT WERE POSSIBLE TO acknowledge all who have contributed directly or indirectly to the publication of this book. It has been a monumental task, and we are grateful to all contributors. We are especially indebted to the superb artist, Judith Tillinger (who shows and *knows* her dogs) and Barbara Reilly, the head instructor of our school, who doubled as our talented photographer.

Their combined talents have materially contributed to the value of our effort. Indeed we think the reader will find that the art work and photography alone are worth the price of the book.

We are also grateful to our instructors and students, as well as the many professional groomers, who told us what they would like to see in this book.

Ben Stone

Pearl Stone

About the Authors

BEN STONE IS THE DIRECTOR of the International School of Animal Arts, the internationally-famous school located in New York City. Mr. Stone is the co-author of several books on dog grooming and has contributed many articles on the subject to magazines such as *Pet Shop Management, Pet Age* and *Dog World*. He has served as President of the New York Groomers' Association and is a member of the Advisory Board of BOCES (Board of Community Educational Services).

PEARL STONE is the author of the best-seller, *Clipping and Grooming Your Poodle*. Mrs. Stone has been involved with dog grooming for over 25 years, first as a salon owner and currently as the Dean of the International School of Animal Arts. Her students have come to her from all over the United States and indeed from all over the world. Mrs. Stone brings her wealth of practical and theoretical experience to this book.

In March 1979, Mr. and Mrs. Stone were awarded a special plaque by the American Society for the Prevention of Cruelty to Animals (ASPCA) which reads as follows:

> For their initiative and support in the design and development of a grooming center for adoptable animals at the ASPCA's Manhattan Animal Shelter.

Another first for the authors and the International School of Animal Arts was the collaboration obtained from the world-famous Animal Medical Center of New York in establishing an internship for students of the school taking the Veterinary Office Assistant Course.

The International School of Animal Arts, owned and operated by Ben and Pearl Stone, is probably the only school of its kind in the world, embracing in its curriculum such courses as Dog Grooming, Cat Grooming, Obedience Training, Kennel Management, Shop Management and Veterinary Office Assistant. The school is licensed by the State Education Department of New York and accredited by the Accrediting Commission of the National Association of Trade and Technical Schools (NATTS).

The authors receiving a special award for their efforts on behalf of animal adoption from Dr. John Kullberg, Executive Director of the ASPCA.

11

Preface

DOG GROOMING IS BOTH ART AND skill, trade and profession. But first and foremost, it is an art form comparable to human beauty culture, for it is indeed the beautification of dogs. To be the complete dog grooming artist, one should know how to make all breeds beautiful and how best to enhance the appearance of each dog.

Thus far we have written three books on dog grooming. Our first, *Clipping and Grooming Your Poodle,* was published in 1965; our second, *Clipping and Grooming Your Terrier,* appeared in 1968; the last of the series, *Clipping and Grooming Your Spaniel and Setter,* was published in 1971. It has been our long-time dream to write a book on grooming all breeds. Many factors beyond our control prevented this dream from becoming a reality for some time. It proved to be a monumental task, and took us two years of hard work to put this work together. Now, at last, the publication of this book by Howell Book House, is that dream fulfilled.

In writing this book one of our first concerns was the format and organization of a work of this scope. How would we give professional and non-professional readers alike instruction in grooming all breeds, in the simplest language and with the clearest explanation. We decided, after much thought, that it would be best to start with the fundamentals of dog grooming, that is, the *Basic Steps* applicable to grooming all breeds, thereby avoiding unnecessary repetition.

For the purpose of this book, the breeds are divided into three main categories; Long-haired, Short-haired and Smooth-haired. It should be noted that a number of Terrier breeds, such as the Kerry Blue and the Bedlington, are naturally long-haired and are listed accordingly. Likewise, a number of Terriers, such as the Smooth Fox and the Manchester, are smooth-haired breeds and fall into our smooth-haired category. Where a particular breed may be on the borderline between long-haired and short-haired, we have simply used our discretion.

While the categories created for this book to distinguish the breeds differ from the American Kennel Club's Group system of classifying breeds, only the 125 breeds officially recognized by the AKC are considered.

Similarly, we have sought to avoid repetition in discussing breeds which occur in more than one size but groomed basically the same way. The Poodle, in three sizes, Toy, Miniature and Standard, or the Schnauzer, also in three sizes, Miniature, Standard and Giant are prime examples.

We have used the step-by-step methodology which proved so successful with our former books. Of course, the reader, especially the professional, will understand that certain breeds, like Poodles, most Terriers and Spaniels, require far more time and skill to groom than smooth-haired breeds, for which only a knowledge of the fundamentals is required.

A number of other considerations have guided us regarding the presentation of the material which follows.

Our primary concern is with those breeds experience has demonstrated require the most frequent grooming.

We have given priority in the respective categories to the breeds in order of their popularity—in the long-haired breeds, the Lhasa Apso (while the Lhaso Apso is fast rising in popularity and ranks among the leading breeds, the Poodle has been and remains the No. 1 breed in the United States. But he is not typical of the long-haired breeds, and his grooming is far more complicated. Thus, the Poodle is given separate and special treatment.); in the short-haired breeds, the Miniature Schnauzer; in the smooth-haired breeds, the Doberman Pinscher.

We have borrowed heavily from the courses of study used at our school. For example, the sequence of study is based on our school curriculum, namely, the Basic Class learns to groom all long-haired breeds; the Advanced Class also learns the short-haired breeds including Terriers; the Comprehensive Class learns the smooth-haired breeds as well as all other breeds.

We have also made extensive use of grooming material kindly provided by many breed clubs and credited in the appropriate sections.

Since one of the aims of this book is in making new and positive contributions to the art of dog grooming, we have incorporated some new styles now gaining popularity with pet owners and professional groomers, (Yorkie/Schnauzer clip, Poodle/Bichon clip, Sheepdog/Puppy clip), as well as introducing some new time-saving tools and equipment (Oster Mat Comb, Wall Dryer, Snap-On Combs).

For the sake of simplicity, the breeds are usually listed alphabetically.

While this book is mainly oriented to pet grooming, many of the breeds are covered for both pet and show grooming, thanks to the material supplied by their breed clubs. With some breeds, especially in the smooth-haired category, there is no real distinction between grooming the pet or the show dog. Moreover, the art of pet grooming is aimed at creating a reasonable facsimile of a normal specimen of a breed. We urge all readers to observe first hand the best specimens of the various breeds by attending, in their areas as often as possible, dog shows.

There are numerous dog shows held throughout the country all year round.

Finally, it should be understood that this book is not meant to be an exhaustive, comprehensive manual on grooming each and every breed, but rather a source of basic information on the *essentials* of grooming all breeds.

We believe the combination of art, photography and detailed text herein is the most definitive work on the subject of dog grooming ever published. Let the reader judge.

One fringe benefit the reader will gain from this book is that it includes the main ingredients of our three former books, in addition to grooming instructions for other breeds not previously covered.

Enjoy.

International School of Animal Arts students at work in the school's theory room.

Part I

History of Dog Grooming

This exquisite bronze, circa 1775, shows a Poodle trimmed in what is very similar to today's Continental clip.

The Sportsman's Cabinet, circa 1803, was a famous book well regarded for its wealth of dog knowledge. It featured among others, this illustration of a "water dog", a breed some believe went into the development of the modern Poodle.

THE DOG, FROM TIME IMMEMorial, has been the closest animal to the human family. The dog's roles as companion, hunter, herder, war dog and many other callings is well documented. However, there is not too much known about the origin and evolution of dog grooming.

Grooming their dogs was the fashion of the aristocracy during the 19th Century, and the art flourished during the reigns of Louis XV and Louis XVI of France. The Poodle, then as now, was the favorite breed, and grooming was largely confined to it. Under Louis XVI, the Toy Poodle became the official dog at court. The first recorded grooming parlors were established in France at about the same time and continued after the fall of the monarchy. Indeed, the Poodle became the national dog of France under the First Republic. So identified did the Poodle become with France that the breed was known as the French Poodle in spite of the probability that it did not originate in that country and long after it became America's favorite breed.

Origin of the Clips

Since the first Poodles were water dogs and retrievers, the clip eventually found most suitable to them resembled what is known today as the *Continental clip*. In this clip a mane of hair was left on the foreparts while the back and hindquarters were completely shaven. Whether by accident or design, this clip made the Poodle resemble a lion, and it was most likely because of this resemblance that this clip became known in England as the *Lion clip*, although it has gone through some modifications since that time.

The American fancy adopted the Lion clip (with some variations of its own) and called it the English Saddle clip. The English Saddle and Continental clips are the only clips in which adult Poodles are shown in the United States. It is, however, the English Saddle clip which calls for the greatest mastery in the art of dog grooming.

Pet Clips

It is not clear, from the historical record, just when *pet clips* originated and became popular. As Poodles became more widely known, to practically all segments of society, the breed achieved unprecedented general acclaim. It became necessary to eventually design new clips for the Poodle coat which would be easier to care for than more traditional clips. Thus, developed the clips known today by such names as the Sporting, Kennel, Dutch, Town and Country, Bermuda clip and other variations.

Blanche Saunders

Just as it is rather difficult to establish precisely the origin of the pet clips, so is it difficult to identify the grooming stylists who created the earlier pet clips. We do know with more certainty of one who did more than anyone else to popularize the pet clips in the United States. That person was Blanche Saunders. Miss Saunders, internationally famous as a breeder, trainer, handler and writer, wrote one of the earliest publications on Poodle trimming, a booklet simply called *The Poodle Chart*. The date of publication is not given; the styles are obsolete, and it may be assumed that it was first published in the 1940s. Miss Saunders did much to popularize the pet clips and for this the pet world owes another debt of gratitude to this early pioneer. Blanche Saunders died in 1964, but her pioneering efforts, her books and famous training movies remain behind as her enduring legacy.

Tom Gately, noted former handler, breeder and judge, is one of the very few who has written anything of substance on the history of dog grooming. In an article for the magazine *Dog World* dated July 1976, Mr. Gately wrote the following:

> In the fabulous work of Vero Shaw, B.A., *The Book of The Dog*, published in London, England, in 1879, a number of references to grooming are made. They stress the importance of the subject as it concerns the animals' well-being and appearance . . . The noted work of Ashmont *Kennel Secrets*, published in Boston in 1893, contains an entire chapter on washing and grooming and another on conditioning the coat . . . Although obscurity exists regarding the exact time when trimming began, the custom traces back centuries . . .

The Wire Coated Breeds

Mr. Gately also has an interesting commentary on the history of the wire coated breeds.

> Early in the history of the wire coated terrier breeds in the British Isles, it was discovered that these terriers could be shaped up and their lines enhanced by the plucking of excessive hairs that hid the body contour. It was learned that these hairs could be removed a few at a time by using the finger and thumb, without pain to the dog. Such removal

An early 16th century German illustration of a water dog. Writers credited this type with being an ancestor of the Poodle and the Irish Water Spaniel.

The Corded Poodle was fashionable before the turn of the century, but in our world this highly unusual coat treatment is virtually unknown.

Blanche Saunders, most famous for popularizing obedience training and competition in the United States, also worked to popularize Poodle pet trims in this country through her writing and personal appearances.

of hairs of a wire coat was likened to the picking of ripe fruit. As experimentation went on, it was learned that complete removal of a stale coat resulted in the growing of a new coat, richer in bloom, color and texture.

It is not only the wire coated terriers whose coats require this type of care, but all of the other wire coated breeds, including German Wirehaired Pointers, Wirehaired Pointing Griffons, Irish Wolfhounds, Scottish Deerhounds, Wirehaired Dachshunds, Brussels Griffons and, of course, all three varieties of Schnauzers. Very few of the professional groomers possess the skill or know-how to properly strip a wire coat. Those few that do find themselves in the happy position of controlling a monopoly.

Certainly we may say that the modern dog and modern dog grooming are both typical of the times. For one thing, the average pet dog has become so "civilized" that he is considered an integral part of the family. Going to the canine beautician is as much a ritual for the family dog as going to the hairdresser is for the lady of the house. Dog styling has also become so professional and sophisticated that dog owners have become as selective about their dog's groomer as they are about their own hair stylist.

ALPHABETICAL LISTING OF ALL BREEDS

1. Affenpinscher
2. Afghan Hound
3. Airedale Terrier
4. Akita
5. Alaskan Malamute
6. American Staffordshire Terrier
7. Australian Cattle Dog
8. Australian Terrier
9. Basenji
10. Basset Hound
11. Beagle
12. Bearded Collie
13. Bedlington Terrier
14. Belgian Malinois
15. Belgian Sheepdog
16. Belgian Tervuren
17. Bernese Mountain Dog
18. Bichon Frise
19. Black & Tan Coonhound
20. Bloodhound
21. Border Terrier
22. Borzoi
23. Boston Terrier
24. Bouvier des Flandres
25. Boxer
26. Briard
27. Brussels Griffon
28. Bulldog
29. Bullmastiff
30. Bull Terrier
31. Cairn Terrier
32. Chihuahua
33. Chow Chow
34. Collie

35. Dachshund
36. Dalmatian
37. Dandie Dinmont Terrier
38. Doberman Pinscher
39. English Toy Spaniel
40. Foxhound (American)
41. Foxhound (English)
42. Fox Terrier
43. French Bulldog
44. German Shepherd
45. Giant Schnauzer
46. Great Dane
47. Great Pyrenees
48. Greyhound
49. Harrier
50. Ibizan Hound
51. Irish Terrier
52. Irish Wolfhound
53. Italian Greyhound
54. Japanese Chin
55. Keeshond
56. Kerry Blue Terrier
57. Komondor
58. Kuvasz
59. Lakeland Terrier
60. Lhasa Apso
61. Maltese
62. Manchester Terrier
63. Mastiff
64. Miniature Pinscher
65. Miniature Schnauzer
66. Newfoundland
67. Norfolk Terrier

68. Norwegian Elkhound
69. Norwich Terrier
70. Old English Sheepdog
71. Otter Hound
72. Papillon
73. Pekingese
74. Pointer
75. Pointer (German Shorthaired)
76. Pointer (German Wirehaired)
77. Pomeranian
78. Poodle
79. Pug
80. Puli
81. Retriever (Chesapeake Bay)
82. Retriever (Curly Coated)
83. Retriever (Flat Coated)
84. Retriever (Golden)
85. Retriever (Labrador)
86. Rhodesian Ridgeback
87. Rottweiler
88. St. Bernard
89. Saluki
90. Samoyed
91. Schipperke
92. Scottish Deerhound
93. Scottish Terrier
94. Sealyham Terrier
95. Setter (English)
96. Setter (Irish)
97. Setter (Gordon)

98. Shetland Sheepdog
99. Shih Tzu
100. Siberian Husky
101. Silky Terrier
102. Skye Terrier
103. Soft Coated Wheaten Terrier
104. Spaniel (American Water)
105. Spaniel (Brittany)
106. Spaniel (Clumber)
107. Spaniel (Cocker)
108. Spaniel (English Cocker)
109. Spaniel (English Springer)
110. Spaniel (Field)
111. Spaniel (Irish Water)
112. Spaniel (Sussex)
113. Spaniel (Welsh Springer)
114. Staffordshire Bull Terrier
115. Standard Schnauzer
116. Tibetan Terrier
117. Vizsla
118. Weimaraner
119. Welsh Corgi (Cardigan)
120. Welsh Corgi (Pembroke)
121. Welsh Terrier
122. West Highland White Terrier
123. Whippet
124. Wirehaired Pointing Griffon
125. Yorkshire Terrier

The All-Important Act of Brushing

This Lhasa Apso is obviously in need of a good brushing.

Hold up the hindlegs when brushing below the hock joint.

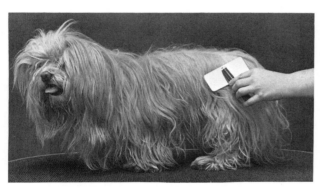

Start at the rear by brushing the hindlegs.

Hold forelegs off the ground while brushing.

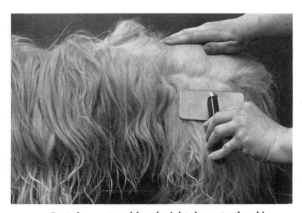

Part the coat and brush right down to the skin.

Continue to hold foreleg up as you brush brisket.

The Fundamentals of Dog Grooming

THE FOLLOWING FIVE STEPS CONstitute the fundamentals of dog grooming and are applicable to each breed. For many breeds these five steps are the entire grooming procedure.

1. Brushing and Combing
2. Bathing
3. Blow Drying
4. Ear Cleaning
5. Nail Trimming

The Lhasa Apso, our first model, is quite typical of longhaired breeds requiring constant coat care and most frequently require the services of the professional groomer. Whatever then applies to the basics of grooming the Lhasa, applies to the basic grooming of all breeds, bearing in mind, of course, the differences in the length and texture of coat.

Brushing and Combing

Brushing out the coat is the most important step in dog grooming. The importance of brushing is underscored by the fact that a dog can be made presentable by brushing alone. It is the foundation for all that follows and much time and effort may be devoted to it, especially when dealing with long-haired, dense and matted coats. While there are a few tricks of the trade which will prove very helpful in cutting down on this time-consuming chore, the main ingredient is manual labor. *Brushing* out the coat is the first and most important step in dog grooming. Thorough brushing before bathing is mandatory since wetting a tangled, matted coat will only cause the coat to tangle and mat even more. *Combing* out the coat runs a close second to brushing. In fact, combing should be considered an accompaniment to brushing, just as a pianist is an accompanist to a singer. The "melody" should be, brush and comb, brush and comb, brush and comb.

Brushing and Combing Techniques

Before going into the specific techniques of brushing and combing, we must first take note of the *approach* to the dog. This consists simply of starting each step from the hindquarters, operating on the theory that if the dog can't see what is being done, he will be less likely to object. So starting with the hindquarters, we proceed to groom the dog systematically and methodically, part by part, step by step.

Now, here is the actual technique of correct brushing and combing. First, grasp the left rear leg and while holding part of the hair in one hand (to reduce tension) brush the other part. To get to the undersides of the leg, lift the leg up and while holding firmly with one hand, brush the undersides. When the leg is completely brushed out, top and undersides, repeat the process exactly with the right rear leg.

At this point you may lay down your brush and pick up your comb. The chief function of the comb is to find and remove any tangles, mats or knots left in the coat after brushing. So, running the comb through the leg coat you just brushed out, whenever you hit a knot, hold the bottom part of the knot firmly with one hand and comb or tease out the knot with the other. The key to doing a good job here are the words, systematically and methodically. You can also add the word patiently, for you will need a great deal of patience if you come across many knots. The more thorough your brushing, the fewer knots you are likely to find when combing. The more thorough your combing, the finer will be your finished job.

After you have finished brushing and combing both hindlegs, do precisely the same with the two front legs. When all four legs are done, start once again at the hindquarters, this time concentrating on the tail. Proceed then to do the entire body coat, first left side, then right side, then underside, then the front or chest areas. The most systematic way of brushing out the body coat is from rear to front, layer by layer, lifting up with one hand a layer of coat and brushing down to the skin with the brush hand.

The final step should be the head, including the ears. With such long-eared breeds as the Poodle, Cocker Spaniel, Afghan and Lhasa Apso, the heavy furnishings on their ears are a part of their beauty, and no effort should be spared in thoroughly brushing and combing this area. If the dog has a beard, then naturally you have the face to do. But once you have mastered the technique of brushing and combing, no area should present a problem. Combing should always be the final, finishing touch.

To review the basic steps of brushing and combing:
1. Start with the hindlegs, brush and comb all four legs.
2. Brush and comb tail, then go forward with body coat.
3. Brush and comb head, face and ears.
4. Proceed step by step, systematically and methodically.

TRICKS OF THE TRADE

Brushing and combing out the long-haired coat is the most laborious and time-consuming chore in dog grooming. However, a knowledge of some "tricks of the trade" will help to cut down on this labor time, especially so in the cases of badly matted coats. Anyone who has seen a badly matted Poodle, Old English Sheepdog, Afghan, Lhasa Apso or Shih Tzu, will appreciate the importance of these special techniques. Obviously, the longer the coat, the greater the potential for matting. With the smooth coated breeds, of course, matting is not a problem.

If an individual dog's coat is so badly matted and tangled that it would take an inordinate amount of time to brush out (we have seen coats so bad that brushing out was virtually impossible) there is no alternative but to strip the coat. This means we must remove the entire coat, with clippers fitted with a fine blade, right down to the skin. Obviously, if the coat is stripped, there is no need for brushing and combing. The techniques for stripping the coat with clippers will be discussed in the clipping section.

Coat Conditioner

Let's assume a dog's coat is not so bad, does not require stripping and can be "saved." But it's still bad enough to require considerable brushing and combing. With an Old English Sheepdog, or similar long-haired breed where clipping is not ordinarily required, we are simply dealing with a great deal of brushing and combing. It has been found that saturating the coat with an oil-based coat conditioner will loosen the knots and tangles and considerably ease the brushing chore. Incidentally, coat conditioners which contain an oil base are beneficial for both the coat and the skin. Mink oil is the best coat conditioner on the market and especially so for matted coats. Some professional groomers and handlers have their own secrets for dealing with matted coats, and this becomes a matter of personal preference.

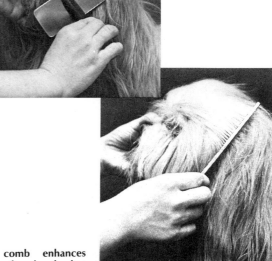

Be extra careful when brushing face furnishings.

The comb enhances what the brush has done.

All areas are first thoroughly brushed to the skin, then the coat is combed through to remove any remaining knots, snarls and mats.

The end result is more attractive, cleaner and less susceptible to illnesses and skin trouble than the animal that is totally neglected.

Coat conditioners neutralize static electricity in the hair for better grooming results.

Grooming powders, like conditioners, are designed to make grooming easier and the results of the work more attractive.

Universal Brush

The Universal brush is a German import and is convex-shaped with fairly long, hard, wire bristles. Its shape and density enable it to pull out the dead hairs more efficiently than any other brush. Unfortunately, it will also pull out the live hairs as well. The Universal brush should, therefore, never be used for show coats.

Oster Mat Comb

Another major product which cuts down on grooming time is called the "Oster mat comb" (not to be confused with "mat splitter"). This comb is a specially designed tool which cuts through knots and tangles and much less time is spent in brushing and combing. This mat comb is used in the following manner:

Grasp the mat comb firmly with thumb resting on the thumbrest and the other fingers around the wooden handle. Then place the mat comb directly behind the mat with the teeth flat against the skin. Then pull the mat comb forward towards you.

If the coat is too heavily matted, trying pulling the comb through the coat with short vertical strokes which should result in slicing the big mat into several smaller ones. Continue this process until you can comb through the coat without catching.

Then using your soft wire slicker or Universal brush, brush, work out all the remaining small mats and comb through once again, until the comb runs through the coat smoothly.

The principle a groomer must establish is that if the owner does not wish to see any loss of coat, he should take appropriate care of the dog. The groomer, meanwhile, will find these tips (tricks) a blessing in dealing with the types of coat described in this section. There are also a number of "detanglers" on the market, which some professional groomers maintain are an aid in the dematting process.

To review these grooming tips for handling matted coats:

1. Use an oil-based coat conditioner.
2. Use the Universal brush.
3. Use the Oster mat comb.

BRUSHES AND COMBS

The Wire Slicker Brush

The brush you use is most important. The brush being used in the accompanying photos is a soft wire slicker brush. We have found this brush to be a happy medium between the too-soft brushes used for show dogs and the too-harsh slicker brushes sold in most pet stores. Other types of brushes, such as the pin brush, natural bristle brush, hound glove and others are used for various procedures that will be explained and illustrated throughout the text.

Universal Brush

In the case of badly matted coats, we also use either the previously described Universal brush or a fairly large slicker brush with hard fibers. This type of brush is harsher than the normal slicker and may take out more hair than is ordinarily desirable, but remember we are dealing with coats which have been long neglected.

Sacrificing some coat is more humane in pet grooming than trying to "tease" out all the knots and tangles over a period of many hours.

Half Fine—Half Coarse Comb

As with brushes, there are several different types of combs. The comb of choice for general use consists of half fine and half coarse teeth and does not have a handle.

The best such combs were formerly manufactured in Belgium but American companies now make equally fine combs. This comb can be used for a variety of purposes, from roughing out to finishing touches.

Mat Comb

Just as the Universal brush is the best tool for coping with badly matted coats, so the mat comb is the companion to the Universal brush. This is heavier with wider-spaced teeth than the comb previously described and is one of the essential tools used for matted coats. This mat comb is not to be confused with the Oster mat comb, which is a special tool designed specifically for dealing with badly matted coats.

BATHING

Bathing a dog may seem like such a simple task as to be hardly worth discussing, much less devoting a chapter in a book to the subject—but again there is a professional way of doing things and an amateur way. Once again we stress that the bathing is done only after the coat is thoroughly brushed and combed.

The soft wire slicker is designed for delicate coats and some show grooming.

The Universal brush is well suited for use on tangled and matted pet coats.

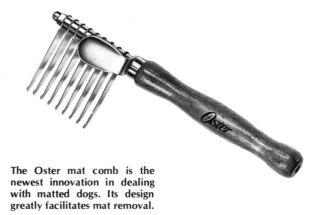

The Oster mat comb is the newest innovation in dealing with matted dogs. Its design greatly facilitates mat removal.

Half-fine/half coarse combs are the choice of many highly experienced groomers for their ease of use and the quality finish they give a coat.

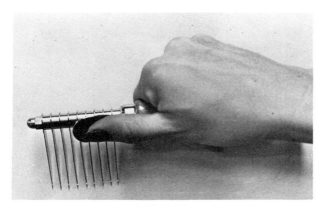

Proper way to hold the Oster mat comb.

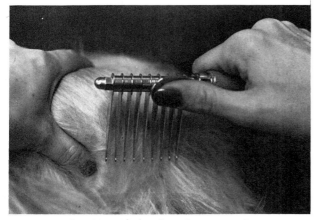

Locate mat before inserting mat comb.

Insert mat comb behind mat, close to skin.

Use a "sawing" motion from the skin out to break up the mat.

The first thing the professional does is prepare all the necessary materials ready at hand before putting the dog in the tub. These materials include a sponge, bristle brush, container of shampoo and a heavy towel. A hose attached to the faucet with a spray for rinsing is most helpful. The water temperature must not be too hot or cold, the ideal temperature being 110 degrees Fahrenheit.

Following the same step-by-step method used in brushing, start at the hindquarters and completely soak the dog. Use your hands if necessary to force the water through the coat as some coats are more water resistant than others. Do not fill the tub with water. Let the water run freely down the drain instead. Correctly bathing the dog is really more like giving it a shower than a bath. Incidentally, since the dog may decide to shake the water off, get a rubber or plastic apron you can slip over your clothes, for protection.

Once the dog is thoroughly soaked, saturate the sponge with shampoo and from the rear to front, shampoo every part of the dog. Areas usually overlooked are the anus and the foot pads. Be especially careful about shampooing around the eyes. Even with shampoos claiming to be tearless, it is best to be careful about getting any shampoo directly into the eyes. One way to avoid this is by using a very small bristle brush rather than the sponge, around the head.

After shampooing is completed, take the bristle brush and work the soap thoroughly into the coat. When this is done, rinse all the soap out, rechecking for the right water temperature. Rinse until the water runs completely clear of any soap. Care should be exercised in rinsing the face, for we do not want any soap or water sprayed directly into the eyes. Cover the eyes with one hand when rinsing the face, and cover the ears (by placing your thumb over the ear canal) when rinsing near them.

If the dog was extremely dirty, one shampoo may not be sufficient, so just repeat the whole process all over again.

When you are certain that the dog is thoroughly clean, squeeze the water out of the coat with your hands, to whatever extent possible. Then with a heavy towel get as much water off the dog as possible. You will then have to use a cage dryer on the coat to get it damp-dry. Our next step will be to blow-dry the dog.

To review the steps in bathing:
1. Soak dog thoroughly.
2. Shampoo with sponge.
3. Brush shampoo into coat.
4. Rinse thoroughly.
5. Squeeze water out of coat.
6. Towel dry.
7. Cage dry leaving coat damp-dry.

25

SHAMPOOS AND RINSES

Shampoos

What is a good shampoo and what is a good creme rinse? By reducing the question to its essence, we may say that a good shampoo is one that cleanses a dog thoroughly and does not contain any harsh detergents harmful to the skin and coat.

Much ado is made by manufacturers of both human and dog shampoos about such ingredients as lanolin base and pH (acidity/alkalinity) factors. These claims may have merit, but *caveat emptor* (let the buyer beware). The authors make no pretension with respect to any chemical expertise, but with over 25 years of grooming experience, we know a good shampoo from a bad one. The case for a good shampoo is quite simple. Does it lather up to a good foam? Does it have a good feel to the hands? Does it have a nice scent? Above all, does it do a good cleansing job? Does it leave the coat free of all dirt, grime and grit? An acid test of a good shampoo is whether or not it leaves a white coat sparkling white. A good shampoo has all these virtues.

If, in addition to the above, the shampoo is well concentrated so that it may be diluted with several parts of water without losing its potency, so much the better (and more economical).

Special Shampoos

All kinds of dog shampoos are manufactured for various specialized needs; shampoos to highlight different colors, shampoos for hard coats and soft coats, tangle-remover shampoos and many more.

We prefer one good, all-purpose shampoo.

The groomer should be aware of the need for a medicated shampoo, and in the flea and tick season, a flea and tick shampoo. The authors have found, to date, that for fleas and ticks it is best to add a "tick dip" after the regular shampoo. Make sure to mix the dip according to the manufacturer's directions.

Creme Rinse

A creme rinse is traditionally used after shampooing coats which are meant to be kept soft and which have a tendency to mat very easily. Afghans, Shih Tzu, Lhasa Apsos, Yorkshire Terriers and Maltese are typical examples. The creme rinse should never be used on a harsh, wire coat. What has been said about a good shampoo applies as well to a creme rinse. Does it perform well? Does it have any negative after-effects? Does the coat feel soft and clean afterward? Again, if the creme rinse can be diluted with several parts of water without losing its potency, so much the better.

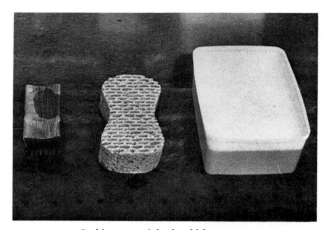

Bathing materials should be assembled before the work commences.

A stainless steel, elevated tub designed especially for use in dog grooming.

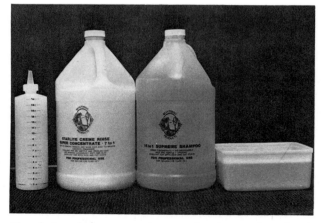

The choice of shampoo and creme rinse is a matter of each groomer's personal preference. There are many excellent formulations on the market.

Recommended Bathing Procedure

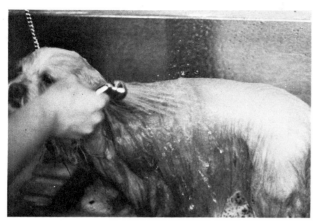

After a thorough brushing out, the coat is rinsed to the skin to remove loose dirt and facilitate lathering.

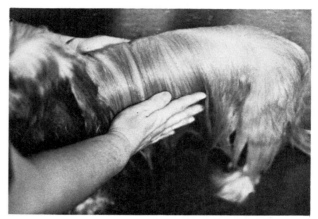

After the final rinse, excess water is squeezed out of the dog's coat by hand.

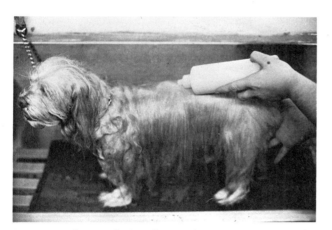

Shampoo is then dispensed into the coat.

The dog is then towelled to blot up additional moisture prior to blow drying.

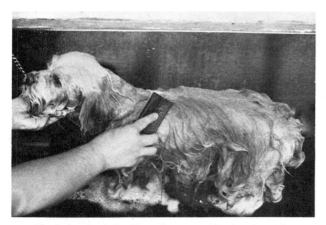

The lather is worked into the coat with a brush. With longhaired dogs, the coat is brushed with the lie.

BLOW-DRYING

The objective of blow-drying is to get the coat as fluffy as possible, to give it that powder-puff look. To blow-dry a coat, place the *damp* dog on the table and:

Always working from rear to front, hold the dryer in one spot, and as the hairs blow apart, brush the coat out once again. Brush until the area is completely dry and there are no kinky hairs. Then move on to the next spot. To get a good blow-dry you must be especially systematic and methodical, otherwise some areas will look kinky and curly. If the coat has dried too quickly, dampen the kinky areas again and blow them dry.

With a heavy coat, of course, a stronger dryer with a more powerful air flow may be necessary to achieve the desired look. It is not necessary to use heavy brushing when blow-drying. Light, quick strokes are all that is needed.

Smooth coats do not require any blow-drying. Regular, cage and towel drying will suffice.

To review the blow-drying procedure:
1. Blow-dry damp coat until all kinks are out and coat is thoroughly dry.
2. Proceed with the same technique as brushing but with faster, lighter strokes.

DRYERS

There are several types of excellent dog dryers on the market. In the professional field we use a cage dryer and a floor or wall dryer. Most pet owners find an ordinary human dryer, with a stand, satisfactory for their needs.

Cage Dryer

After the bath the dog is towel-dried and placed in a cage. The professional cage dryer has hooks on it, and the dryer is simply hooked onto the cage door. The dryer is then set to warm or hot and, within a short period of time, the dog is dried.

Floor Dryer

The floor dryer is used for blow-drying. It usually has a stronger "blow" than the cage dryer and a different technique is used (see Blow-Drying). The floor dryer is mounted on a movable stand and may be maneuvered in a variety of positions.

Wall Dryer

A recent innovation in blow-drying equipment is a wall-mounted unit. All the maneuvering for blow-drying

28

Some groomers prefer to use a cage dryer prior to blow drying.

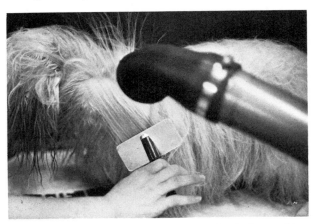

By directing a stream of air at the area being brushed, we achieve the elegant finish we seek. This technique is known as blow drying.

Where blow drying is not needed cage dryers are useful.

A floor dryer is most often used in blow drying and is suitable for use on all dogs. It permits the operator the use of both hands as he works.

The wall dryer is a recent innovation in drying equipment.

The Oster *Airjet* is designed for home use by nonprofessionals who work on their own pets.

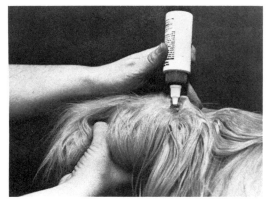

Checking ears for the presence of wax or developing infection is very important. Use of a proprietary ear powder is sometimes indicated with certain dogs.

is done with a hose. The advantages of this type of drying are several. First, there is no space taken up on the floor. Second, the hose is much easier to maneuver. Third, since the "blow" is much stronger through the hose, the dryer requires very little amperage, and there is a considerable saving of electricity.

Pet Dryer

The Oster Corporation manufactures the *Airjet*, a dryer for the individual pet owner. It is mounted on a small stand and has a certain limited maneuverability. This dryer is fine for home use on small and some medium-sized breeds. The Airjet can also double as a dryer for human hair.

EAR CLEANING AND NAIL TRIMMING

Ear Cleaning

Ear cleaning is a rather simple chore, but it is essential for all breeds. With the long-haired breeds, problems can arise if ears are not cleaned regularly. The hair in the ears will grow long, knot up, mat and eventually interfere with proper functioning of the ear canal. Infection can result, with serious consequences and the need for a veterinarian's attention.

A can of ear powder easily obtained in any pet shop or supermarket is an excellent preventative against ear problems. Squirt some powder directly into the ear. The hair will become dry and brittle and is easily plucked out with the fingers. Pluck the hairs out with a quick, firm motion until the ear looks clean. If you find that there are hairs you cannot reach with your fingers, use a hemostat to reach them. These can usually be obtained in any medical supply house.

An incidental benefit of the ear powder is that it helps control canker and ear mites. Make sure to ask for ear canker powder. For those breeds, especially the smooth coats, where there is very little hair growing in the ears, the only ear cleaning which may be necessary is swabbing with cotton dipped in mineral oil or rubbing alcohol.

Always be careful to clean the ears gently.

Nail Trimming

The nails of any dog will grow too long if left unattended. Some dogs will wear their nails down themselves if they have unlimited access to hard ground. Most, however, need some attention paid to their feet. Without regular trimming, nails may grow so long that they can actually throw the dog off his natural balance and act as a source of general irritation. Neglected nails also detract from the look of an otherwise well-groomed dog.

29

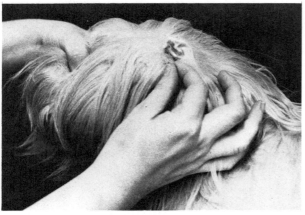

In some cases it is possible to remove hair from the ear canal by plucking with finger and thumb.

In trimming nails, every effort should be made to avoid cutting the quick, or vein.

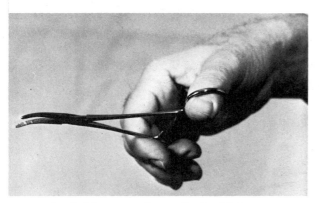

Surgical hemostats do an effective job in removing ear hair where fingers cannot reach.

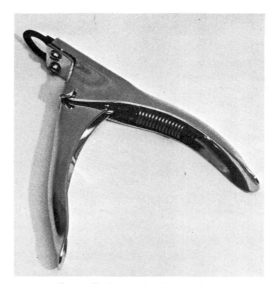

The guillotine nail trimmer is the most popular tool for cutting nails.

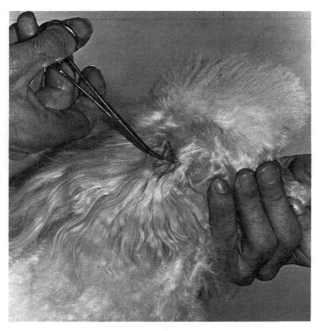

When using hemostats, the dog's head must be held very steady.

The proper way to hold the guillotine nail trimmer.

Trimming front nails.

The motorized nail grinder does a fast, effective job of shortening nails and is particularly in demand by those who work with show dogs.

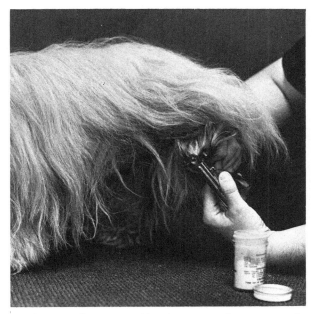

Accidents can happen, so this wise groomer keeps a coagulant close by in case a nail is cut too close.

Nail Trimmers and Techniques

Guillotine type nail trimmers are the best and, like all tools, there is a correct way of holding and using the trimmers. Hold the trimmers vertically, in the manner illustrated in the accompanying photo. Grasp the foot firmly, and holding the leg up towards you, carefully trim each nail. You may sometimes find it unnecessary to trim the nails on the hind feet because they always seem shorter than those on the fore feet. If dewclaws are present, their nails should be trimmed at the same time.

The shorter the nail the better, and frequent trimming will, in time, help tighten the feet and improve the dog's balance. Trim off a little at a time until you get the feel of it and acquire some skill. Be careful about the *quick,* a vein which can be easily observed in most white and light-colored dogs but may be rather difficult to see in darker dogs, so the latter will require closer observation and extra caution.

Nail Bleeding

If the nails should bleed, there is no cause for alarm. Always have on hand one of the antiseptic coagulants which you can purchase in any drug store. These substances will quickly stop any bleeding. Incidentally, the best time to trim the nails (or clean the ears) is before bathing, so that any trace of blood or powder will be washed away.

Nail Grinding

A finishing touch in trimming nails is the use of the nail grinder. The chief function of this tool is to polish off the rough edges of the nails. The Oster Corporation makes a nail grinder favored by those who prefer such tools. Caution is advised when using a grinder on dogs with long ear fringes. If the dog were to bend his head, some part of the fringes could get caught in the grinding wheel causing the dog considerable pain.

It is important to note that while some dogs will not object to the grinding (especially if trained from puppyhood), others will object most strenuously. Since the grinding is mostly for cosmetic effect, it would not seem advisable to force the issue unduly.

REVIEW OF FUNDAMENTALS

Brushing, bathing, blow-drying, ear cleaning and nail trimming are the fundamentals of dog grooming for all breeds. Each step must be learned systematically and methodically, step by step, slowly mastering the art each step of the way. Patience is of the essence, and while it may sound like another cliché—practice does make perfect.

The "tricks of the trade," (coat conditioner, Universal brush, mat comb and the Oster mat comb) will help reduce the labor time involved, but in general it is mostly physical labor, which hopefully is a labor of love.

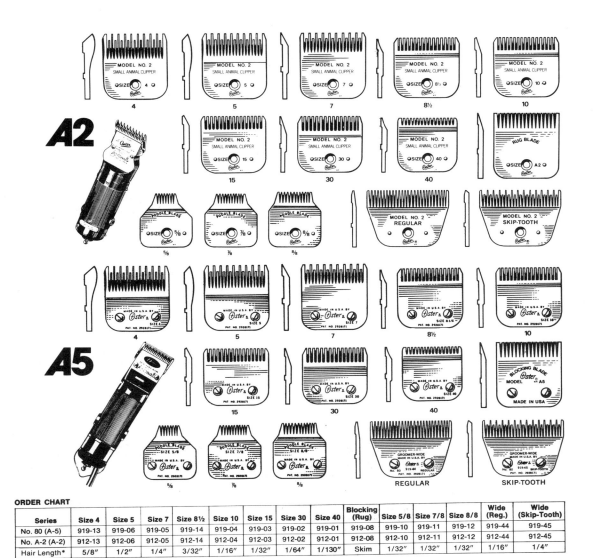

ORDER CHART

Series	Size 4	Size 5	Size 7	Size 8½	Size 10	Size 15	Size 30	Size 40	Blocking (Rug)	Size 5/8	Size 7/8	Size 8/8	Wide (Reg.)	Wide (Skip-Tooth)
No. 80 (A-5)	919-13	919-06	919-05	919-14	919-04	919-03	919-02	919-01	919-08	919-10	919-11	919-12	919-44	919-45
No. A-2 (A-2)	912-13	912-06	912-05	912-14	912-04	912-03	912-02	912-01	912-08	912-10	912-11	912-12	912-44	912-45
Hair Length*	5/8"	1/2"	1/4"	3/32"	1/16"	1/32"	1/64"	1/130"	Skim	1/32"	1/32"	1/32"	1/16"	1/4"

*(When cut with grain)

The Oster Company manufactures clipper blades for the A5 and the older A2 models to meet any need from roughing out to surgical shaving.

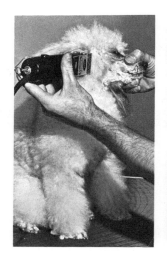

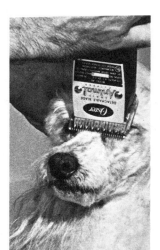
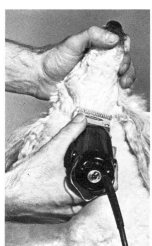

A clipper always cuts closer when used against the lie of the coat as shown in these photographs.

Clipping and Scissoring

A MAJOR ELEMENT IN DOG grooming is the proper use of clippers, although with many breeds there is little or no clipping involved. With other breeds, however, like the Poodle, clipping is one of the main features of grooming. The other essential skill is scissoring.

Clippers

The clipper is a form of automatic scissors with which we set the patterns for such traditional Poodle clips as the Kennel, Dutch, Town and Country and Sporting, as well as all the show clips. The clipper is also used for a variety of other purposes on different breeds, which will be explained as we proceed.

The best known and probably the best-quality clipper in the world is the Oster clipper, manufactured by the company of the same name. Two models are used by professional groomers. One is the A5 and the other is the A2. The principal difference between them is that the A5 has detachable blades while the A2 has a detachable head. Most professional groomers today use the A5 because of the ease with which the blades are interchanged.

The Oster Company also manufacturers and markets a pet clipper for the individual pet owner which may be sufficient for the novice or non-professional.

Blades

It is well to study the accompanying blade chart since a familiarity with the whole range of blades will pay great dividends. There are 14 different blades that come in a variety of sizes, ranging from the #4 blade to the #40 blade. The #4 blade has the widest spaced teeth while the #40 has the closest set teeth. As the chart indicates, the #4 blade will leave a 5/8″ coat, the #15 blade a 1/32″ coat, while the #40 blade will leave a 1/130″ coat. The #30 and #40 blades are used in show clips for Poodles. Veterinarians use the #40 blade for surgical operations.

The Oster A5 small animal clipper is widely used by dog groomers, handlers, veterinarians and anyone who does any amount of serious grooming.

Hold the clipper as you would a pencil.

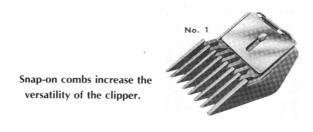

No. 1

Snap-on combs increase the versatility of the clipper.

Snap-On Combs

A fairly recent innovation in grooming techniques is the use of snap-on combs. These snap-on combs were developed because manufacturers found it impractical to make a coarser blade than a #4. The #4 blade, you will recall is the blade with the widest spaced teeth and leaves on more coat after clipping (⅝″) than any other blade.

While snap-on combs are available in different sizes, only one size is important to us, size #1. When the #1 snap-on comb is snapped onto a #10 or #15 regular blade, it will leave a one-inch coat—considerably more than any regular blade. This opens up several possibilities for reducing clipping time. For example, the #1 snap-on comb attached to the #10 blade, leaving a 1″ coat, is equivalent to the coat left on a modified Puppy clip or Sporting clip. Theoretically, no scissoring need be done on the body. Likewise, the coat of a Shih Tzu, Lhasa Apso, Bichon or Old English can be trimmed down to "puppy" length without scissoring.

The object of the snap-on combs, when correctly used, is to reduce clipping and scissoring time. The professional groomer would do well to improvise and experiment along these lines. The technique for using the snap-on comb is described and illustrated in the next chapter under THE SPORTING CLIP.

Clipping Technique

The clipper should be held in a certain position for greatest efficiency of use. In the correct position, the clipper is held like a pencil. There are times when some pressure must be exerted, but in general the clipper should be held easily and lightly, yet firmly. With the correct blade attached, the clipper can remove any coat from any breed (even the most matted) right down to the skin, or the coat can be shaped and blended into almost any style desired.

Oster A5 and A2 clippers can provide practically a lifetime of useful service, providing proper care is taken of them. All Oster clippers are packed accompanied by a booklet of maintenance instructions. If these are carefully followed, the clipper will give optimum efficiency for many years. Care must also be taken that the clipper is not dropped, for this can cause serious damage.

SCISSORING

The most artistic component of grooming lies in the scissoring work. The perfection of finish required can only be achieved through skillfully applied scissoring. It is the scissor work, above all, which separates the real professional from the novice. If, therefore, one's objective is top-quality, professional grooming, then it is essential to develop the scissoring technique to the nth

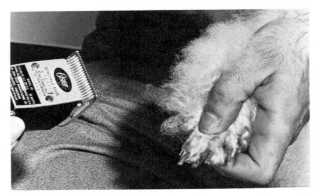

Clipping the feet of a Poodle calls for skill and a very light touch. Here the toes are gently spread to allow the clipper entry.

Clipping top of paw.

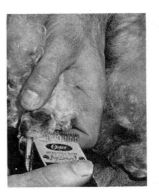

Clipping between foot pads.

Clipping underside of tail. Always clip this with the lie of the coat.

Clipping side of paw.

Clipping top of tail between pompon and body.

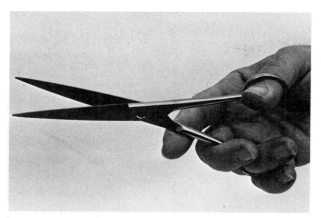

Proper position for holding the scissors.

Intent on her practice.

Scissoring around the pastern.

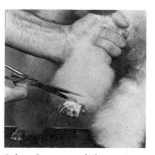

Scissoring sides of legs.

Blending hair on neck and shoulder.

degree. It is an education in itself to watch the really great professional groomers and handlers at work with the scissors.

Technique of Scissoring

While scissors may be held in different ways with varying degrees of success, the technically correct way of holding the scissors is to place the tip of your thumb in the thumb rest, the little finger under the open shank, the tip of the third finger in the finger hold; the second finger rests on the handles, while the index finger braces the scissors. Scissor by holding the lower section as still as possible, letting your thumb do the work. In our school novice students practice the scissoring technique on human wigs before actually scissoring the dog, and we recommend this method of trial and error to the beginner. Just get any old Afro wig and practice.

Scissoring the Poodle

Just as in clipping the Poodle, where the basic techniques described may be used in clipping any breed where clipping is required, so the basic scissoring techniques described here may be applied to the scissoring of all breeds. Only the particular application may differ from breed to breed.

Scissoring the Legs

Our method is to start the scissoring on the legs and work upward, leaving the head for the last. The first step is to comb the hair down around the pastern so that all straggly hairs clearly hang over the clipped area. Then scissor straight across the narrowest part of the pastern and uniformly all around it. Then, holding the leg up with one hand, scissor along the inside leg silhouette in a straight vertical line right up to the elbow. Do the same thing on the other side of the leg. Scissor in a circular fashion with overlapping strokes so that there are no ridges, and the final result will resemble a cylindrical column. All four legs should be trimmed in the same fashion.

Blending with Scissors

Looking at the body coat in perspective you may see uneven lines. Blend these lines with the scissors so that the whole coat is even and uniform. Scissor more closely and carefully in the anal area.

Scissoring the Tail

The Poodle Standard calls for a pompon on the tail. This "pom" should approximate a ball. The better the coat, the rounder the ball. To achieve the desired effects, comb out the pom and scissor in a circular fashion. Even

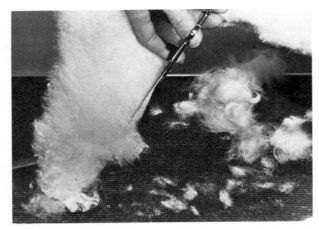

All wispy hair is trimmed away and the legs are nicely outlined.

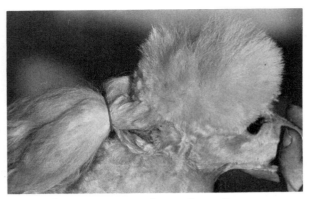

Some groomers prefer to tie up the ears with a latex band while trimming the head.

Here the topknot is being formed.

Take care to keep the topknot in balance with the trim.

The topknot must be blended into the neck.

Rounding out the topknot with curved scissors.

All hair around the anal opening is trimmed as short as possible.

Trimming down back of neck.

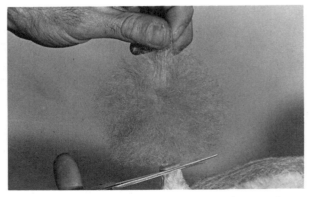

The pompon on the end of the tail is scissored to roundness.

scissoring and uniformity of coat texture will contribute to the roundness and beauty of the pom. Some professional groomers find that curved scissors achieve better results.

Scissoring the Head

The head furnishing or "topknot" is scissored to achieve a domelike effect. The first scissor cut on the topknot should be along the top line of the ear. Do the same on both sides. Then scissor the whole topknot in proportion to the size of the head. The top should be in proportion to the sides. The ear furnishings may be scissored just to remove any straggly hairs. Whenever ear furnishings get in your way, put them up with a latex band.

Decoration

In pet Poodle grooming, ribbons are sometimes used as decorative effects. Ribbons can be bought in a variety store, or they can be homemade. Instructions for making your own ribbon appear later in this book. Before the ribbon is applied, look the dog over carefully to see if a little touch of trimming is needed here or there, then attach the ribbon. Traditionally the ribbon is placed on the hip for the male dog while it is placed at the ear separation for the bitch.

SCISSORS

Barber Scissors

Professional dog groomers, barbers and beauticians all use the same type of scissors. These are usually made in Germany, in the city of Solingen, which for generations has been famous for its manufacture of fine scissors. The best German scissors are expensive, but they are superbly made, hollow ground, with almost razor-like edges, which must be kept sharpened regularly.

There are basically two different-size scissors used in dog grooming—7½" and 8¼". In the formative years of dog grooming the 7½" scissors was most often used; today the majority of professional groomers use the 8¼" size. This size helps combine quality with production. The 7½" size is still used principally by the non-professional or for Toy breeds. Curved scissors are used by some professional groomers for making pompons and bracelets on Poodles.

Thinning Shears

As the name implies, thinning shears are used basically for thinning out the coat rather than doing any substantial cutting, as with regular scissors. The technique for both is virtually the same. Like scissors, there are basically two different types of thinning shears, the single serrated edge and the double serrated edge. Most professional groomers use the single serrated edge thinning shears, which contain 30 teeth. Thinning shears are traditionally used only for those breeds whose coats call for thinning of certain areas, not for heavy cutting.

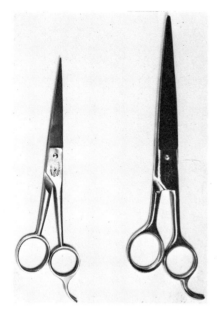

Quality barber's scissors are available in various lengths to satisfy any preference or application.

Curved scissors are useful for any trimming in the round and some like them for trimming between pads of the feet.

Thinning shears are widely used for blending and getting out unwanted hair without leaving cut marks.

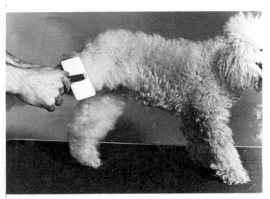

When brushing hindlegs, hold leg straight out behind dog.

Essential grooming for the Poodle includes the bath. Without it, results will not be fully satisfying.

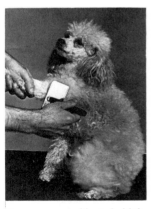

Many groomers like to hold the hair with one hand as they brush with the other. This technique is said to result in a fuller look to the leg furnishings.

Wring and towel out as much moisture as possible before blow drying.

If a dog will lie down during brushing, it will be more relaxed during grooming sessions and will generally come away from them looking better than "standers only."

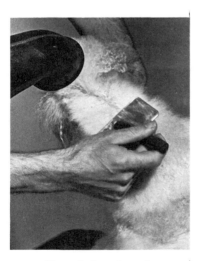

Blow drying gives the Poodle an extra measure of beauty and charm.

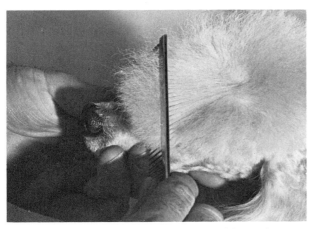

The topknot should be combed up and forward.

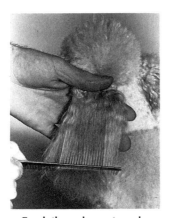

Comb through ears to make sure no snarls are present.

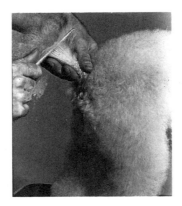

The pompon is combed through before being scissored.

The Poodle

Standard Regarding Coat

Coat—Of naturally harsh texture, profuse and dense throughout.

Breed Note

The Poodle's origin is controversial, claims having been made by Germany, Denmark, France and even Russia as his original birthplace. His most likely place of origin is Germany and the name Poodle is probably derived from the German *Pudel* which means to splash in water. In France the Poodle was called *Caniche*, a derivation of *canard* or duck and described his chief function there.

Among the Poodle's many attributes are his boldness, intelligence and sensitivity. He is extremely gentle with children. Being easily trained, he was much in demand as an acrobat and performer with circuses and variety shows.

Part of the Poodle's popularity stems from the fact that he is bred in three sizes—Toy, Miniature and Standard—and a variety of colors ranging from black to white with many distinctive hues in between. He may also be trimmed in an infinite assortment of appealing styles for pets or in formal, traditional show clips.

Because of his variety of sizes, colors, trims and universal appeal, the Poodle has been the most popular breed in the United States for the past twenty years.

The Poodle is the only breed whose coat is traditionally styled in a variety of ways. These range from a host of different pet clips to the formal clips seen almost exclusively in the show ring. So adaptable and versatile is the Poodle coat, that trimming him is like trimming many breeds all rolled into one.

The Poodle is also the one breed endowed by nature with the kind of profuse coat which can grow over eight inches long, an extraordinary length for any breed of dog.

For all of the above reasons we are using the Poodle as our model for a demonstration of the whole range of clipping, but the *techniques* of clipping are basically the same for all breeds wherever clipping is required. The following stages are the proper sequence of Poodle clipping.

1. Clipping the face, feet and tail (Basic clip)
2. Clipping the pattern
3. Shaping and blending

THE POODLE PET CLIPS

When Poodle popularity started zooming out of sight in the 1960s, many clips were specially fashioned for the breed, many of them bizarre and exotic. In recent years the fad character of grooming the Poodle has given way to such traditional clips as the Kennel, Sporting, Dutch, Town and Country and others. By far the most popular clip is the Kennel Clip. But first, we start with the Basic clip.

THE BASIC CLIP
(Face, Feet and Tail)

Face

The traditional blade used for the Basic clip (face, feet and tail) is the #15 blade. A #10 blade is used on dogs with light-colored coats and/or sensitive skins. Start by clipping the face, using as your first guideline the middle of the ear to the corner of the eye.

Then with parallel strokes clip down the face to the corner of the lip. Next place the clippers at the stop and bring them down the nose. Again with parallel strokes clip the muzzle clean. Proceed to follow the same procedure on the other side of the face. The area on the face to be most concerned about is the lips. In order not to nick the lips with the clippers, it is necessary to stretch the lips taut while clipping in this area. The guideline for ending the clipping of the face is the Adam's Apple (where the neck begins).

Feet

The Poodle, once again, is the only breed where the feet are shaven clean. The feet, or more accurately, the paws, are the most difficult part of clipping, and once this area is mastered, everything else in clipping becomes easy. The paw of a Toy Poodle especially, is very small and dainty, and clipping these paws requires a great deal of skill and dexterity. The following procedure will make things a lot easier. The guideline for clipping the paws is the pastern, which roughly corresponds to the human ankle. The clipping should not start any higher than this point. Clip the paw (still with a #15 blade) top, sides and underneath (the pads). The most difficult part of clipping the paw is getting between the toes. This requires

a side-to-side clipping technique using the end of the clippers, with care being taken not to dig into the web. Clipping the hair out of the pads (bottom of paws) requires a kind of scooping action, and it may take a little practice to master this.

Like the face, it is desirable to clip the paws as clean as possible. Any straggly hair destroys the clean, tidy look the paws should have and detracts from the elegant finish of a well-groomed Poodle.

Tail

There is no guideline for clipping the tail as each dog is an individual. The length, thickness and curve (if any) of the tail will affect how it will be clipped. Most professional groomers do not measure but do it by eye. Care must be taken not to clip into the anal area itself. A pompon is left on the tail fashioned as much as possible into a ball.

THE PUPPY CLIP

The clipping of the face, feet and tail (the Basic clip) is all that is done on the Poodle puppy until the coat matures enough to be put into a pattern for one of the adult clips. Before the puppy reaches its first birthday, the coat may be scissored or tipped. This is called the Puppy clip.

THE KENNEL CLIP

The Kennel clip is the most popular clip of all. It is a fairly close clip, uniform all around, easy to maintain and easy on the pocketbook, since it retains its clean appearance longer than most other clips.

Pattern

The first step in executing the Kennel clip is the clipping of the face, feet and tail (#15 blade). The next step is to put on the pattern. Switch to the #5 blade. The guideline for the first stroke is the backbone or spine. Starting from the base of neck, clip down the back to the base of the tail. Then with parallel strokes *overlapping* each other, clip down the right side, going no further than the elbow on the forequarters and the thigh on the hindquarters. Repeat the entire procedure on left side.

Next, clip the chest and brisket area with the #5 blade down to the point approximating the upper arm. The rear should be clipped to the point approximating the upper thigh. Forelegs and hindlegs should not be touched by the clippers. The legs should be scissored to match the overall trim. When clipping is finished, the

The Puppy Clip

The Kennel Clip

entire body coat should be an even, uniform blanket, ½″ in length.

Neck

Consider the neck as part of the overall pattern. Just bear in mind that the closeness of the trim on the neck must correspond to the closeness of the body pattern. This means that you are still using the #5 blade and will blend the neck coat into the body coat always being careful not to clip into the legs,

So, starting at the base of the skull, clip down to the base of the neck. Clip the neck uniformly all around.

Shaping and Blending

Shaping and blending with the clipper is both a time-saving technique and also removes the line left by the clipper in making the pattern. Clipping the pattern for the Kennel clip with the #5 blade leaves ½″ coat on the body while a longer coat is left on the legs. The object then of shaping and blending is to graduate the body coat into the legs so there will be no perceptible line separating the two. To do this, round off the edges of that coat, holding the clipper at a 45-degree angle so that you don't dig into the leg coat. All we want is to shape and then blend the body coat into the leg coat so there is no visible line.

After you have clipped off the edges with the #5 blade and have developed some skill in shaping and blending, you can graduate to the #7 blade—a finer blade and will do the job more quickly. Some professional groomers get so carried away with their skill in shaping and blending with the clipper that they tend to let the clipper do the work which should be left to the scissors.

You may leave the basic clipping of the face, feet and tail for the last step or you may do it as the first step, as many professional groomers seem to prefer.

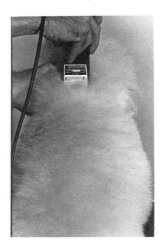

In setting most pet patterns, clipping commences from the base of the skull.

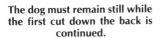

The line is continued down to the tail.

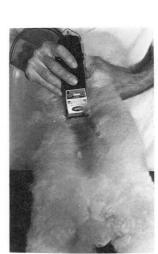

The dog must remain still while the first cut down the back is continued.

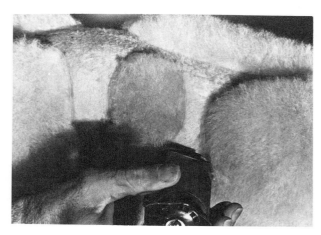

After the back has been clipped, the specific pattern can be set.

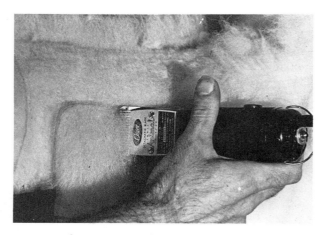

The groomer continues setting the pattern.

Clipping sides of the neck.

Applying the snap-on comb.

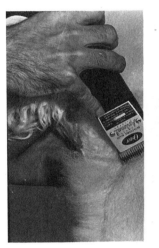

Rounding off edges of longer hair.

Shaping and blending hindquarters.

The snap-on comb in position.

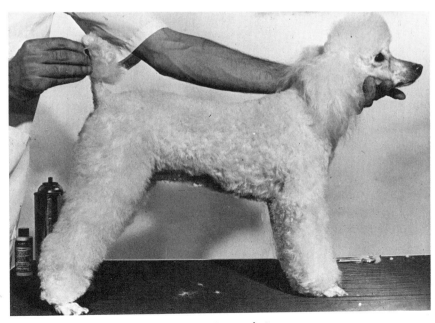

The finished Kennel clip.

43

THE SPORTING CLIP
(formerly the Lamb clip)

The most popular clip after the Kennel clip was previously called the *Lamb clip*. However in June, 1979 the Poodle Club of America, revised the breed Standard to allow the *Sporting clip* in the show ring in stud dog and brood bitch classes. In almost every respect this Sporting clip resembles the Lamb clip; the only difference is that the coat in the new Sporting clip is a little fuller on the body. In the interests of simplicity and uniformity, and in deference to the Poodle Club of America, we have decided to adopt the newly approved Sporting clip to replace the old Lamp clip.

The Sporting clip, like the Lamb clip, differs from the Kennel clip only in the length of coat left on the body after clipping. It can, therefore, be properly considered a pet clip. So it is only logical that the Sporting clip hereafter be included in the available choice of styles offered to Poodle owners who patronize grooming shops.

The Sporting clip can be used for pet or show and is executed in identical fashion for both (except the #30 or #40 blade is used for show only on the face, feet and tail).

The #1 snap-on comb is attached to a #10 or #15 blade. Then the same procedure is followed as for the Kennel clip, except that the clippers are used against the grain *after* being used with the grain. This leaves the body coat with the one inch blanket which the Standard calls for. The whole coat, body and legs, is then scissor-finished, leaving the legs fuller than the body.

Some purists may prefer to completely scissor the body coat rather than resort to the faster method of the snap-on comb. There can be no objection to this. The only point to stress is that everything should be scissor-finished, even when the snap-on comb is used.

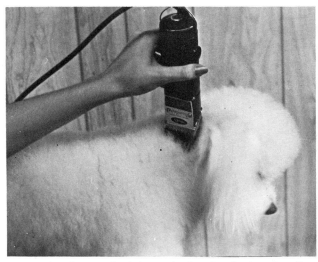

For pet trimming, much of the work of setting the Sporting clip is done with the snap-on comb. Here the groomer blends neck into shoulder.

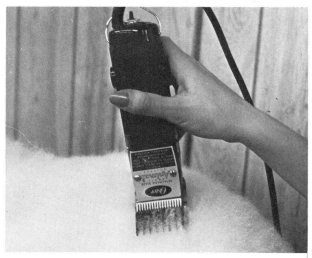

In the same manner as above, the snap-on comb is used to blend and round out hair over the rear.

When the snap-on comb on a #10 or #15 blade is used *against* the grain after clipping with, the result will be an even, one inch blanket all over the dog.

The finished Sporting clip with the addition of an appealing moustache.

THE TOWN AND COUNTRY CLIP

Setting the pattern for the Town and Country clip calls for a #10 blade on the clipper for the body pattern. We start the pattern out in the same way as the other clips, going down the back from the base of the neck to the base of the tail. The next step is to clip down in the rear, starting at the last rib and clipping down to the abdomen. Then clip down from the withers to the elbow. The remaining coat between the forelegs and hindlegs is now removed. The only outstanding feature left is the full legs contrasting with a closely clipped body.

Unlike the Kennel clip, where the edges are clipped off the leg coat, in the Town and Country the legs are left full and the only remaining work is the scissoring of the legs, the tail and topknot. The technique is basically the same as for the other clips, the only difference being that the legs are high and full and the scissoring is required to achieve clean, straight lines on the legs and clean, round lines on the topknot and tail pompon.

The Town and Country looks best on the Standard Poodle although the trend for all three Poodle varieties (Standard, Miniature and Toy) is toward the Kennel clip. The best effect for the Town and Country on a Standard Poodle is achieved when there is a sharp contrast between the closely clipped body pattern and the full, high coat left on the legs.

THE DUTCH CLIP

The Dutch clip is more complicated and time consuming than any other pet Poodle clip, and professional groomers are probably thankful that its popularity has been declining in recent years.

The Dutch pattern requires a ⅝" blade (Oster calls it the Poodle blade). It is the narrowest of all the Oster blades. Once again we go down the back to the base of the tail. The line must be perfectly straight. Use the backbone for your guideline. The next step is to make a band around the loin area of the body. Starting at the topline in the approximate area of the loin or last rib, clip down to the abdomen. Do the same thing on the other side. You should now have a pattern resembling a cross.

Four coat areas are scissored in the Dutch clip, and this consequently calls for more hand work than other pet styles where the body coat is clipped in the desired pattern.

Indeed, the Dutch clip looks good only on Poodles with very full coats which, by the same token, require the greatest amount of scissoring. While the end product is much fancier than any other clip, most Poodle owners are shying away from it.

Setting the pattern in the Town and Country clip.

Setting the pattern in the Dutch clip.

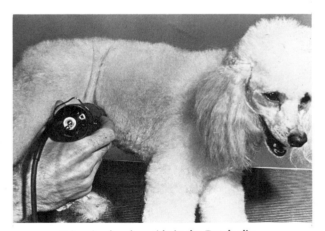

Trimming band on side in the Dutch clip.

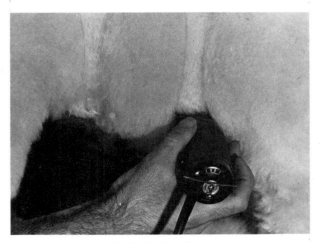

Completing the Dutch pattern.

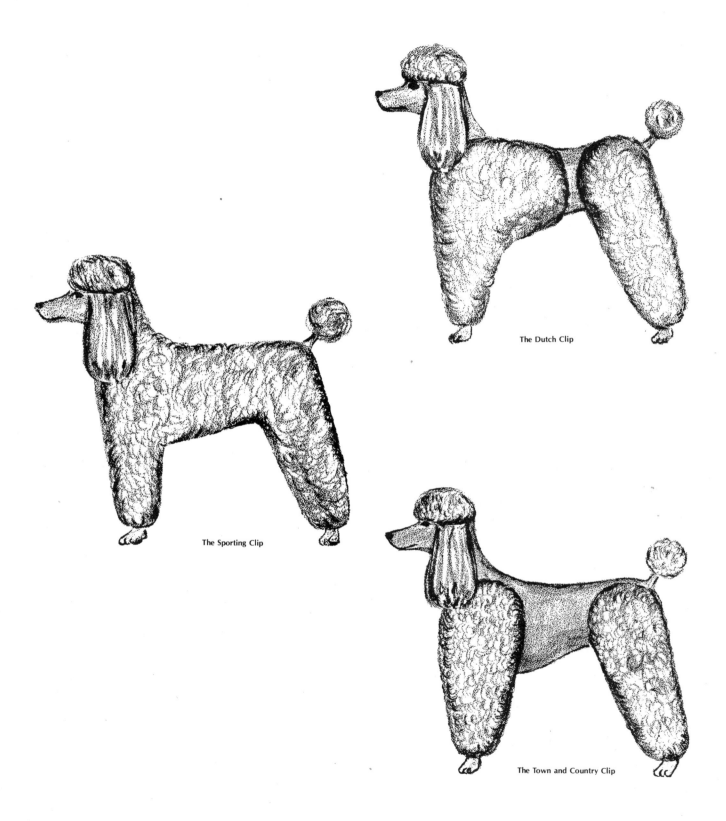

The Dutch Clip

The Sporting Clip

The Town and Country Clip

The Bichon/Poodle Clip.

The Teddy Bear clip.

From the German book, *Mein Freund, Der Pudel.*

The topknot and tail are fashioned the same as in the other clips.

The edges on the forelegs and hindlegs, like the Town and Country clip, are not clipped off but are left high and full.

THE BICHON/POODLE CLIP

This clip is for Poodle owners who like the look of the Bichon Frise. Since the Bichon resembles the Poodle in many respects and since the Poodle coat lends itself to the Bichon look, it is a fairly simple variation of the traditional Poodle clips.

Perhaps the simplest way of describing the Bichon/Poodle clip is as follows:
1. No clipping at all is done. It is all scissor work.
2. The head is fashioned in the Bichon style (See photo).
3. The body coat is scissored as in the Puppy clip.
4. The paws are not clipped, and the legs are left full.
5. The legs are scissored to blend in with the body coat.

Professional groomers have become so proficient in executing the Bichon/Poodle clip that experts are hard put to tell the difference between a Bichon and a white Miniature or Toy Poodle, without looking at the tail. (The Bichon Frise's tail is naturally long while the Poodle's is docked.)

THE TEDDY BEAR CLIP

The Teddy Bear clip is a relatively simple clip for anyone who has done a Puppy clip. The only differences are:
1. The paws are not clipped.
2. The hair on the ears is taken off with a #15 blade, and the edges of the ears are then scissored.

Although the Teddy Bear clip is a relatively recent innovation in grooming styles, a study of an old German book on the Poodle reveals that it is, in fact, an old German grooming recipe. Interestingly enough, the book, entitled *Mein Freund, Der Pudel,* published in 1958, illustrates some Poodle styles remarkably similar to our own.

THE BIKINI CLIP

The pattern for the Bikini clip is the easiest to put on. It is the nearest thing to stripping the coat off completely. In fact, the basic difference is that bracelets are left on the legs, giving the clip some style.

Scissoring bottom of rear bracelet in Bikini clip.

Shaping rear bracelet with scissors.

Scissoring top of rear bracelet in Bikini clip.

Stripping a badly matted coat with the clipper.

In some cases a neglected coat can be stripped off in one piece.

The trick is to shape this hair into a ball or "bracelet". The following is one method used:

1. Comb the hair down and scissor straight across, removing all straggly hairs at the bottom.
2. Comb up and scissor straight across, removing all straggly hairs at the top.
3. Comb all the hair together towards the middle and scissor to achieve a round ball effect.
4. Do the same on all four legs.

The topknot and tail remain to be scissored the same as all other clips.

STRIPPING THE PET COAT

Now that we have learned something about the art of clipping, it should be a fairly simple procedure to strip a coat with the clippers. Before discussing the technique, it must be restated that we strip a coat only as a last resort when all else has failed, when the coat is very matted or is so far gone that it is virtually one piece of felt. Under these circumstances, stripping becomes the only humane way to handle the coat. The accompanying photos show an extremely matted coat.

To strip off a badly matted coat, only certain blades can be used. For example, a #4 or #5 blade with their widely spaced teeth will not go through the matted coat. A #7 blade will go through some matted coats. A #10 blade will go through almost any matted coat. Only rarely will it prove necessary to use a blade as fine as a #15.

Assume then we are using a #10 blade, the procedure of choice is to clip/strip the body coat. Clipping slowly and carefully will have a less traumatic effect on most dogs. By working slowly, the groomer will be better able to find sores or other symptoms of neglect on the skin. The moment this is detected, stop. It then becomes a veterinarian's job.

After the body coat is stripped, proceed to strip the legs, always clipping with the grain. It would be nice to try to "save" the hair on the head and the tail, if it doesn't prove to be too much of an ordeal, so that the dog will not appear to be completely naked. Discretion is called for in this circumstance, even though the owner may be entirely at fault.

Lazy pet owners who habitually neglect their dogs for long periods of time and are known to professional groomers as "oncers" or "twicers" (meaning they have their dog groomed only once or twice a year) invariably wind up having their dogs stripped. It must, however, be mentioned that there are some professional groomers who strip the coats all too readily, who are more interested in the "production" angle than quality work. In the long run, educating the pet owner to take care of the coat will pay off.

Incidentally, it is merely coincidence that the same term is used to describe the procedure and the manner of trimming harsh-coated breeds for the show ring. The stripping done in each case is entirely different, as will be apparent in subsequent chapters.

48

The Bikini Clip.   After clipper stripping.

From the German book, *Mein Freund, Der Pudel.*

The English Saddle Clip

The Puppy Clip

The Continental Clip

The Poodle Show Clips

Standard Regarding Coat

Coat—Curly: of naturally harsh texture, profuse and dense throughout.

The Poodle Standard states that dogs may be shown in the ring in four different clips—the Puppy, Continental, English Saddle and the Sporting. As explained in the chapter on pet clips, the Sporting clip became an officially recognized show clip as of June 1979 for certain classes only. Prior to that time it was considered a pet clip and was more familiarly known as the Lamb clip.

THE PUPPY CLIP

The Standard states that a Poodle may be exhibited in the Puppy clip up to a year of age. The Puppy clip has, in effect, also been described before since it consists of clipped face, feet and tail plus a uniformly scissored coat to present an even, symmetrical line all over.

There are a few important differences between the Puppy clip for pets and the Puppy Clip for exhibition. First, a pin brush is used to brush out the coat in place of the wire slicker brush for the pet. The pin brush will not pull out the hairs the way the slicker brush does. Second a #30 or #40 blade is used for the face, feet and tail in place of the #15 blade. Third, the topknot is not trimmed into a round dome but rather the head hair is allowed to grow long and flow into the back. Fourth, the front part of the topknot is wrapped in a latex band to prevent it from falling over the face. The *technique* for scissoring the show puppy is the same as for the pet.

THE ENGLISH SADDLE CLIP

Standard Regarding Coat

In the "English Saddle" clip, the face, throat, feet, forelegs and base of the tail are shaved, leaving puffs on the forelegs and a pompon on the end of the tail. The hindquarters are covered with a short blanket of hair except for a curved shaved area on each flank and two shaved bands on each hindleg. The entire shaven foot and a portion of the shaven leg above the puff are visible. The rest of the body is left in full coat but may be shaped in order to insure overall balance.

Setting the English Saddle Pattern

There are several areas requiring the use of clippers in executing the English Saddle clip, although the major part of the work is done by scissoring. The areas to be clipped beside the face, feet and tail are (1) the *kidney patch* on the flank and (2) the forelegs from the wrist to the elbow. These areas are clipped with the #30 or #40 blade. The face, feet and tail are clipped using exactly the same techniques as in the pet clips.

Clipping the Kidney Patch

Before you can clip the kidney patch, you must do a little scissoring first. It is necessary to form a dividing line, or a part, between the *mane* and the *pack*. This line, or band, is trimmed at a point slightly behind the last rib. The internal organ in this area is the kidney, hence the term kidney patch.

1. Part the hair in the area of the last rib with a comb. Then scissor up the part to make the band sharp and distinct.
2. Right past the rib, directly in the center on each side of the body, clip a crescent shaped patch. For the Miniature Poodle this patch should not measure more than 1½ to 2 inches in circumference.

The AKC Standard does not specify any precise measurement for the kidney patch. It is used more as a matter of tradition and ornament in the American show ring. In England the kidney patch is not formed at all, and the English Saddle clip is known as the Lion clip. Otherwise, the English Saddle and the Lion clips are identical.

Clipping the Forelegs

When clipping the forelegs, place the clipper at the point slightly above the wrist and clip upward to the

51

elbow. You will find the mane in your way, so just hold the mane up with your free hand while you are clipping. After clipping, let the mane fall back, extending about one inch below the elbow. Follow the same procedure with the other foreleg. When you have finished clipping the forelegs, you are finished with your clipper. The rest of the work will be with the scissor.

Scissoring the English Saddle Clip

Pack—The pack is formed on the hind part of the dividing line, and this is scissored to about a two inch depth. The pack should be trimmed as uniformly as possible all around. It extends backward from the part or dividing line and down to the stifle joint. The objective in trimming the pack is a solid, plush look.

Mane—The mane covers the foreparts of the dog and extends to the last rib. The show coat is demonstrated through the mane, which should be as thick, dense and profuse as possible. If the mane does not grow to a length of at least five inches, the dog will not be in serious contention in the show ring. The best show coats grow to a length of seven or eight inches and more.

The mane is the heavy part of the coat, covering most of the dog, including the shoulders, ribs and chest, and coming down to about one inch below the elbow joint.

1. Start scissoring the mane from the rear, and trim in a circular fashion. Starting at the top of the dividing line that separates the mane from the pack, scissor downward and come around the undersection. Continue trimming around to the front area. You will have trimmed around in a sort of semi-circle.

2. When you have trimmed around one side, do the same thing on the other side until you meet the side you have already done in the center of the front area. The lines should meet symmetrically and uniformly. When you have finished trimming both sides, you have come full circle.

3. You must now trim the balance of the mane, removing all straggly ends, scissoring until you achieve an even, plush look throughout the coat.

Bracelets—The techniques for scissoring the bracelets in the English Saddle clip differ somewhat from that of the pet Bikini clip, although the principle is the same.

1. Make your parts with the scissors. Starting in the rear again, trim a part all around the stifle joint. This part should be slanting downward. Then trim another part around the hock joint. This part should be trimmed at about a 45-degree angle. Repeat the same thing on the other hindleg. You do not have to make any part for the forelegs, since you did this in effect when you clipped the forelegs up to the elbow.

2. When you have trimmed all the parts on the hindlegs, proceed to fashion the bracelets. The bracelets at the stifle joint differ slightly in shape from the bracelets at the hock joint. The bracelet at the stifle joint is trimmed into a sort of cup or U-shape. The bracelet at the hock joint is more angulated, trimmed into almost a V-shape,

52

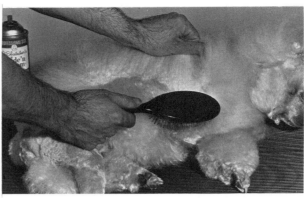

All show Poodles are brushed with the pin brush rather than the slicker.

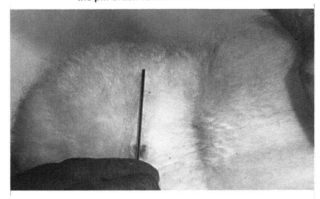

In setting the English Saddle pattern, the coat is parted to trim in the pack.

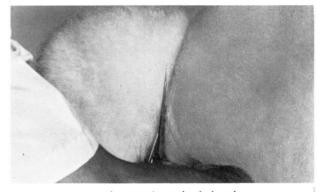

Once the part is made, it is scissored to set it apart prior to clipping.

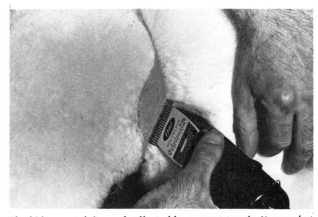

The kidney patch is much affected by current trends. Know what is popular before executing the English Saddle clip.

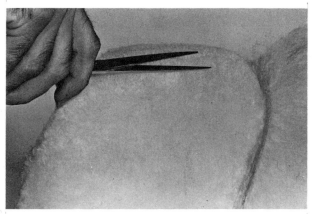

When scissoring the pack, be sure to keep the topline perfectly level.

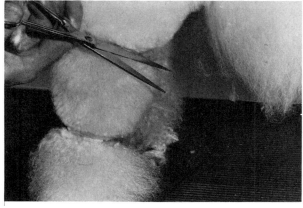

Form rear bracelets with scissors.

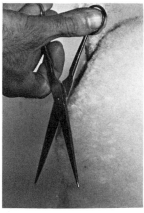

Scissor the hindquarters to roundness.

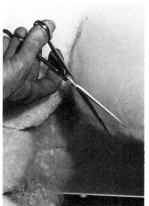

Round out the mane.

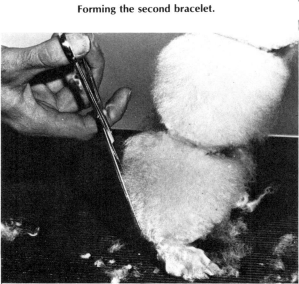

Forming the second bracelet.

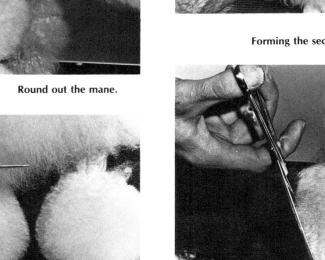

Neaten bottom of mane to set it off from forelegs.

Shaping bracelets.

with the V being a cross between a U and a V, or another way of saying it is that the V curved at the bottom, rather than angling sharply. First comb down. Then shape into V.

3. Moving to the forelegs and starting at the top of the bracelet (first combing up) scissor straight across the top. Then do the same thing at the bottom of the bracelet. The rest of the sequence of scissoring the front bracelets is to shape each into a round ball.

Tail—The last stage in scissoring is the pompon on the tail. This is done with practically the same technique for pet or show clips.

Comb out and scissor into a round ball.

Finishing

You have now completed the basic clipper and scissorwork of the English Saddle clip. Go over every area, the face, feet and tail, the kidney patch, pack, mane and bracelets. Check and double check. There is always a little more clipping needed here, a little more scissoring there. The English Saddle clip is the epitome of the groomer's art, and here one should strive for perfection.

The final touch is to brush the mane against the lay of the coat with the pin brush. The pin brush will not split or break the hairs. Brush the mane straight back so that it fans out at the topknot, giving it a halo-like effect. The front of the topknot is tied with a clasp or a latex band. Simply pick up the front part of the crown and twist the band down to the base. Then bring the hair back to blend in with the mane. This method or procedure with the topknot applies to all the show clips. The Poodle is now in the English Saddle and ready for the show ring.

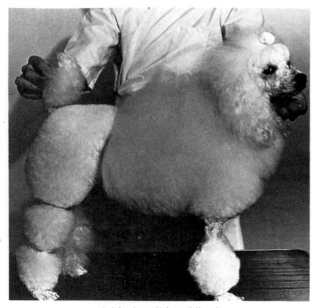

Finished English Saddle clip.

THE CONTINENTAL CLIP

Standard Regarding Coat

In the "Continental" clip, the face, throat, feet, and base of the tail are shaved. The hindquarters are shaved with pompons (optional) on the hips. The legs are shaved, leaving bracelets on the hindlegs and puffs on the forelegs. There is a pompon on the end of the tail. The entire shaven foot and a portion of the shaven foreleg above the puff are visible. The rest of the body is left in full coat but may be shaped in order to insure overall balance.

Setting the Continental Pattern

The Continental clip is quite a bit simpler to execute than the English Saddle. There is no pack on the hindquarters, and pompons on the hips, while traditional, are optional. The only set of bracelets on the hindlegs are fashioned at the hock.

As in the English Saddle clip, the hindquarters are divided from the point behind the last rib. The difference is that the entire hindquarters are clipped with the #30 or #40 blade. If you are going to leave pompons on the hips, as is customary, the poms should be styled before the hindquarters are clipped. The following method of fashioning the poms is probably the simplest, although professional handlers are more apt to use eye judgment. This method applies to Miniature Poodles, so for Standards and Toys, proportions should be adjusted accordingly:

1. Place a drinking glass at least three inches wide at the top over each hip joint, and clip around the glass.
2. Clip the rest of the hindquarters clean down to the point slightly above the hock, which will be covered with a bracelet. Then scissor the poms on the hips into round rosettes.
3. The forelegs are clipped exactly the same as in the English Saddle clip, starting slightly above the wrist and clipping up to the point of the elbow.

Bracelets

You now have the guidelines for scissoring the bracelets of the hindlegs and the forelegs. The rear bracelets are shaped exactly like the rear bracelets in the English Saddle clip, with the modified V-shape. The front bracelets are also identical with the bracelets on the English Saddle clip.

Since the pompons on the hips are considered more desirable than none at all, and since most professional handlers exhibit the Continental clip with hip poms, the tradition to show the Continental in this fashion has been reinforced accordingly. The topknot, as with all the show clips, is put up with a latex band.

To summarize, the English Saddle and the Continental clips are very similar. However, since the Continental has no pack, optional hip poms and only one set of bracelets on the hindlegs, it is that much easier and faster to execute. However, the Continental clip exposes much more of the dog's hindquarter assembly, so to wear it a Poodle should boast excellent rear conformation.

THE SPORTING CLIP

Standard Regarding Coat

In the Sporting clip a Poodle shall be shown with face, feet, throat and base of tail shaved, leaving a scissored cap on the top of the head and a pompon on the end of the tail. The rest of the body and legs are clipped or scissored to follow the outline of the dog leaving a short blanket of coat no longer than one inch in length. The hair on the legs may be slightly longer than that on the body.

The Sporting clip is executed in almost exactly the same way for pet or show. The only difference is that for show the face, feet and tail are clipped with a #30

or #40 blade where the pet is done with a #15 blade. See the section, Poodle Pet Clips in Chapter 4 for detailed instruction on the Sporting clip.

THE PIN BRUSH

The pin brush, as previously explained, is used to brush out Poodle show coats, as well as other breeds with long, flowing coats.

As the name implies, these brushes are made of pins and mounted on a rubber-backed cushion with a plastic or wood frame. The pins are flexible and pliable and have rounded edges so cannot break or pull out hair. The coat must be free of all mats so that the pin brush can do its job of keeping the hair sleek and glossy.

The best method of using the pin brush is to work with the lay of the coat in long, sweeping strokes. Brush section by section, layer by layer, remembering the maxim, systematically and methodically.

Use a drinking glass to help set the hip pompons in the Continental clip.

After clipping, refine the shape of your poms with scissors.

The finished pom should be in good proportion to the trim and the dog wearing it.

The finished Continental clip.

The pin brush is used on show Poodles as it does not pull out or break live hairs in normal use.

Part II

THE LONGHAIRED BREEDS

Afghan Hound
American Water Spaniel
Bearded Collie
Bedlington Terrier
Belgian Sheepdog
Belgian Tervuren
Bernese Mountain Dog
Bichon Frise
Borzoi
Bouvier des Flandres
Briard
Brittany Spaniel
Chihuahua
Clumber Spaniel
Cocker Spaniel
Collie (Rough)
Chow Chow
Dachshund (Longhaired)
English Cocker Spaniel
English Setter
English Springer Spaniel
Field Spaniel
Gordon Setter
Great Pyrenees
Irish Setter
Irish Water Spaniel
Irish Wolfhound
Japanese Chin

Keeshond
Kerry Blue Terrier
Komondor
Kuvasz
Lhasa Apso
Maltese
Newfoundland
Old English Sheepdog
Otterhound
Papillon
Pekingese
Pomeranian
Poodle
Puli
Saint Bernard
   (Longhaired)
Samoyed
Scottish Deerhound
Shetland Sheepdog
Shih Tzu
Silky Terrier
Skye Terrier
Soft-Coated Wheaten
   Terrier
Sussex Spaniel
Welsh Springer Spaniel
Tibetan Terrier
Yorkshire Terrier

The Longhaired, Parted-Coat Breeds

Lhasa Apso   *Skye Terrier*
Shih Tzu   *Tibetan Terrier*
Yorkshire Terrier *Maltese*
Silky Terrier   *Afghan Hound*

      THE BREEDS LISTED ABOVE HAVE their long coats parted in the middle as an element of their fundamental grooming pattern, and we call them the parted-coat breeds. With the Afghan Hound the top-knot depending on individual taste, is parted in the middle.

      All eight breeds are groomed alike regarding body coat. Their headpieces distinguish their grooming. Of the eight breeds, three have their topknots tied up with ribbons, the Shih Tzu, Yorkie and Maltese. Traditionally, the Shih Tzu and Yorkie wear one ribbon, the Maltese two ribbons. The topknots of the Lhasa, Silky, Skye, Tibetan and Afghan are not tied up.

      The pin brush is used on all regularly-groomed parted coats. For coats which have been neglected or not groomed on a regular basis, either the soft wire slicker brush or the Universal brush may have to be used.

      The feet on all eight breeds are trimmed round to give an even, level appearance. The table surface itself is used as a leveller. Foot pads may be either scissored or clipped. For pets, the stomach area may be clipped, and scissors or thinning shears used for trimming excess coat. Only thinning shears should be used on show dogs and then only very sparingly.

      For breeds where pet and show grooming are virtually the same, no separate, special treatment is required.

The Lhasa Apso

Standard Regarding Coat

Coat—Heavy, straight, hard, of good length, very dense, neither woolly nor silky.

Breed Note

The Lhasa Apso's vision is partly obscured by the heavy fall over his eyes, but he is compensated by extremely good hearing, and makes an extraordinary watchdog. The Lhasa Apso originated in Tibet and was a watchdog in the homes and temples of that rugged, mountainous land. In recent years he has steadily gained favor in the United States, and presently ranks twelfth among all breeds.

Grooming Procedure

A Lhasa coat is parted from the tip of the nose to the base of the tail. To make the part, use the end tooth of a comb or a knitting needle. Whatever you use, the parting instrument should be pointed and narrow enough not to catch more than a few hairs at a time. Like every-

thing else, this will take some time to perfect. Spray the coat lightly with a coat dressing, which will help "set" the coat in place, then brush the coat down on both sides of the part.

Probably the most difficult step in grooming the Lhasa or any of the other parted-coat breeds is to make a perfectly straight part down the center of the back. Your position as you make the part is important. Stand squarely *behind* the dog so that you are standing over and behind him. Now lean over with your knitting needle or comb and start making the part, section by section. Starting at the very top of the back, work your way right to the base of the tail. Take your time until you pick up some skill and experience.

The feet are trimmed to give an even, level appearance, the table top being used as the leveller. The legs and feet should look larger than they are because of the profuse coat. The nails should not show, and the foot pads may be either scissored or clipped to remove any excess hair. For pets the stomach area may be clipped.

The only difference in grooming the Lhasa pet or show dog is in the extra care required by the show coat.

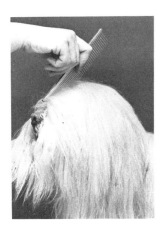

The Lhasa Apso's coat is parted from nose to tail. A knitting needle or the end tooth of a comb is used to make the parting.

A good coat dressing is essential to any grooming for the Lhasa Apso.

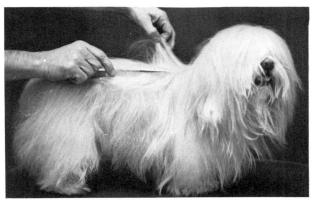

The coat is brushed and combed in layers.

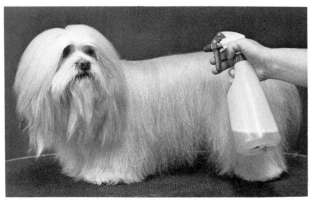

The coat dressing conditions the hair and retards hair loss.

Here the groomer brings the part to the base of the tail.

A side view of the finished Lhasa Apso.

A bird's eye view of a well-executed Part.

The head of a finished Lhasa Apso.

Some owners like to have their Lhasas' topknots caught up in a bow as here.

The Shih Tzu

Standard Regarding Coat

Coat—A luxurious long, dense coat. May be slightly wavy but not curly. Good wooly undercoat. The hair on top of head may be tied up.

Breed Note

The Shih Tzu and the Lhasa Apso are so similar in appearance that even experts may be fooled in distinguishing them—especially poor specimens. Both breeds have similar origins, the Lhasa coming from Tibet, while the Shih Tzu reached its greatest development in China. Today the Shih Tzu is high on the popularity list in the United States.

The Shih Tzu, a member of the Toy group, has a lively and a dignified carriage and is a joy to all around him.

Grooming Procedure

The Shih Tzu is a little lower at the withers and slightly shorter-bodied than the Lhasa Apso, and his coat is a bit softer. Both breeds have almost identical grooming requirements.

When brushing and combing have been completed, the Shih Tzu coat should have a sleek look. The beard comes to a point and a long, luxuriant moustache flows over the beard.

To fashion the Shih Tzu topknot, part the hair from the ear on both sides of the head. Next, gather up in one hand the hair in the middle and slip on a latex band at the base. The band may have to be wrapped around twice to make it secure, but the topknot should not be drawn so tight as to cause the dog discomfort. Finally, a ribbon or barrette may be attached to the latex band, but this point is purely optional.

Before grooming, this Shih Tzu is not very attractive.

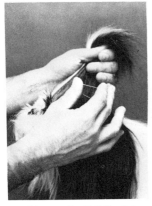

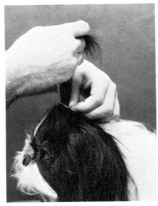

Catching up the Shih Tzu's top-knot with a latex band.

The latex band in proper position.

Most pet owners like a bright colored ribbon bow on their Shih Tzus' topknots.

The finished Shi Tzu.

Headstudy of the finished Shih Tzu.

Some owners prefer their dogs in shorter coat. This pet Shih Tzu was photographed before trimming.

After trimming, the same dog still bears essential breed characteristics, but is easier to look after.

The Yorkshire Terrier

Standard Regarding Coat

Coat—Quality, texture and quantity of coat are of prime importance. Hair is glossy, fine and silky in texture. Coat on the body is moderately long and perfectly straight (not wavy). It may be trimmed to floor length to give ease of movement and a neater appearance, if desired. The fall on the head is long, tied with one bow in center of head or parted in the middle and tied with two bows. Hair on muzzle is very long. Hair should be trimmed short on tips of ears and may be trimmed on feet to give them a neat appearance.

Breed Note

The beauty of the Yorkshire Terrier belies his original purpose—ratting. He has long, silky hair throughout and an outstanding specimen can be spectacular when conditioned and groomed to perfection.

The Yorkie makes a great apartment pet but given the right circumstances will still prove a capable ratter.

The Yorkshire Terrier originated in the Northern English county that gave him his name. For many years he has been a favorite Toy breed in the United States, currently ranking 11th in popularity.

Grooming Procedure

The Yorkie, as he is familiarly known, has a profuse coat of long, silky hair. His body coat is groomed parted down the middle of the back from the occiput to the base of the tail. The topknot, being so profuse, is tied up with one ribbon set in the center of the head. Although the Standard makes it optional to use one or two bows, traditionally only one bow is used on the topknot.

The body coat is long and its entire length may reach to floor level. Coat dressings which help set the part should also enhance the shining, healthy coat.

The top half of the ears are clipped with a #10 blade on both sides. The edges are then scissored to neatness. With thinning shears, scissor around edges of feet to give a cat-like, rounded look.

The Schnauzer Trim in the Yorkshire Terrier

In recent years one pet grooming innovation which has taken hold is the Schnauzer clip in the Yorkshire Terrier. The Schnauzer clip is executed on a Yorkie in the same fashion as on Minature Schnauzers, as described in Part III in the section on Terriers.

One advantage the Yorkie owner has with the

Schnauzer look is that the coat is much easier to maintain. Moreover, it seems to bring out the Terrier nature of the Yorkie even though the Yorkie is officially classified in the Toy group.

The Schnauzer trim makes sense. For the pet owner whose time is limited and who would have no need to maintain a Yorkie in a long, show coat, the Schnauzer trim is the perfect answer. Better a shorter, neat coat than a long, tangled mess.

Under certain circumstances even serious fanciers can find application for the Schnauzer trim. The brood bitch whose showing days are behind her is better off trimmed short for her role as the producer of the next generation. The old, retired show dogs can be comfortable and cute while being spared the long, arduous grooming routine of a full-coated show dog. For many Yorkies and their owners the Schnauzer trim is the smart move in the good looks department.

A Yorkshire Terrier badly in need of a groomer's attention.

The fully groomed, well-kept Yorkshire Terrier is a dog of surpassing beauty.

The part down a Yorkshire's back.

The Schnauzer trim—appealing and practical.

The Silky Terrier

Standard Regarding Coat

Coat—Flat, in texture fine, glossy, silky; on matured specimens the desired length of coat from behind the ears to the set-on of the tail is from five to six inches. On the top of the head the hair is so profuse as to form a topknot, but long hair on face and ears is objectionable. Legs from knee and hock joints to feet should be free from long hair. The hair is parted on the head and down over the back to the root of the tail.

Breed Note

The Silky Terrier was developed by crossing Yorkshire and Australian Terriers. A dog of pronounced terrier character, he has become, over the years, an excellent housepet and watchdog. The Silky's place of origin is Sydney, Australia.

Grooming Procedure

The Silky Terrier is similar to the Yorkshire Terrier in quality of coat and grooming style. The breed name indicates correct coat texture. The parting of the head and body coat is identical to that of the Yorkie, except that the topknot is not tied. The parted hair falls over the sides of the face and combines with the beard. The center part extends from the stop and continues over the middle of the back to the base of the tail. The Silky's body coat, like the Yorkie's, drapes the body like a cloak.

To enhance the characteristic Silky expression, the hairs on the inside corner of the eyes should be plucked or stripped, leaving the eyes fully exposed. The erect ears are carefully trimmed around the edges for a neat, tidy look.

Unlike the Yorkie, the Silky has sparse leg furnishings. From the knee and hock joints to the feet, the legs should be trimmed of any long hair. The paws are trimmed closely to give a cat-like effect.

Grooming the Silky for the Show Ring

Comb the muzzle back, toward the jaw, in the direction of its growth. It seldom needs shortening. However, if it is so long that it forms a "fall" or "goatee," it may be shortened using the same procedure as with the legs; stripping knife or thinning shears. In no instance should the muzzle ever be shaved.

By the way, many dogs are quite sensitive around their "snoots," so be gentle.

The hair above the eyes, toward the top of the head, becomes part of the topknot. However, if it is so excessive in length as to fall forward and cover the eyes, it may be plucked in the same manner as the ears, to a shorter length. A Silky's eyes are dark and piercingly

Like the Yorkshire, the Silky Terrier's part should extend from the nose to the base of the tail and be as straight as possible for its entire length.

The Silky's body outline is greatly enhanced by neatly trimmed legs and feet.

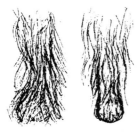

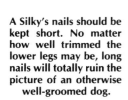

Excess feathering on the feet, up to the first joint, should be carefully removed.

A Silky's nails should be kept short. No matter how well trimmed the lower legs may be, long nails will totally ruin the picture of an otherwise well-groomed dog.

His expression is one of the Silky's chief aspects of breed type. Proper trimming brings this out and enhances this little dog's charm and appeal.

keen in expression—and should always be clearly visible.

Feathers on the feet up to the first joint only should be shortened to about one-quarter to one-half inch (¼″ to ½″) in length, not clipped to the skin. Brush the hair up (opposite direction of growth) and shorten the hair using the stripping comb. Feathers growing on the legs above the first joint should not be removed, as this is part of the body coat. The long hair above the first joint should then be brushed down over the lower leg and checked for length of overhang. In no case should it touch the ground. Before, or after, the feet and lower leg portions have been trimmed, use small blunt-nosed scissors and trim the hairs that extend beyond the outline of the foot. What you want is a tidy appearance and a rounded outline to the foot. Also, with care, you will want to tidy up hairs that grow between the pads.

Long hair on the inside and outside of the ears, extending past the outline and the back of the ears, should be plucked. Plucking is done using your thumb and forefinger. The hair is usually "dead" and breaks off quite easily. The backs of the ears should have a smooth, velvety appearance. A better grip is obtained if you lightly coat your fingers with precipitated chalk. Start when they are puppies, then grooming becomes part of their life. Once again, take your time, plucking only a few hairs at a time.

Clean inside parts of the ear you can see with flexible stick Q-Tips about once a week. This will prevent an accumulation of wax which can irritate the ear. Use caution and don't probe too deeply into the ear.

A "well coated" tail, as called for in the Standard, is one that has sufficient fall to appear balanced. The fall, or feathering, on the tail should be no more than an inch or two, and never shaved or trimmed to less than one and one-half to one inch (1½″ to 1″) in length. Hold the tail horizontally and use the stripping knife or thinning shears to shorten the excess feathering. Having the tail in a horizontal position will give you a better perspective of the actual length of the hair. Take only a little at a time, comb through, and check for proper length and a natural look, rather than a "fresh cut" appearance. Don't get carried away, remember it's to be "well coated."

Courtesy, Silky Terrier Club of America

Judith J. Tillinger

The Skye Terrier

Standard Regarding Coat

Coat—Double. Undercoat short, close, soft, and woolly. Outer coat hard, straight, and flat, 5½ inches long without extra credit granted for greater length. The body coat hangs straight down each side, parting from head to tail. The head hair, which may be shorter and softer, veils forehead and eyes and forms a moderate beard and apron. The long feathering on the ears falls straight down from the tips and outer edges, surrounding the ears like a fringe and outlining their shape. The ends of the hair should mingle with the coat at the sides of the neck.

Breed Note

The Skye Terrier originated in Scotland and was originally a working hunter. Eventually his special beauty made him a favorite of Queen Victoria and members of British nobility. The Skye's coat is so long and thick that it falls to the ground and covers him completely, like a cloak. It is curious that given the Skye's small size and beauty, he is not listed amongst the most popular breeds.

Grooming Procedure

The Skye Terrier's profuse, hard coat is groomed somewhat like the Lhasa Apso's. It can become easily matted if not brushed regularly, so should be kept up on a regular basis. Brushing two or three times a week with a natural bristle brush or a pin brush, making sure to brush down to the skin will keep a Skye Terrier's coat in good shape. Finish off with a wide-tooth comb. Remember that the parting extends from the tip of the nose to the base of the tail.

Grooming for the Show Ring

Good grooming is essential to the beauty and well-being of a Skye Terrier, but the "how-to's" are controversial. When to bathe. How often. What kind of brush to use. All are a matter of personal preference and experience; no two breeders will feel the same way. We believe in bathing—keeping a dog in good coat means a bath at least once a month.

The only tools used are a pin brush with stainless steel pins set in rubber, and a wide-tooth comb. Pull apart mats with your fingers and brush out. Try not to cut with scissors unless the coat is in very bad condition, then cut in the direction of the hair and try separating with your fingers.

When totally dry, part him with the comb from head to toe.

Courtesy, Skye Terrier Club of America

The Tibetan Terrier

Standard Regarding Coat

Coat—Double-coated. The undercoat fine wool, the top coat profuse, fine, but not silky or woolly; long; either straight or waved.

Breed Note

The Tibetan Terrier shares a common origin with the Lhasa Apso and the Tibetan Spaniel, and, like them, is an ancient breed. He is not a Terrier and probably acquired the name in the West as a matter of convenience. Neither is he a hunter or watchdog but exclusively a family pet.

The Tibetan Terrier has a double coat. The undercoat should be fine wool. The top coat should be profuse and fine, but not silky or woolly; and it may be either straight or wavy.

Grooming Procedure

Regular, thorough grooming is the key to a manageable, good-looking coat for both the pet and the show dog.

Tools needed for the routine grooming procedure should include a pin brush, a slicker brush and a metal comb.

Care of the pet Tibetan Terrier should include a daily inspection of the dog and at least a weekly grooming session. Bathing is needed periodically.

The daily inspection should include cleaning the eye corners of any accumulated matter, an examination of the coat for mats and foreign objects, a cursory inspection for injuries or signs of health problems and a check of both ears. Any mat or foreign object found during the daily inspection should be removed by gently separating the snarled hair with the fingers, followed by gentle brushing or combing out of the hair in the mat. The slicker brush, used last, is handy to pick out all the fine undercoat tangled together into small knots in the matted area. Applying corn starch, grooming powder or a spray to the mat may ease removal of the dead coat.

The weekly grooming session should begin like the daily routine, followed by a thorough brushing of the entire coat with a pin brush and an equally thorough combing. Using a slicker brush on the Tibetan pet after brushing and combing will remove any dead coat missed before and will make the next grooming session easier. It should never be necessary to cause the dog pain during grooming if a regular schedule of thorough grooming is maintained. Most Tibetan Terrier coats will do very well with a weekly grooming session, but some dogs may need to be completely groomed more frequently.

Some trimming of the Tibetan Terrier coat may be

necessary at times. Because of the heavy headfall characteristic of the breed, some people thin the "bangs" a bit with thinning shears to help the dog see better. Trimming the hair on the feet may also be necessary occasionally. This should be done whenever the furnishings around the feet become too long; otherwise dogs can trip over their own hair. The foot is trimmed to keep the large, round appearance characteristic of the breed. Thick hair also grows between the pads of the feet. This hair may be cut level with the pad, but should not be removed from between the pads because it, too, is required by the Standard. Trimming is also done around the anus and reproductive organs, but should not be obvious on show dogs.

Most Tibetan Terriers carry long coats throughout their adult lives. Some pet owners, however, prefer to have the coat trimmed occasionally for ease of upkeep. A badly matted Tibetan Terrier must be clipped down almost to the skin to remove the mats with minimal discomfort to the dog. These procedures are best done by an experienced dog groomer.

When the Tibetan Terrier is trimmed or clipped down, the groomer should try to preserve, as much as possible, the unique character of the breed. Therefore, the whole head, including the eyes, should remain covered with hair; the feet should remain covered with hair and looking relatively large; and the entire tail should remain a plume. The length of the hair in these areas may, however, be somewhat shortened cutting to balance with the rest of the coat. The effect should resemble a six-month-old Tibetan Terrier puppy. Extreme trims like Schnauzer or Poodle clips should be avoided.

The show dog needs more careful grooming than the pet, of course. Special care must be taken to remove mats as soon as they develop. The daily inspection for mats is mandatory to keep the coat at its best. All foreign bodies must be removed from the coat during the daily inspection. With practice, mats can be detected by touch before they have actually developed and can be removed at the earliest possible moment to prevent coat damage. A spray or grooming powder should be used when brushing the dog, and care in the use of grooming tools is needed to avoid damaging the coat during grooming.

As with all show dogs, the Tibetan Terrier should be carefully bathed and completely brushed before appearing in the show ring. The correct Tibetan Terrier coat will part naturally as it matures and exhibitors may straighten the part before entering the show ring. Most mature Tibetan Terriers being shown today have parted coats.

Courtesy, Eileen D. Wilk

Mrs. Wilk kindly agreed to write this article on grooming the Tibetan Terrier in the absence of any club-approved material on the subject. She is a successful breeder of Tibetan Terriers, having bred some twenty champions including three Best in Show winners.)

Judith J. Tillinger

The Maltese

Standard Regarding Coat

Coat—The coat is single, that is without undercoat. It hangs long, flat, and silky over the sides of the body almost, if not quite, to the ground. The long head-hair may be tied up in a topknot or it may be left hanging. Any suggestion of kinkiness, curliness, or woolly texture is objectionable.

Breed Note

The Maltese derives his name from the island of Malta, off the coast of Italy. The Maltese is a very ancient breed, and was known in the Mediterranean before the time of Christ. He is a handsome, intelligent dog, always inquisitive, and makes a wonderful pet. He is very popular in the United States, currently ranking 26th in registrations.

Grooming Procedure

In comparing one breed to another, regarding grooming, the Maltese may be compared to the Yorkshire Terrier. Like the Yorkie, the Maltese coat is long, flat and silky. The body coat is parted along the topline from the base of the skull to the base of the tail. The hair on the headpiece should be parted in the middle from the tip of the nose to the base of the skull and the head part should meet the body part.

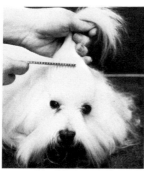

Catching up the head hair is the first step in fashioning the Maltese's double topknot.

The comb is used to divide the untied topknot in two.

Before grooming, this Maltese is just a shaggy little dog.

Each half is doubled over and caught up with a latex band, then dressed with a bright-colored bow.

With grooming comes the wondrous transformation, and the shaggy little dog becomes an elegant toy jewel.

The Maltese's topknot is usually tied up with two ribbons. It is the only breed where this is a standard procedure. This requires a little variation from the one-ribbon topknot. The topknot has already been parted in the middle. Make another part at the corner of the eye on the right side. Gather up a handful of hair and slip a latex band onto the base. Then do the same thing on the left side. The ribbons are then tied around the bands or a barrette may be used in place of the ribbons.

The long, white coat of the Maltese should fall like a silky cloak over the body, covering the legs completely. The legs, similar to the Shih Tzu, should look big because of the abundant hair. The Maltese coat requires constant care, and a more than average bathing schedule may be required to keep the coat spotlessly white. The gleaming, dark eyes and black nose of the Maltese form a stark contrast to the gorgeous white coat.

Judith J. Tillinger

The Afghan Hound

Standard Regarding Coat

Coat—Hindquarters, flanks, ribs, forequarters, and legs well covered with thick, silky hair, very fine in texture; ears and all four feet well feathered; from in front of the shoulders; and also backwards from the shoulders along the saddle from the flanks and the ribs upwards, the hair is short and close, forming a smooth back in mature dogs—this is a traditional characteristic of the Afghan Hound. The Afghan Hound should be shown in its natural state; the coat is not clipped or trimmed; the head is surmounted (in the full sense of the word) with a topknot of long, silky hair—that is also an outstanding characteristic of the Afghan Hound. Showing of short hair on cuffs on either front or back legs is permissible. **Fault:** Lack of shorthaired saddle in mature dogs.

Breed Note

The Afghan Hound originated in Afghanistan and surrounding areas as a first-class hunter. The breed is very ancient and was a favorite of desert and mountain tribesmen. Only during the Twentieth Century did the Afghan become popular in Europe and America. Of regal appearance, the Afghan ranks 40th in total AKC registrations.

Grooming Procedure

Well, you finally bought that aloof, regal, sophisticated-looking, longhaired dog seen with all the best models in all the best magazines. You say he doesn't look much like that now, and the seller told you there would be no problem keeping his long hair "combed" when he got his long hair. Well, even if there are no grooming problems today, tomorrow or even next month, when that bouncing ball of fuzz starts growing and growing and growing, so does his coat. As babies lose baby hair, so puppies lose their puppy coats. Did anyone ever tell you Afghans don't shed? Know why? Because they *mat*. All the hair that falls out falls into the coat below and gets more snarled and tangled all the time. What to do about it? We groom. Don't be fooled—there is no easy, one-step, foolproof method of grooming. To become proficient in grooming, you must study how best to cope with the type of coat on your own dog. This comes with time, practice and experimentation.

If you don't plan to show your dog, you may want to purchase an Oliver Mat and Tangle Splitter, which does exactly what the name indicates. It cuts through a mat and also some of the coat (and sometimes a finger if you don't watch out). It should always be used carefully, and only when *absolutely* necessary.

Now let's groom!! Your dog has some coat, and he's table-trained and agreeable. Start by standing him on the table and using the grooming post. I like to start grooming on the dog's left, or "show," side. Working *up* the side of the front leg, pushing the coat up with one hand, brush the coat out from under your hand. Use your pin brush for an adult coat, a slicker for a puppy coat. After you have done a small section, run your comb through to double check for mats. Listen to the sound of your brush—you'll be able to tell when you hit a mat. When you find that lovely little bunch of tangled hairs, don't be discouraged. Take some long hair clips to hold the upper coat up out of the way. Carefully pull the mat apart with your fingers. A bit of coat spray will help, but never saturate the area. Use the tip of the comb to pick carefully at the mat. If you find some really bad mats, work from the outermost edges, carefully separating the hairs from the rest of the mat. Gently run the slicker or pin brush over the combed-out or pulled-apart area to pick up the loose hairs. Remove the hair clips and continue working all the way up the side of the leg until it is completely groomed and mat-free. Next, move to the front of the leg and work all the way up, and continue with the back of the same leg, following the same procedure. The back leg on the same side comes next. Do the right front and back legs in the same manner, always making sure you are getting right down to the skin. This is an excellent time to check for fleas, ticks and foreign matter.

You may choose to do the ears and topknot either first or last, or you may groom the side of the head which is exposed while the dog is lying on the table. I find that by very carefully picking with the tip of the comb at those ever-present mats behind the ears, I can save more of the coat than I do by trying to brush the mats out. (Get your dog used to wearing a snood to keep his ears out of his mouth and food. A snood can be anything from the top of old pantyhose, cut very long, to one of the more expensive models you can purchase through a pet supply dealer.)

Remember, a happy dog is a clean dog. Grooming helps to keep a dog clean, but a bath will be in order periodically. *Never, never* bathe a matted dog. Use a good dog shampoo, and a creme rinse, if desired. Experiment until you have found which shampoo and which creme rinse are best for your dog's type of coat. Stay away from fads and far-out suggestions, and use only those products which have worked successfully for others. Establish a rapport with your Afghan so that grooming is enjoyable for both of you. Grooming should be a labor of love—not an unpleasant chore.

Courtesy, Finger Lakes Afghan Hound Club
by Carol A. Strong.

An Afghan Hound before being groomed.

The Afghan carries a saddle of smooth hair down the back. This must always be completely natural, never cut in or simulated with thinning shears or stripping knife.

Fully groomed, the Afghan Hound is one of the most spectacular beauties in the entire dog world.

74

LONGHAIRED BREEDS

Most longhaired breeds' coats are not parted. But the basics or fundamentals of grooming all longhaired breeds remain the same. A good rule of thumb to follow when in doubt about the type of brush for a particular coat is to use the pin brush or the natural bristle brush on a non-matted or show coat. For pet grooming, the soft wire slicker or the Universal brush, depending on condition of coat is the tool of choice. To a large degree, common sense and experience dictate how much can be done with a particular coat.

It should be stressed again, that wherever the instruction includes the techniques of stripping and plucking, this is usually intended for dogs which are being shown. For pet owners, clipping is almost always used in place of stripping and plucking.

In this section on grooming longhaired breeds, the breeds are presented alphabetically within their AKC variety groups. This same arrangement is followed for shorthaired breeds and finally for smooth breeds.

The classifications herein were made with the dog groomer in mind and the type and amount of work required on each breed. So, these classifications will not always accord with traditional categories in which breeds are usually considered.

Longhaired Sporting Dogs

The English Setter

Standard Regarding Coat

Coat—Coat should be flat and of good length, without curl; not soft or woolly. The feather on the legs should be moderately thin and regular.

Breed Note

The English Setter is among the most beautiful and gentle-natured of all dogs. Developed in England several centuries ago to hunt upland birds, the modern English Setter embraces two distinctly different types—one for bench and one for field. The Llewelin, or field type, is a favorite breed at pointing dog trials while the Laverack is a much admired companion and show dog. The English Setter is as much esteemed for his wonderful temperament as for his beauty and makes a particularly good companion for small children.

Grooming Procedure

Good trimming for any dog makes the most of its best and the least of its worst. But no trimming, however skillful, will improve any dog beyond its individual endowments. Furthermore, trimming alone is only the first step. Top condition is only achieved through long hours of careful grooming.

Start trimming under the neck using an Oster clipper with a #7 blade. Clip to about the breastbone and as far

as the ridge of hair found on each side of the neck. Now clip excess hair off sides of the neck, running the clipper with the lie of the hair. Bring the clippers right to the base of the ear to remove the hair that would otherwise prevent the ears from lying flat.

The clippers should not be used on the back of the neck. This hair is longer and is trimmed by hand, using a Duplex Dresser.

Use clippers on the cheeks and under the eyes, removing as much hair as possible. Blending into the longer hair left on the adjacent areas will come later.

When using the clippers on the underside of the ear, be especially careful not to accidentally cut into the double fold. If this double fold (found on the underside of the ear at the outside edge) is cut, it bleeds profusely and a coagulant is required to stem the flow. It is best to take the time and care to avoid accidents as a dog, so injured once, is likely to be permanently difficult about having the ears approached with clippers again.

Clip underside of each ear, going against the lie of the hair. Some of the coat here can be clipped, but some must be trimmed with sharp, curved-blade scissors.

The English Setter's ear set will be greatly enhanced by careful trimming at the junction of ear and skull. To achieve a pleasing blending, start with the clipper working against the grain from a quarter way down the ear almost to where it joins the skull. Pull the clipper back at this point to avoid any harsh, abrupt lines.

In trimming ears, be sure to leave the hair on the front edges intact. This hair, working with the eyes, gives the gentle expression so important to the breed.

Now, using a stripping knife, smooth out hair on the skull from above the eyes to past the occiput. Do this in overlapping swaths, taking only a small amount of hair each time. This will give a smoother, finished look.

In smoothing the backskull, you will return to the junction of head and ear. This is the point at which the stripped area is usually blended into the dog's clipped parts. Again, remove only a few hairs each time for a more satisfactory end result.

Trimming the neck and shoulder is very important as, properly done, it greatly enhances the overall picture the dog makes. Poorly done, it spoils the impression of a smooth, flowing harmony of parts the English Setter should always mirror.

Many English Setters will grow unruly, difficult-to-groom hair on the dividing line between the chest and the body. A great deal of patient hand stripping as well as brush and comb work will be needed for this hair to lie in the desirable, smooth fashion.

On the shoulders themselves, hair should lie smoothly to make this feature sleek and fine. In grooming, remove excess hair between withers and shoulders with a Duplex Dresser or a stripping knife. Trim with the lie of the coat as this will heighten the impression of more sloping shoulders. After excess hair is removed go over the dog's shoulders sparingly with thinning shears and follow with the judicious application of a stripping knife.

Proceed carefully in the area between shoulder and rib cage as taking out too much will make a dog appear out at the elbow. Cut a few hairs, stop, observe and repeat this procedure as indicated. If you can work at training the hair over a period of several days or longer to lie as desired, the results will be most gratifying. Otherwise you will probably need to remove more hair.

English Setters often grow considerable amounts of excess hair on the hindquarters. These curls are best removed with the Duplex Dresser, going with the lie of the coat. As with other body areas, it is best to remove only a small amount of hair on the quarters each time.

Next remove unwanted hair from the rear and under the tail to the upper thigh with the Duplex Dresser. This important part of the grooming, properly executed, will preclude a ''trouser'' effect. Then scissor excess around anus for the sake of hygiene and to enhance correct tail carriage.

What is done with the tail will greatly influence the entire picture. If an English Setter is perfectly trimmed but the tail is unkempt or untouched, the entire effect fails utterly. Great care should be taken to achieve the typical ''flag'' effect associated with all setter breeds.

Start by thinning the hair with the Duplex Dresser to give a graceful taper from root to tip. Be sure to avoid any suggestion of bushiness with the tail coat. In order to achieve the typical, triangular shape, some hair is removed from its longest point back to the anus.

Trim all but ½" of hair extending past the tail tip. That little fringe you leave protects the tail tip from injury when the dog beats his tail enthusiastically or travels through any thorny cover. All hair growing on the underside of the tail is now trimmed to the triangular shape required. Both top and undersides of the tail are trimmed with scissors, but following initial shaping, the tail is trimmed with a stripping knife. This is also the right time to trim the hair between the dog's toes. Some prefer to use curved scissors for this, but whatever tool is used, great care should be taken to avoid cutting into the pads or the webbing between them. Clean out enough hair to avoid discomfort and potential infection to the dog and trim the outside of each foot to neat roundness.

A well-groomed English Setter will also not show any whiskers on muzzle, cheeks and eyebrows. Some veteran groomers will use an ordinary safety razor to get whiskers off while others prefer curved scissors or even clippers for this work. It's mostly a matter of personal preference.

After being roughed out, an English Setter is bathed, blanketed and crated. Bathing follows the same plan described in the Fundamentals of Grooming except for blanketing. The process of blanketing entails wrapping a large towel around the dog's body after bathing and drying to make the coat lie flat. This is most often used with setters and spaniels, but is also occasionally used in hardcoated terriers.

The towel is secured to the dog's body with large safety or blanket pins secured at the chest and under the loin. A dog is usually blanketed before its coat has dried completely and the drying process continues naturally while the blanketed dog is crated. Show dogs should always be bathed, and blanketed the night before a show.

The natural color of an English Setter's coat will be altered somewhat by trimming, but the normal color will be restored by new coat growth in two to three weeks. In this connection, timing the coat is particularly important for show dogs. Several trimming sessions may be needed for some animals. The pet or the field dog however, can be well served by an ''all at once'' grooming.

Trimming an English Setter is really not as tedious as it may sound. Once a dog is in trim, weekly sessions at home are sufficient to keep a dog in good shape. Puppies should be familiar with the grooming routine by three months old. In this way, it is easier to accustom a pup to unfamiliar actions and strange sounds like the buzz of the clippers and the hum of the dryer than when the dog is older.

Judith J. Tillinger

The Gordon Setter

Standard Regarding Coat

Coat—Should be soft and shining, straight or slightly waved, but not curly, with long hair on ears, under stomach and on chest, on back of the fore and hind legs, and on the tail.

Breed Note

The Gordon Setter, from Scotland is the ideal personal shooting dog. He differs from the English and Irish Setters in the color of his coat, which is black with mahogany-colored markings and also in his more robust body and shorter, silky, wavy hair. The Gordon, like the other Setters, is both a good hunting dog and an enjoyable housepet.

Grooming Procedure

The purpose of trimming any dog is to make it resemble as closely as possible the Standard of its breed. For instance, if a particular Gordon has a large head and light body, it would be best to trim the head closely and leave the body coat thick. On the other hand, a dog with a small lightboned head would be trimmed more closely on the body and not as fine on the head. These are extreme examples, just chosen to give the idea behind the suggestions which follow. The end result of the advice is to enable you to trim your dog so it presents the appearance of a well-balanced Gordon type.

In order to do a good trimming job, the dog must be accustomed to the procedure and stand reasonably still while you are working on him. So, it is important to start with the puppy, beginning as early as three months of age. Place the puppy on a slip-proof table or crate top. It is not advisable to use a grooming arm on a restless animal. Such a one may slip off the table and either break its neck or hang itself, even though you are right there.

Using a #7 blade in the Oster electric clipper, begin at the chin and run the clippers down under the throat to a point about two inches above the breast bone. (If you put your two thumbs on the point of the shoulder blades and bring your hands together till they meet on the dog's throat, where they touch is the point to mark end of trimming.) Then, working back, clean out hair around and under the ears. For the sides and top of the neck, start clippers directly behind the occiput and bring back in one continual sweep, in a slanting line down the neck and across the shoulder to the back of the shoulder blade. If there are any clipper marks on the shoulder or neck after this, they should be removed with thinning shears. Avoid pushing in with the clippers where the neck joins the body as that gives a "bottle-brush" appearance. Do not use the clippers at all on the very top of the neck. Clean entire face with a #10 blade. This is the best way to remove the whiskers which should be taken off to give a clean outline to the jaw. Go over the sides of the head also and slightly on the top, to give a "nicely rounded skull."

As you become more proficient with the clippers and your dog is completely used to the trimming procedure, you can use a #15 blade and trim on top of the muzzle and make a "clearly indicated stop" and at the back of the occiput to make the neck "arched to the head." Ears are trimmed with the #10 blade, one-third of the way down and blended into the longer hair. The above treatment is to make the dog conform to the sections of the Standard which refer to the head as "lean and the cheek narrow" . . . "lip-line shows a well defined square contour" . . . "ears set low on the head, well-folded and carried close to the head" . . . "neck long, lean, arched to the head, and without throatiness" and shoulders "when viewed from behind, the neck appears to fit into the shoulders in smooth, flat, lines that gradually widen from neck to shoulders."

Never stop a trim abruptly—always finish off using the coarser blade or thinning shears to blend into the longer hair. Thinning shears are always used in combination with a comb. Holding thinning shears pointing in the direction of the hair, thin and comb out hair as you go along. It is better for beginners to use #10 and #5 blades which do not cut too closely and advance to the #15 and #7 blades as they become more proficient.

Feet should be trimmed with the dog standing up. Lift one foot at a time and trim hair on bottom of feet even with the pads. Do not take out any hair between the toes, the feet should be "well-arched with plenty of hair between." Using regular barber's shears, trim to achieve a rounded, high-appearing foot "cat-like in shape." Working with shears pointed toward the ground at a slight angle, trim off excess rough hair around foot. Nails should be trimmed so that they clear the floor at least. It may be necessary to do a little at a time several times to get the desired length if the nails have been allowed to grow. The back feet are done the same and the hair on the back of the hock is combed down, and holding scissors perpendicular to the floor, make a nicely rounded shape to the hock to fit the description "short, strong hock."

Courtesy, The Gordon Setter Club of America
by Fred Itzenplitz

Judith J. Tillinger

The Irish Setter

Standard Regarding Coat

Coat—Short and fine on head, forelegs and tips of ears; on all other parts, of moderate length and flat. Feathering long and silky on ears; on back of forelegs and thighs long and fine, with a pleasing fringe of hair on belly and brisket extending onto the chest. Feet well feathered between the toes. Fringe on tail moderately long and tapering. All coat and feathering as straight and free as possible from curl or wave.

Breed Note

The Irish Setter became a popular favorite in the United States soon after being introduced here. He ranks 10th in AKC registrations at this writing.

The Irish Setter is a dog of great beauty and grace. He is also endowed with a winning personality and unwavering loyalty to home and family. The breed is very successful in the show ring and is steadily gaining as an accomplished gun dog.

Grooming Procedure

The following has been prepared by the Irish Setter Club of America to assist the fancy in proper grooming of the Irish Setter. To some, grooming is considered, fundamentally, a requisite for appearance in the show ring. To others grooming is required maintenance for making the dog a "livable" housepet. In either case, good grooming is essential, and in many circumstances the same procedures apply to both the show dog and the housepet.

The Neck—With an Oster electric clipper (fitted with a #7 blade) and held like a pencil, start at the chin and cut a swath down the center of the neck to just above the breast bone (how far down you go depends on how long you wish the neck to appear). Always cut with the lay of the the hair. Using a line along the lower edge of the jaw, underside of the ear, the cowlick line where the hair changes direction on the side of the neck, and the center of the neck, trim all hair evenly. A technique recommended only in isolated instances where a dog with very heavy undercoat needs special attention, includes clipping beyond the cowlick line. This trimming technique helps achieve a smooth, well-defined, well-balanced neck, and helps eliminate the problem area where the humerus joins the scapula. At that joint, excess hair may need to be removed, and the area itself defined and shaped to emphasize as much angulation as possible. This technique is very difficult to do well, and should be used only in extreme circumstances by experienced groomers. It is essential to know what effect is desired when trimming any dog. Stand back and examine the work often. Removal of too much coat is as objectionable as failure to remove enough.

When clipper work is complete, use thinning shears to blend from the short hair into the long. Never cut across the grain of the hair. Work into the direction of growth or with the grain. Basically, try to layer the hair evenly and gradually so that there is a smooth transition from the 2″ to 3″ hair on the back of the neck to the ⅛″ clippered hair on the front of the neck. All this must be accomplished within a space of from ½″ at the ear to approximately 4″ at the shoulder. In a well-groomed dog there should be no trace of a ''break'' between the longest and shortest hair. Mastery of the thinning shears is indispensable here, but part of the trick is trimming ahead of time enough so discoloration, which occurs in dogs with light undercoats, will have time to grow out or darken. Some dogs take longer to grow out than others. Others have such dark, even coloration that no lightening occurs at all. A light undercoat which does not darken as it grows in can be helped by more frequent trimming. The more frequently the hair is clipped with the grain, the darker it will become. Remember, the goal is the dog's appearance at the show. Each dog is different, and a trimming schedule should be established for him so that the dog is always at his peak when shown. What he looks like a week before or the day after is immaterial. It is possible to trim an Irish Setter so that he does not look trimmed at all, yet every feature has been enhanced to its maximum.

The Ears—The ear is, perhaps, less difficult to trim than the neck and shoulders. Again, clipping, using a #10 blade, should be done in the direction of hair growth. Holding the ear leather near the bottom, stretch it. Starting just below the highest extremity of the cartilage area, clip downward approximately one-third the total length of the ear leather. Note that the ear has a fold along the front edge. Do not trim that. Trim into the underside of the fold only. Be very careful not to run up onto the head itself or the side of the neck with the clippers.

Turn the ear over and remove all the hair from the inner surface, including the burr at the front. Cutting here can be against the grain so as to remove as much as possible. Make sure when finished that all long hair under the ear, as far down as the cut on the top of the ear, has been removed. Now, very carefully, trim the front edge of the upper ear until reaching the fold area. Clipper only a narrow triangle here. Using the same technique as on the neck, blend the short hair into the long hair of the head and neck using the thinning scissors. Also blend around the jaw, and shape the face and skull as necessary.

Feet—The feet are shaped by using thinning scissors to remove excess feathering around the toes. Do not remove the hair from between the toes themselves. Trim around the pads with barber scissors and cut the excess hair on the bottom of the feet flush with the pads. Clippers may be used for this task if desired, but avoid cutting hair from between the pads.

Toe nails should be kept short. Long nails can cause the feet to spread and, if left unattended too long, can break the pasterns. Whether the nails are cut, filed, or ground, it is preferable to angle the nail up and back. The bottom of the nail will take care of itself. If properly attended, the nails can be worked shorter and shorter without cutting the quick. Trim, file, or grind around the quick, leaving it slightly exposed. It will gradually recede by itself if the task is repeated on a weekly basis.

Tail—The tail may be trimmed to show a blunt, triangular appearance, and to remove excess hair from the end to bring it to proper length to balance the rest of the dog. To trim the end of the tail, grasp the hair near the end of the tail by wrapping the hand around it. Then gently pull it all toward the end. When the desired length to be cut protrudes from the hand, cut the hair at ninety degrees to the tail with thinning shears. The result will be a·nicely tapered and pointed tail.

Whiskers—Using the curved-blade scissors, remove all whiskers as close to the skin as possible. The best way to do this is to place the fingers inside the flew and push the individual whisker out. Then cut.

Finishing Touches—Some thinning may improve the topline of a dog that is high in the rear if the work is done in the hip area. But don't expect miracles. The back of the hock joint should be thinned to eliminate any bushiness, but should not look scissored.

The top of the head can be effectively shaped by using thinning shears, cutting into or with the grain, or by using stripping combs or a Duplex Dresser. Do not use clipper on either the top of the head or the top of the neck. If additional attention to the shoulder is needed, skillful use of the thinning shears can effect false highlights and shadows to give the illusion of improved shoulder angulation.

Summary—Remember that each dog is different. His conformation and coat quality are different from that of other dogs. Some products work well on some dogs, and cause problems on others. Experimentation may be necessary on a given dog, and so it is important to start well ahead of time to get him ready for the show ring. Finally, the adage that what appears on the outside of a dog is more often than not the reflection of what went into him is worth remembering. Grooming a well-conditioned dog is always easier than grooming a poorly conditioned specimen.

Courtesy, The Irish Setter Club of America

Judith J. Tillinger

The American Water Spaniel

Standard Regarding Coat

Coat—The coat should be closely curled or have marcel effect and should be of sufficient density to be of protection against weather, water or punishing cover, yet not coarse. Legs should have medium short, curly feather. Faults—Coat too straight, soft, fine or tightly kinked.

Breed Note

The American Water Spaniel is one of the few breeds developed in the United States. He is particularly favored by sportsmen in the Midwest. Like his cousin, the Irish Water Spaniel, he is a great duck retriever but is also excellent for use on upland birds. Like all the Spaniels he is a good watchdog and family pet.

Grooming Procedure

Since the American Water Spaniel closely resembles the Irish Water Spaniel, particularly in coat, the reader is referred to the section on the Irish Water Spaniel for appropriate grooming instructions.

Judith J. Tillinger

The Clumber Spaniel

Standard Regarding Coat

Coat and Feathers—Coat silky and straight, not too long, extremely dense; feather long and abundant.

Breed Note

The Clumber Spaniel was named for Clumber Park, the Estate of the Duke of Newcastle and was developed from an older French strain. Possessed of tremendous dignity, the Clumber is a rather slow-moving gun dog. While this last has not helped his popularity in America, he would be a wise choice for an older gunner.

Grooming Procedure

The Clumber Spaniel is one of those borderline breeds which did not easily fit into the longhaired category. His coat, while extremely dense, is not too long. With his long, low body, he differs considerably from most other Spaniels. But his grooming is fundamentally the same. Like the Springer, the head area is smoothed out, the body lines are evened out, the legs are scissored clean, the feet are cleaned out and tightened up. The Clumber is one of those Spaniels where less trimming is called for rather than more.

Judith J. Tillinger

The Brittany Spaniel

Standard Regarding Coat

Coat—Dense, flat or wavy, never curly. Texture neither wiry nor silky. The ears should carry little fringe. The front and hindlegs should have some feathering, but too little is definitely preferable to too much. Dogs with long or profuse feathering or furnishings shall be so severly penalized as to effectively eliminate them from competition.

Breed Note

The Brittany Spaniel is the only AKC-recognized spaniel breed that points game. He is equally at home as a house pet or hunting dog. One peculiarity of the Brittany is that he is born with a very short tail or no tail at all. The "Brit" is a great favorite with hunters for his great ability afield, convenient size and pleasant personality.

Grooming Procedure

While many of the more popular Spaniel breeds appear very glamorous at the present time, the Brittany should retain the working hunter look that has always been his legacy.

The Brittany should be groomed to show his structure to best advantage and minimize his weak points as much as possible. Dogs that will be shown should be trimmed with thinning shears rather than clippers. The thinning shears method is much slower, but the results are more satisfying and the correct coat texture is not sacrificed for speed in preparing a dog. Once the use of thinning shears is mastered, your results can be as clean as with clippers and more natural-looking.

On the head, snip off the heavy whiskers with scissors and blend the hair at the tops of the ears where they join the skull. Use your thinning shears to smooth and blend the coat on neck and shoulder. The hair on the underside of the neck to the breastbone should be brought down closer than on the back of the neck.

From the shoulders, the hair should be blended into the body coat without any abrupt transition and on the tail a little may be left to give it a merry air in the field or the ring.

The Standard dictates that feather on the backs of the front and rear legs should be minimal, so if you have a dog with very heavy furnishings, it is wise to trim these back. The feet must also come in for a share of attention. Scissor any excess hair around each foot and between each toe pad. A Brittany with unkempt feet is particularly unsightly.

A steel comb, natural bristle brush and a hound glove will handle most of a Brittany's grooming requirements. There are many models of all these available. Which you like best is a matter of personal choice. The important consideration is that the dog looks well.

If a bath is required for a show, it should be given at least two days in advance and it is best to pin a large towel on the dog while it is drying. The towel is pinned with large safety or blanket pins at the chest and loin. Blanketing helps the coat remain properly flat after the bath.

Some who show their dogs like to use a little whitener on the day of the show to enhance their dogs' appearance. This works well but should be thoroughly removed before the dog enters the ring or it may be excused. A liquid coat dressing sprayed onto the hair as a final touch further enhances a beautiful coat that should come from excellent, hard condition, and overall good health.

Standard Regarding Coat

Coat—On the head, short and fine; on the body, medium length with enough undercoating to give protection. The ears, chest, abdomen and legs are well feathered, but not so excessively as to hide the Cocker Spaniel's true lines and movement or affect his appearance and function as a sporting dog. The *texture* is most important. The coat is silky, flat or slightly wavy, and of a texture which permits easy care. Excessive or curly or cottony textured coat is to be penalized.

Breed Note

The Cocker Spaniel, in his American development derives from the English Cocker Spaniel, but he has been bred smaller and with a fuller, more beautiful coat. When properly groomed, the beauty of his body coat and long ear furnishings can be spectacular. The American Cocker's sweet, happy disposition, good looks and convenient size make him an ideal housepet, which explains why he is by far one of the most popular of all breeds in the United States.

Grooming Procedure

The main difference between grooming the pet Cocker Spaniel and grooming the show dog is that clippers are used on the pet while thinning shears are used on the show Cocker.

The Cocker Spaniel

The pet trimming of the American Cocker Spaniel proceeds as follows:

Body—Using a #7 blade, clip down the backbone from the base of the skull to the base of the tail. Then clip both sides of the body going down to the shoulder joint in the forequarters and down to the thigh in the hindquarters. Overlap your strokes to make sure no ridges or clipper marks show.

Tail—Clip the tail with the same #7 blade. Always clip from base of tail to tip (in the direction of coat growth) tapering toward tip.

Head, Ears and Throat—Switch to a #10 blade for the head and clip with the grain or lie of the coat. Clip from the midbrow (leaving a small crown just above the eyebrows) to the base of the skull. Then with parallel strokes clip the cheeks, the muzzle under the jaw and under the throat. Clip the front and back of the ears about one third of the way down. The most comfortable way to do this is to lay the ear furnishings in the palm of your hand and clip the front. Then turn the ear over and clip the other side. The ear furnishings should be long and abundant. After clipping the throat, clip a U-shape in front of the chest going down to the breastbone. Do not clip any further down and above all avoid clipping into the legs.

Shaping With Thinning Shears—Shaping the body into the furnishings of the apron and skirt is best done with thinning shears. Starting with the crown on the brow, blend the crown into the clipped area of the skull. Then shape the clipped portion of the body into the apron

The Cocker Spaniel before grooming.

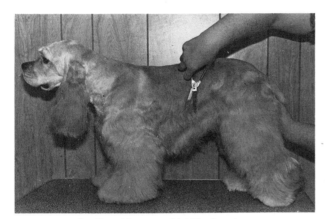

Blending side coat with thinning shears.

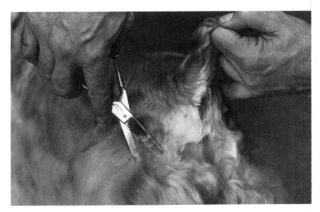

Blending short to long coat at hindquarters.

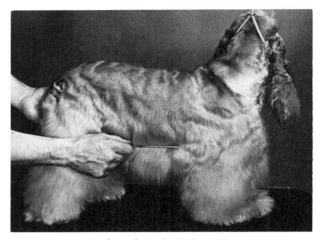

Combing through the furnishings.

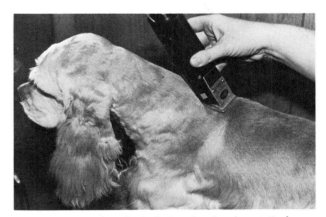

Clippers are used on the body for trimming the pet Cocker.

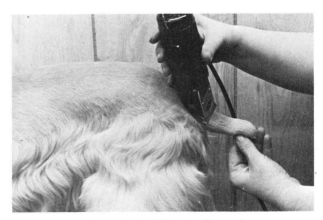

The Cocker's tail is also clippered.

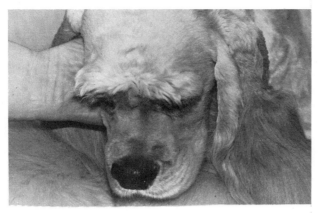

If left untrimmed, the Cocker's skull becomes very overgrown and even develops heavy eyebrows.

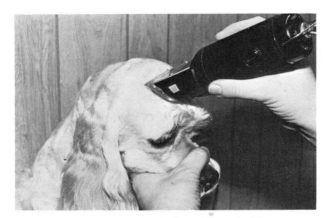

The skull is clipped with show dogs and with pets.

Clipping the top part of the ear makes it appear lower set.

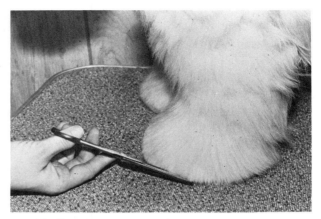

With all Cockers, the feet must be trimmed to roundness.

The finished pet Cocker Spaniel.

Pet Trimming for the Cocker Spaniel.

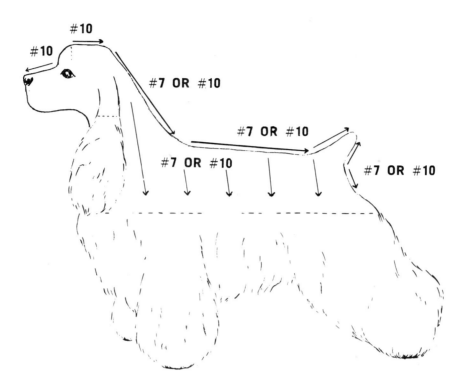

on the chest and the back portion into the skirt and the rump into the hindquarters. The objective is to blend the body into the skirt and legs so that no uneven lines of separation or ridges are visible.

Legs and Feet—The legs should be shaped with thinning shears blending from the body so that they appear full and abundant, but trim. Follow around the contour of the leg eliminating all straggly hairs. The apron should resemble a perfect arch when viewed from the rear.

Scissor the feet around in a tight circle using the table top as a leveller. The nails should not be exposed. Then scissor any excess hair from the pads.

Skirt—The skirt should fall as naturally as possible. All that should be done is a little trimming if this coat is too profuse and the shaping and blending from the body.

Grooming the Cocker Spaniel for Show

The fundamental difference between trimming the Cocker Spaniel for show and pet trimming is in the use of thinning shears for the entire body including legs and tail. The only areas clippers are used in the show trim are the head, ears and throat, which are clipped as already described.

Thinning shears are used exactly like barber shears. They do cut differently and it is usually necessary to get used to their different "feel".

The thinning shears should follow the same path for the show trim as the clippers did for the pet trim. From the base of the skull to the base of the tail, the neck, shoulders and hips, hindquarters and legs. Thin the tail in a tapering effect from the base to the tip and trim the rectal area as closely as possible.

Proficiency in using thinning shears may take some time to develop; perfection doesn't come overnight. As with any skill, common sense, patience and practice usually brings the desired skill. Thinning the coat reduces bulkiness and pleasingly blends the areas of longer and shorter hair. The overall effect in a properly executed show trim will show smooth transition from shortest to longest hair throughout.

Grooming the Cocker Spaniel, for pet or show, as described herein, is the basic spaniel trim. All spaniel trimming may be said to conform to this basic pattern.

Judith J. Tillinger

The English Cocker Spaniel

Standard Regarding Coat

Coat—On head, short and fine; on body, flat or slightly wavy and silky in texture. Should be medium length with enough undercoating to give protection. The English Cocker should be well feathered but no so profusely as to hide the true lines or interfere with his field work. **Faults**—Lack of coat; too soft, curly or wiry. Excessive trimming to change the appearance and coat should be discouraged.

Breed Note

The English Cocker Spaniel is larger and higher on leg than his American counterpart. He carries much less coat and has a longer, narrower head. An excellent housepet, he is greatly admired as a show dog and first-class shooting companion.

Grooming Procedure

Pet grooming the English Cocker Spaniel is very similar to pet grooming the English Springer. The main difference between the two breeds' grooming concerns the English Cocker's generally more abundant feathering.

Clipping the English Cocker's body is done with a #7 blade in precisely the same way the American Cocker is trimmed. Likewise with the head where a #10 blade is used. Ears and throat use the same #10 blade in the same way.

The legs can be left natural with little or no trimming since the furnishings tend to be sparse. Thinning shears may be used just for evenness and uniformity. The paws should be trimmed for a tight, tidy look, with the nails showing slightly. The English Cocker's tail is trimmed from base to tip evenly all around and should be tapered to conform to its natural contour.

Grooming The English Cocker Spaniel For Show

Though the following material primarily concerns show trims, it is just as good for a so-called "pet trim." The main point is that English Cockers especially dark roans and blacks, often grow as much coat as an American Cocker. Notwithstanding, they should NOT be trimmed like American Cockers with all the coat hanging off the legs. There are many English Cockers with natural coats that do not grow hair on the front of the forelegs. In spite of comparisons, an English Cocker is trimmed more like a Springer than an American Cocker.

Coat color can make quite a difference—what one can do with a black or dark roan the day before a show, one cannot pull off with reds, orange roans or other light colors. Of course, this doesn't matter to the pet groomer, but it certainly makes a difference in a show trim.

As far as using clippers on an English Cocker's back—it's a cardinal crime of course to purists, but fanciers indulge even so. An Oster clipper with a #7 blade does about the best job without being too drastic, but a finer blade is necessary for a dog with a skin problem that needs special help.

A #7 blade is also good for the fronts of the forelegs on very heavy-coated dogs, even though the hair will tend to grow back curly ever after! Some English Cockers can be clipped on the back and others need never be touched. It's all a matter of the coat texture.

Courtesy, The English Cocker Spaniel Club of America
by Kate Romanski

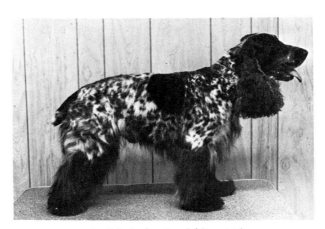

English Cocker Spaniel in pet trim.

Judith J. Tillinger

The English Springer Spaniel

Standard Regarding Coat

Coat—On ears, chest, legs and belly the Springer is nicely furnished with a fringe of feathering of moderate length and heaviness. On head, front of forelegs and below hocks on front of hindlegs the hair is short and fine. The body coat is flat or wavy, of medium length, sufficiently dense to be waterproof, weatherproof and thornproof. The texture fine, and the hair should have the clean, glossy, live appearance indicative of good health. It is legitimate to trim about head, feet, ears; to remove dead hair; to thin and shorten excess feathering particularly from the hocks to the feet and elsewhere as required to give a smart, clean appearance. **To be penalized:** Rough curly coat. Overtrimming, especially of the body coat. Any chopped, barbered or artificial effect. Excessive feathering that destroys the clean outline desirable in a sporting dog.

Breed Note

The English Springer Spaniel is a dog of numerous assets. Developed to hunt or "spring" upland game, he is a modern specialist on the wily ringneck pheasant. His abundant good looks have earned him a high place in the show ring and as a family pet. In this department he scores also on his steady temperament and easy-to-live-with size.

Grooming Procedure

The English Springer is groomed very like the English Cocker. But the main point to stress in grooming the Springer is the importance of the "natural" look. The tendency should be toward less trimming rather than more. The trimming which is done (mostly with thinning shears) should be more in the nature of tidying up rather than overtrimming. Smooth out the head hair, even out the body lines, trim the legs neatly, tighten up the feet, and generally follow procedures as detailed for English Cockers.

One important area to trim is the back of the hocks, which should be free of long hairs.

The Irish Water Spaniel

Standard Regarding Coat

Coat—Proper coat is of vital importance. The neck back and sides should be densely covered with tight, crisp ringlets entirely free from wooliness. Underneath the ribs the hair should be longer. The hair on lower throat should be short. The forelegs should be covered all around with abundant hair falling in curls or waves, but shorter in front than behind. The hind legs should also be abundantly covered by hair falling in curls or waves, but the hair should be short on the front of the legs below the hocks.

Breed Note

The Irish Water Spaniel is the tallest member of the Spaniel family and is, in reality, an excellent retriever. He is especiallly suited for hunting water fowl, and was a favorite with "market" hunters before the turn of the century. A very ancient breed, the Irish Water Spaniel has been mentioned in Irish records and literature for centuries.

Grooming Procedure

A happy, healthy, well-groomed Irish Water Spaniel is one of the handsomest of dogs. The information that follows will help you keep his beautiful, double coat in top shape. There is nothing difficult about this if you follow a few simple steps.

Start by giving the coat a good brushing with a coarse brush. A nautral bristle scrub brush removes much of the top dirt. Follow the brushing by going through the whole coat with a wide-tooth comb. If you come across a mat, try to break it apart gently with your fingers and comb it out. A mat is a combination of dead hair and dirt. There are several ways to get at mats which do not come out easily. You can use the mat separator, which is a wooden paddle with rows of nails. It is used as a rake and will often pull the mat apart. You can also slip the lower blade of scissors through the mat and, pushing outward, force the mat apart. A mat splitter is a special tool that works basically the same way. And the latest weapon in the war against mats, the Oster mat comb, is described in an earlier chapter. Liquid detanglers are widely used preparations made to facilitate mat removal. A little vinegar worked into it can also soften a mat. Never try to cut a mat out. This leaves a hole in the coat which is hard to hide.

After you have combed through the coat and gotten rid of any mats, take the slicker brush, and holding the dog's hair down lightly, brush against the fall of the hair. Start at the back of the topknot, holding the topknot forward, flat to the head. Brush lightly toward the rear of the dog, catching a bit of the topknot with each stroke. Do the same to the ears, brushing against the fall of the hair. Get right down to the skin but be gentle. Now brush the ears straight down again. See how much longer it makes them look. This little trick can be useful when getting a dog ready for the show ring. Brush the topknot forward again.

When you are sure all the dead hair is out of the coat, you are ready to use the scissors. Hold them point down when cutting. This minimizes the danger of scissor marks.

To finish the face, trim the coarse whiskers off the muzzle and also any fuzz. This will give the face a cleaner look. Be careful not to touch the head or sideburns, which are a characteristic of the breed. Many now trim this off to make a cleaner neck. The beard is not mentioned in the Standard. There is very little to do on the face, but a bit here and there can make a great difference.

Put the dog's foot flat on the table. Hold the scissors flat against the foot as if you were using it for a pattern and cut around it. Hold the leg and shake it to fluff out the hair of the foot. Hold the scissors point down and cut straight down. You are trying to make the foot look like a powder puff. You can stay a bit away from the foot so as not to make it look too small and show the nails too much, but this is the general idea. Put the foot down on the table, slant the lower blade inward and trim a bit so that the foot looks as if it were good and tight and the dog is up on his toes. The hair between the pads should be trimmed close.

To shape the body, trim off sunburned or frizzy ends, making the coat even. Trim flat on the sides but round out the rear. In front of the hind legs, in that hollow, trim a bit shorter. This gives the body a bit more shape. If your dog is a little heavy, take more off the sides. If a little too high in the rear (our breed has an even or slightly elevated topline) trim a little closer there. Neck a little thick? Take off more there. You get the idea. Stand back and look at your dog and then look at the accompanying drawing. Go slowly—you can't glue the hair back on.

Now you have the head, feet, top and sides of the body done. Look at the legs. Stand at the side of the dog. Trim the coat on the back of the front legs so that the hair is even. Keep a full leg coat but blend it into the body. Is there a thick bunch of hair at the elbow? Get in there with the thinning shears and take a couple of cuts. Comb. Does it look right or does it need more? One or two more cuts, then comb and look. Trim the rest of the leg.

Look at the dog from the side. Even off the "apron," the side hair which hangs down and the underneath hair. Our breed is not supposed to have a tucked up appearance, but it makes the dog's chest look deeper if you slant the apron up slightly toward the rear. Look at your dog before cutting. If the dog is too leggy, trim the apron shorter.

This is a good time to clean the dog's ears, even though you have been doing it regularly. Take a bit of cotton with a few drops of oil and wipe the ear. Don't be afraid to get down there. You can't get to the eardrum. It makes a bend. Be gentle but keep the ears clean. Any dog with long drop ears can have problems because air doesn't get into the canal. From time to time you can use any of the good preparations available for cleaning ears and killing anything that gets in them. Be sure you clean out all this solution with cotton after you use it.

Courtesy, The Irish Water Spaniel Club of America

Judith J. Tillinger

The Field Spaniel

Standard Regarding Coat

Coat—Flat or slightly waved, and never curled. Sufficiently dense to resist the weather, and not too short. Silky in texture, glossy and refined in nature, with neither duffleness on the one hand, nor curl or wiriness on the other. On the chest, under belly and behind the legs, there should be abundant feather, but never too much, especially below the hocks, and that of the right sort, viz. setterlike. The hindquarters should be similarly adorned.

Breed Note

The Field Spaniel originated in England and was introduced into the United States in the late nineteenth century. While he appears to have all the qualities of a good sporting dog, the breed never attained any great popularity in the United States.

Grooming Procedure

Like the Clumber Spaniel, there is very little required in trimming the Field Spaniel—as long as the coat is kept free of mats and is brushed regularly.

The instructions appearing earlier for trimming the English Springer Spaniel are applicable for the Field Spaniel.

Judith J. Tilinger

The Sussex Spaniel

Standard Regarding Coat

Coat—Body coat abundant, flat or slightly waved, with no tendency to curl, moderately well feathered on legs and stern, but clean below the hocks.

Breed Note

The Sussex Spaniel is an excellent if slower-paced, hunting dog. His liver-colored coat with golden high-lights is an important, identifying hallmark of the breed. The Sussex Spaniel is a very rare breed but with a long list of positive qualities.

Grooming Procedure

The instruction for trimming the Clumber Spaniel also apply to the Sussex. No special instructions are needed and would indeed be repetitious. The Sussex, like Clumber and Field Spaniels should not be overly trimmed and the natural look is desirable.

The Welsh Springer Spaniel

Standard Regarding Coat

Coat—Straight or flat and thick, of a nice silky texture, never wiry nor wavy. A curly coat is most ob-jectionable. **Color**—Dark rich red and white.

Breed Note

The Welsh Springer Spaniel, like so many breeds, takes his name from his homeland. This is a tough, de-termined hunter and an excellent retriever, even in ice cold water. A favorite hunting and farm dog in Wales, the breed is a rarity at the present time.

Grooming Procedure

The Welsh Springer, is very similar to the English Springer and the reader is referred to the instructions for grooming the English Springer as a guide for work on the Welsh Springer.

Longhaired Hounds

The Borzoi

Standard Regarding Coat

Coat—Long, silky (not woolly), either flat, wavy or rather curly. On the head, ears and front of legs it should be short and smooth; on the neck the frill should be profuse and rather curly. Feather on hindquarters and tail, long and profuse, less so on chest and back of forelegs.

Breed Note

The Borzoi, was for centuries, the favorite hunting dog of Czarist Russia. He is one of the tallest and most majestic-looking of all sight hounds, measuring, 28 inches at the withers. Justly famous as a hunter of wolves and coyotes, he is possessed of incredible strength and speed. Today the Borzoi is most often found in the role of gentle, beautiful companion.

Grooming Procedure

The Borzoi Standard does not address itself to grooming and no specific requirements or recommendations are made. Thus, any grooming (other than the obvious bathing, brushing and combing) is a matter of personal taste.

In general, any grooming done should only accentuate, or complement the natural lines of the dog. Most exhibitors remove the whiskers and the tuft of hair at the ears. They tidy the pasterns and hocks, and "clean up" the feet. Occasionally, exhibitors will remove some hair from the underline to accentuate the brisket and tuck-up. If done, thinning shears should be used so the area will not appear shorn.

Courtesy, Borzoi Club of America
by Asa Mays, Jr.

Judith J. Ellinger

The Longhaired Dachshund

Standard Regarding Coat

Coat—The soft, sleek, glistening, often slightly wavy hair should be longer under the neck, on the underside of the body, and especially on the ears and behind the legs, becoming there a pronounced feather; the hair should attain its greatest length on the underside of the tail. The hair should fall beyond the lower edge of the ear. Short hair on the ear, so-called "leather" ears, is not desirable. Too luxurious a coat causes the longhaired Dachshund to seem coarse, and masks the type. The coat should remind one of the Irish Setter, and should give the dog an elegant appearance. Too thick hair on the paws, so-called "mops" is inelegant, and renders the animal unfit for use. It is faulty for the dog to have equally long hair over all the body, if the coat is too curly, or too scrubby, or if a flag tail or overhanging hair on the ears are lacking; or if there is a very pronounced parting on the back, or a vigorous growth between the toes.

Breed Note

The Dachshund's native land is Germany and the literal translation of his name means *badger dog*. This reflects the fact that the Dachshund excels at tracking and confronting the savage badger in his natural earth.

The Dachshund is an ancient hunting dog and is bred in three varieties—Longhaired, Wirehaired and Smooth. The Longhaired Dachshund differs from the others only in his coat, which is long and silky and covers him completely.

The Dachshund was brought into the United States in the nineteenth century, primarily as a family pet. With the exception of the years of World War I, this long bodied, short-legged, droll hound captured the fancy of the American public and continues to rank among the top ten of all breeds in popularity.

Grooming Procedure

The Longhaired Dachshund's coat should be rather long and silky, reminiscent of the Irish Setter. When bathing a Longhaired Dachshund, a good creme rinse should follow each bath to enhance the silkiness of the coat. Regular brushing and combing will loosen and remove any dead hair, stimulate the skin, distribute the natural oils throughout the coat, and allow for a new coat growth. The bath water should be tepid to cool in temperature—water which is too warm or hot, will cause damage and breakage of the coat.

Grooming the Longhaired Dachshund is done to enhance his elegance and body shape. The most difficult Longhairs to groom are the reds and chocolates because of their lighter-colored undercoats. With the lighter undercoat, areas that have been recently scissored are very obvious in the show ring. Reds and chocolates which are being shown should be groomed about six to eight weeks before the show date. Finishing touches and neatening can be done during the last week before the show.

The dappled Longhaired Dachshund presents a unique challenge in that the silver or white hairs of the dappled areas are generally coarser in texture, and feel harsher when freshly cut. It is best to do the major part of any dapple's grooming six to eight weeks before the show date. The black and tan Longhair can be groomed closer to the show date since its coat texture and color are uniform all over the body.

Use barber shears with rounded tips to cut whiskers on the muzzle, cheeks, over the eyes and under the chin. This should be done the day before the show, and the whiskers should be cut very close to the skin.

Some dogs have longer hair on their heads and, therefore appear unkempt. This excess hair should be removed by either plucking with the thumb and index finger, or by using a pumice stone, brushing with the lie of the coat.

Ears—Coat on the ears should be long and flat-lying. Some dogs, particularly puppies, have excess hair where the ear joins the skull. This hair makes the head look overly wide thus detracting from the desired elegant appearance. You can pluck out this hair, or you can use thinning shears. In using thinning shears, place the blades under the coat near the top of the ear and cut only *once or twice*. Comb the hair where you have just cut and determine whether or not you should thin the area further. Too many cuts in the same area will create a bald spot! Continue to cut, comb, and evaluate until you create the desired effect.

Hair on the inside of the ear at the cheek and around to the small flap on the inside back of the ear should be cut *very* close to allow the ear to lay flatter against the head and to outline the ear against the neck.

Neck—The neck should be long, lean, and taper elegantly into the shoulder. Heavy coat growth tends to make the neck look too short. Thinning shears should be used from the back of the jaw down the front of the neck to a point just above the point of the breastbone. Hold the dog's head up with one hand and place the thinning shears under the coat against the skin and in line with the coat growth (never across the direction of coat growth). Cut once or twice, comb and see if more thinning is needed. Thin the hair from the underside of the jaw down into a long, full coat beginning just above the breastbone. Thin the total neck area to the point where the coat growth coming from the back of the neck joins the hair on the front of the neck on each side.

To groom the back of the neck, I prefer to begin with a MAGNET STRIPPING BLADE. This gem of a tool has a very fine serrated edge and, when used like a comb, will remove an amazing amount of dead hair and undercoat without affecting the longer outercoat. Because of the magnet stripper's very fine edge, use it slowly, and keep the skin taut in the area you are using it. It is possible to have the tiny "teeth" catch in the small fold of skin.

Comb with the magnet stripping blade until no more coat comes out. If the neck area still looks too thick, use the thinning shears to achieve a sleek, elegant, lean look. Be sure to cut, comb and evaluate. The back of the neck should blend smoothly into the shoulders.

Body—Again, use the magnet stripping blade like a comb down the length of the body and the sides to remove dead guard hair and undercoat. The body coat should lie flat and taper into a flowing coat on the sides and underside of the body. Thinning shears can be used judiciously on the body to enhance the topline and sleekness of the dog.

The hair behind the front legs should form a pronounced feather. Heavy hair growth on the front legs can make the dog look out at the elbows. To correct this, use thinning shears on the sides of the front legs, particularly at the elbows. This gives elbows a nice tight look. Furnishings on the back of the front legs should be combed backward. If they are too profuse and tend to protrude sideways, use thinning shears until the coat does comb back. It is also helpful to dampen this hair frequently and comb it back. By doing so, you train the hair to lie in the desired fashion.

The hair on the back of the thighs should also be long and full, but not protruding outward to the side of the back legs. Use the thinning shears to blend this coat into the upper thigh.

Cut the hair on the bottoms of the feet even with the pads.. With the dog standing securely on a firm surface, trim the foot with straight scissors. The desired look is a rounded, compact foot. You may have to scissor the top of the foot near the nails to remove the wispy hairs which stick up here. *Do not* cut the hair in an outline around the nails; rather, cut so as to blend this hair into a fully-coated, rounded appearance.

The Longhaired Dachshund's coat should reach its greatest length on the underside of the tail. Many Longhairs are shown with a setter-like flag on the underside of the tail. The shape is easily achieved with scissors. If the tail feathers are especially profuse, it is wise to trim them for about an inch off the underside of the tail and thin the breeches to avoid accumulation of fecal matter. Little else is done to the tail other than combing, brushing and to maintain its shape and condition.

Pet Grooming the Longhaired Dachshund

Combing the back of the neck and the body with the MAGNET STRIPPING BLADE regularly will remove dead hair and excess undercoat and keep the coat in good condition. Scissor the hair on the bottom of the feet even with the pads to keep dirt and debris from accumulating. Use thinning shears to shorten the hair on the sides and front of the neck.

Regular, but *not frequent*, bathing, followed by a creme rinse and lots of brushing will keep the coat in good, shining condition.

Courtesy, The National Miniature Dachshund Club and The Dachshund Club of America
by Jeanne A. Rice

The Irish Wolfhound

Standard Regarding Coat

Hair—Rough and hard on body, legs and head; especially wiry and long over eyes and underjaw.

Breed Note

The Irish Wolfhound is Ireland's ancient sighthound. He is the tallest of all breeds, measuring up to 32 inches at the shoulder. This shaggy giant is an effective guard and an excellent companion for the person with sufficiently spacious property.

Grooming Procedure

Grooming, essential in caring for any dog, is relatively simple with the Irish Wolfhound. A daily five-minute brushing under ordinary circumstances will insure a clean, healthy coat. While brushing, one should check for skin lesions, bumps or parasites. Ears should be inspected and gently cleaned with moistened cotton swabs when necessary. Any excessive wax accumulation or offensive odor emanating from the ear needs the attention of a veterinarian. Nails should be trimmed at least twice a month. An Irish Wolfhound's nails are naturally thick and heavy. If allowed to become too long, the nails will throw the feet back and downward, upsetting natural balance, especially in the front. Elbows and shoulders may be affected once balance is disturbed.

Grooming for the show ring cannot be accomplished without following the aforementioned basics. However, additional attention and readying for showing should include head and neck finger stripping. Using thumb and forefinger pull out dead hair inside and outside the ears. The object is to keep the excess hair from making ears appear any larger than they actually are. Thin out, gently and evenly, excess ruff along both sides of the neck. Use either thinning shears or a stripping blade. Do not use clippers or straight scissors. The purpose is to show a long powerful neck. A thick, coarse, foreshortened appearance and a false semblance of a too-small head for overall balance may result when a heavy ruff is present. The feet should be free from mats and burrs or other material between toes and pads. Long hair hiding the shape of the feet when the dog is standing should be trimmed around the toes in front and also up the back, to prevent a look of weak pasterns. Any spiky point of hair present on the elbows should be trimmed. Soiled or unsightly hair beneath the base of the tail should be washed and trimmed. If long coat disguises the natural underline of the tuck up, trim cautiously, reasonably close to the skin. If there is no tuck up because the dog is fat, only diet and exercise can remedy this problem.

Occasionally, a bath may be necessary, but the Irish Wolfhound coat requires at least a week to regain its natural body after being shampooed. Bathe the dog, if you feel it is required, a week to ten days before showing. The Irish Wolfhound should never look manicured. He is not a canine fashion plate, but is a rugged, rough-coated coursing hound. However, he should be clean and groomed sufficiently so that he is at his best. *He should never be groomed to the point of looking like an outsized terrier.*

Courtesy, The Irish Wolfhound Club of America

Authors Note: The *pet grooming* of the Irish Wolfhound, like any other pet, includes the use of clippers in place of the stripping and plucking. To the layman's eye, however, there should not appear to be any difference.

The Otter Hound

Standard Regarding Coat

Coat—The rough outer coat is three to six inches long on the back, shorter on the extremities. It must be hard (coarse and crisp). A water-resistant inner coat of short woolly hair is an essential feature of the breed. A naturally stripped coat lacking length and fringes is correct for an Otter Hound that is being worked. A proper hunting coat will show the hard outer coat and woolly undercoat. *Faults*—A soft outer coat is a very serious fault as is a woolly-textured top coat. Lack of undercoat is a serious fault. An outer coat much longer than six inches becomes heavy when wet and is a fault.

Breed Note

The Otter Hound is another English breed with a very long history. Related to the Bloodhound, he has been called the ''Bloodhound in sheep's clothing.'' The Otter Hound's oily coat and webbed feet permit him to spend unbelievably long hours in the water while hunting his quarry. He is also an excellent, devoted family companion.

Grooming Procedure

The Otter Hound, beyond needing the fundamentals, requires only the most minimal grooming. He is another of those breeds which must be presented as naturally as possible. There is no clipping, scissoring or stripping involved. In fact, there is no trimming of any kind, just the fundamentals previously referred to. For show dogs, some extra brushing and fine combing is in order.

The Scottish Deerhound

Standard Regarding Coat

Coat—The hair on the body, neck and quarters should be harsh and wiry, about three or four inches long; that on the head, breast and belly much softer. There should be a slight fringe on the inside of the forelegs and hind legs but nothing approaching the "feather" of a Collie. A woolly coat is bad. Some good strains have a mixture of silky coat with the hard which is preferable to a woolly coat. The climate of the United States tends to produce the mixed coat. The ideal coat is a thick, close-lying ragged coat, harsh or crisp to the touch.

Breed Note

The Scottish Deerhound traces his origin into the mists of antiquity. He was, for centuries, regarded as the "Royal Dog of Scotland"; he was admired as a companion and an integral part of the hunt. Speed, strength and courage are all exemplified by this rare, beautiful hound. Once dangerously close to extinction, the Scottish Deerhound is still a rarity, but his future is quite secure.

Grooming Procedure

According to the breed Standard, the ideal Deerhound coat is thick, close-lying and ragged, harsh or crisp to the touch. It is actually the ideal coat for a housepet or a show dog, as it requires minimum care. A thorough, brushing daily with a pin brush will keep it healthy and clean. Foreign objects are easily removed with a metal comb, and mud tends to dry quickly and flake off easily. Toenails should be kept short enough so that they don't "click" as the hound walks, but long enough to offer traction while running. A weekly trim with heavy duty clippers is a *must*. Deerhounds do not mind having their nails clipped if it is done often and gently. As a matter of habit, the Deerhound owner should occasionally check the teeth for plaque accumulation and the ears for wax. Some Deerhounds are prone to anal gland problems, so it is wise to keep them emptied and the anal area trimmed and clean.

As for show grooming, again there is little work to do. If the hound in question needs a bath, give one several days before the show and use a shampoo especially for wire coats. The Deerhound coat softens and becomes fluffy when newly washed and takes a few days to settle down again. For showing, many people *hand strip* the silvery hairs that grow on the ears. It is also acceptable to hand pluck any ragged hairs along the belly to tidy up the profile. *Never* strip out the mane or the hairs on the top of the head. Cleaning up the long hairs around the ears, however, is permissible.

The only place that scissors are used is on the feet. Trimming the long hairs from between the pads and around the nails help to show off the feet.

It takes no more than a brush and comb to ready the Deerhound for the ring once you are at the show site. The Deerhound is shown "au naturel" which is one of its redeeming qualities.

The only grooming "problems" are the elbows which can become calloused and unsightly. To prevent this, the hound should have a soft place to lie down. To keep the skin from drying out, should this problem arise, use Corona ointment or bag balm.

Courtesy, The Scottish Deerhound Club of America
by Mrs. Parker B. Field

Longhaired Working Dogs

The Bearded Collie

Standard Regarding Coat

Coat—The coat is double with the undercoat soft, furry, and close. The outercoat is flat, harsh, strong and shaggy, free from woolliness and curl, although a slight wave is permissible. The coat falls naturally to either side but must never be artificially parted. The length and density of the hair are sufficient to provide a protective coat and to enhance the shape of the dog, but not so profuse as to obscure the natural lines of the body. The dog should be shown as naturally as is consistent with good grooming but the coat must not be trimmed in any way. On the head, the bridge of the nose is sparsely covered with hair which is slightly longer on the sides to cover the lips. From the cheeks, the lower lips and under the chin, the coat increases in length towards the chest, forming the typical beard. An excessively long, silky coat or one which has been trimmed in any way must be severly penalized.

Breed Note

The Bearded Collie was developed in Great Britain on either side of the Scottish-English border. He was basically a sheepdog and drover and was a vigilant guard of the flocks. Today he is mostly a good companion.

Grooming Procedure

The Bearded Collie is shown naturally. There is to be no cutting, plucking, stylizing or thinning in any way. Even the part down the center of the back is frowned upon.

Courtesy, The Bearded Collie Club of America
by Emily Holden

The Belgian Sheepdog

Standard Regarding Coat

Coat—The guard hairs of the coat must be long, well-fitting, straight, and abundant. They should not be silky or wiry. The texture should be extremely dense, commensurate, however, with climatic conditions. The Belgian Sheepdog is particularly adaptable to extremes of temperature or climate. The hair is shorter on the head, outside of the ears, and lower parts of the legs. The opening of the ear is protected by tufts of hair. **Ornamentation**—Especially long and abundant hair, like a collarette, around the neck; fringe of long hair down the back of the forearm; especially long and abundant hair trimming the hindquarters, the breeches; long, heavy, and abundant hair on the tail.

Breed Note

The Belgian Sheepdog is the quintessential watchdog and shepherd and is incomparable at the tasks for which he was bred. This explains his great popularity in Europe and his rising popularity in America. He has often been compared to the German Shepherd.

The Belgian Sheepdog has a long, thick, shiny, black coat. The coat distinguishes him from the Malinois and Tervuren varieties of Belgium's development of the sheepdog.

Grooming Procedure

The instructions in the next section, on the Belgian Tervuren, are applicable for grooming the Belgian Sheepdog.

Judith J. Tillinger

The Belgian Tervuren

Standard Regarding Coat

Coat—The guard hairs of the coat must be long, well-fitting, straight and abundant. They should not be silky or wiry. The texture should be a medium harshness. The undercoat should be very dense, commensurate, however, with climatic conditions. The Belgian Tervuren is particularly adaptable to extremes of temperature or climate. The hair is shorter on the head, outside the ears and on the lower part of the legs. The opening of the ear is protected by tufts of hair. **Ornamentation**—Especially long and abundant hair, like a collarette, around the neck, fringe of long hair down the back of the forearm; especially long and abundant hair trimming the hindquarters, the breeches; long, heavy, and abundant hair on the tail.

Breed Note

The Belgian Tervuren's coat carries a distinctive black ''overlay'' on a reddish coat which can be very striking, especially in mature males.

Grooming Procedure

Brush coat thoroughly in sections down to the skin, paying particular attention to the soft hair behind the ears and the heavy feathering of the tail, breeches and collarette (males). Follow this through with combing the entire coat with a steel comb. When the Tervuren is shedding, it may be necessary to use a curved slicker to remove all the dense, soft undercoat.

Clean the ears using cotton moistened with alcohol—not too wet. Do not put your fingers in deeper than you can see down. Wipe dry with another cotton ball, and dust lightly with a medicated ear power.

The Tervuren should have a tight, cat-paw foot. The nails should not touch the floor, nails should be cut monthly to prevent splitting nails and to keep a good tight paw. A motorized nail tool may also be used to bring the nails down closer.

Bathe and fluff dry. Coat should be brushed forward and away from the body from approximately mid-rib cage. Hair should be brushed down from that point back.

Scissor the whiskers and any long hair on the muzzle and face for dogs to be shown. This step is optional.

With thinning shears remove any hair around the paws that touches the ground or grows out between the toes. This gives them a neat, natural look. Trim excess feathers on hocks to evenness with thinning shears.

Use a lanolin coat conditioner, first putting a small

amount on hands and rubbing it into the coat, down to the skin. This gives the coat a clean, healthy look and prevents breaking guard hairs during brushings.

The Belgian Tervuren should be bathed and groomed following the steps above every three to four months. To keep his coat under control and free from mats and tangles, the Tervuren should be thoroughly brushed once a week. A spray bottle of water applied to his coat during this brushing will keep down on the amount of dirt and dust that will accumulate in his coat. When a Tervuren is shedding it may be necessary to brush him daily.

Courtesy Of American Belgian Tervuren Club
by Dana B. Plaskowitz

Bernese Mountain Dog

Standard Regarding Coat

Coat—Soft and silky with bright, natural sheen; long and slightly wavy but may never curl.

Breed Note

The Bernese Mountain Dog has, for centuries, accompanied milkmen to market in the Canton of Berne, Switzerland. He has also been used as a watchdog, rescue dog and sheepdog. A true working dog, he is held in the highest esteem by those who know him.

Grooming Procedure

Thorough combing is the first item. Then toenails should be checked and cut if necessary. Pick up a foot. Trim all hair growing beyond the pads evenly with the pads. Do not spread the pads and trim in between them as this could cause a dog to limp. Place the foot back on the table and with the scissor resting horizontally on the table, trim around the foot. Trim any excess or unruly hair at the back of the foot. Now we have a nice, neat looking foot. Repeat the process for all four feet.

Next remove all whiskers from the head—over the eyes, at the base of the jaw, under the chin and on the muzzle. This may be done with a clipper or with a pair of sharp scissors. If you use pointed scissors, be sure you know what you are doing and be very careful. If you use clippers, be careful not to nick a hole into the hair on the dog's muzzle. Just clip the whiskers. Go from front to back. For the novice, a pair of scissors, with rounded tips, is best.

The next step is to *bathe him, dry him* and *to see* that he does not roll in the dirt before he is thoroughly dry.

At this point you may wish to blow him dry, or let him dry naturally. If you wish him to dry naturally, confine him to a clean, warm area—a crate with towels, or your living room, covered in blankets. During the summer he can be confined outside to dry providing the area where he will be lying is clean. This is the fastest drying method. If you let him dry naturally in a heated house, allow at least 12 hours for drying. In some cases it takes longer.

To prepare a dog for a show, remove any dust he may have picked up by spraying him with water and wiping him down with a clean, dry towel. Comb him thoroughly and chalk all white areas. Make sure to brush out all chalk before going into the ring. A dog may be excused from the ring if loose chalk billows when the dog is patted, or has been sprayed with any substance which might alter the texture of his coat. You may wish to check his whiskers for any stragglers you missed or any he retracted when you cut them originally. Bring a clean towel to ringside with you for any last-minute touch up or emergency.

Now your Bernese looks absolutely gorgeous. He is ready to walk into the show ring and knock them dead. Whether he wins, loses or draws, you know he is being exhibited looking his best.

Courtesy, Bernese Mountain Dog Club of America
by Gloria E. Henes

The Bouvier Des Flandres

Standard Regarding Coat

Coat—A tousled, double coat capable of withstanding the hardest work in the most inclement weather. The outer hairs are rough and harsh, with the undercoat being fine, soft and dense.

Topcoat—Must be harsh to the touch, dry, trimmed, if necessary, to a length of approximately 2½ inches. A coat too long or too short is a fault, as is a silky or woolly coat. It is tousled without being curly. On the skull, it is short, and on the upper part of the back, it is particularly close and harsh always, however, remaining rough.

Undercoat—A dense mass of fine, close hair, thicker in winter. Together with the topcoat, it will form a water-resistant covering. A flat coat, denoting lack of undercoat is a serious fault.

Mustache and Beard—Very thick, with the hair being shorter and rougher on the upper side of the muzzle. The upper lip, with its heavy mustache and the chin with its heavy and rough beard gives that gruff expression so characteristic of the breed.

Eyebrows—Erect hairs accentuating the shape of the eyes without ever veiling them.

Breed Note

The sturdy Bouvier des Flandres was developed as a cattle dog by the Flemish although the breed has been used with outstanding success as a guard dog, military dog and guide dog for the blind. The two World Wars were damaging to the breed, but today the Bouvier is well-regarded as a personal companion and a good show dog.

Grooming Procedure

It is only common sense to realize that for both the dog's and owner's comfort the dog must be kept clean and well groomed. The term grooming does not necessarily mean excessive trimming of hair or shaping of coat, but simply a few minutes of brushing each week to keep the coat from becoming tangled and matted as well as to remove all loose hair.

The unique qualities of the Bouvier coat keep shedding problems to a minimum. The longer, harsh guard hairs of the outercoat tend to keep the shedding undercoat from falling out or being deposited on furniture or clothes. Instead, the dead hairs become matted in the coat if weekly grooming is not performed. This grooming is a simple, enjoyable matter for owner and dog. All that is required is a brushing, followed by a combing.

Grooming, WHICH IS BEST BEGUN AT AN EARLY AGE, is most easily done with the dog on a raised platform or grooming table about 30″ in height, 24″ wide, and 30″ long. The time spent in grooming can also double as a training session to teach your dog such helpful commands as "stand," "stay," "sit," and "down" and is an important time for man and dog to build a greater rapport based upon mutual love and dependence.

As an introduction to grooming, keep in mind the description of the breed in the official AKC Standard. The Standard is a reliable description the groomer should work toward.

The most important ingredient in grooming is a healthy coat best gained through good nutrition, exercise, and weekly brushing. The tools needed are a pin or wig brush, a bristle brush, stainless steel or aluminum coarse-toothed comb, stripping knife, three or four tiered rake, nail clippers, file and scissors. Flat, wiry coats require more use of the bristle brush to encourage undercoat growth. Dense coats are greatly improved by frequent plucking with thumb and forefinger. Plucking controls the soft undercoat and prevents it from choking out the top coat, giving way to the woolly appearance. The rake is also useful in controlling any prolific growth of undercoat.)

Begin grooming with an efficient brushing. Start at the head with a stiff bristle or pin brush forward toward the head, making sure the coat separates to the skin and that you are not just brushing the surface. Next start at the rear and brush the hair back into place. Legs should also be brushed up and then down. This method assures good stimulation of the skin and removal of loose hair.

With the coat clean and free of mats, using thumb and forefinger, pluck all but the shortest (about ½") hair from just above the eyebrows, back across the skull blending into longer hair behind the ears at about the collar. This may also be done with a stripping knife. Also shorten the hair on the outside of the ears and clean along the amputated part with scissors. With stripping knife clean and flatten the cheeks from the back corner of the eye and corner of the mouth blending into the heavy beard. With heavily bearded dogs it is often helpful to rinse out the beard and apply a bit of hair conditioner to keep the beard from matting with food.

If the head is particularly well furnished, it may be necessary to thin the sideburns under the ears to avoid a "stuffed chipmunk" appearance of the jowls. The head should look massive, yet dignified and powerful, but never as clean shaven as a Schnauzer's. The head must be kept in proportion to the body, neither overbearing nor too small. Clean excess and wild hairs from hocks, elbows, and tail.

When finished grooming, the ideal length of coat is 2½" but considerably shorter on the head except for eyebrows, mustache, and beard. The coat should be shorter but denser on legs. One must be careful to avoid the appearance of the "Kerry Blue" (over-trimmed), the "Briard" (shaggy head), or the "Old English" (profuse undercoat and squared-off rump). The general appearance when finished should be that of a cared-for, but not coiffured dog.

Courtesy, American Bouvier des Flandres Club, Inc.

Author's Note—For pet trimming of the Bouvier, clippers and scissors are used instead of stripping and plucking.

Pet Bouvier Des Flandres in the rough.   Same dog after grooming and trimming.

The Briard

Standard Regarding Coat

Coat—The outer coat is coarse, hard and dry (making a dry rasping sound between the fingers). It lies down flat, falling naturally in long, slightly waving locks, having the sheen of good health. On the shoulders the length of hair is generally six inches or more. The undercoat is fine and tight on all the body.

Breed Note

The Briard comes from the Brie region of France, famous for its delicious cheese. He somewhat resembles the Bearded Collie, with whom he shares a common ancestry. He is a working sheepdog, but has also shown an aptitude for numerous other tasks. And, of course, he is a fine companion for the right person.

Grooming Procedure

The first rule to success in grooming a Briard is regularity. If the dog is groomed out carefully once a week, there is little need for bathing and it is not likely the dog will develop serious mats. These are tedious to remove and damaging to the coat.

The Briard is a rustic, working dog and the correct coat texture is usually described as a ''goat's coat.'' It should fall naturally into smoothly waving locks with a natural part on the head and some tendency to part on the neck and back. The coat does not require trimming and contrary to what can be found in some grooming books it would be inexcusable to cut off the forelock or square it off with scissors. If any scissor work is done to the coat at all, it must never appear that the coat has been trimmed. It is permissible to trim between the foot pads, however, and this should be done for the pet and show dog alike.

The Briard has a double coat. The outer coat is long and is not inclined to be shed. It also grows more slowly than the undercoat and, once lost, especially on the ears, neck or tail, outer coat can be very slow to return.

The undercoat is softer than the outer coat and about three to five inches long. It is shed out periodically and tends to cling to the outer coat instead of dropping off. For this reason it is important to groom the dog regularly or the coat can eventually become matted or even felted (one solid mat).

The puppy coat is softer than the adult coat. Sometime between the ages of nine and 18 months of age the puppy coat is shed and serious matting can result if regular grooming is not pursued. It may even be necessary to groom the dog daily with a wire pin brush to prevent mats from forming. Once the adult coat is in, grooming the Briard is much easier. It is also wise to groom the pup regularly, even if there is no need in order to accustom the dog to this routine.

Some Briards, especially those in colder climates may develop very heavy undercoats, which destroy the outline of the dog. Rather than thin or trim the coat, it is wiser to comb out the excess undercoat on the neck, around the base of the tail and wherever mats tend to form. A comb, a slicker or grooming "rake" can be used for this but any tool that cuts the coat should be avoided. The secret is to keep as much of the longer outer hair as possible while removing some of the dense undercoat. A Briard should never be stripped or groomed like a terrier.

The forelock can become too heavy. It should lightly veil the eyes but not obscure the vision or the shape of the head. This is a fault which can be corrected by thinning the forelock. To do this, the hair should be combed back from the dog's face and the underneath layers, especially between the eyes, cautiously thinned with thinning shears. The top layers must not be cut but can be combed to reveal more eye.

No dog is perfect and with the coated dog, there is always the temptation to "improve things a little" by working with the dog's coat. This is frowned upon by the Standard—but if the temptation is too great for you to bear, remember that the finished product *must* look as though it grew that way—a natural dog with a natural coat.

Courtesy, Briard Club of America

The Rough Collie

Standard Regarding Coat

Coat—The well-fitting, proper-textured coat is the crowning glory of the rough variety of Collie. It is abundant except on the head and legs. The outer coat is straight and harsh to the touch. A soft, open outer coat or a curly outer coat, regardless of quantity is penalized. The undercoat is very abundant on the mane and frill. The face or mask is smooth. The forelegs are smooth and well feathered to the back of the pasterns. The hind legs are smooth below the hock joints. Any feathering below the hocks is removed for the show ring. The hair on the tail is very profuse and on the hips it is long and bushy. The texture, quantity and the extent to which the coat ''fits the dog'' are important points.

Breed Note

The words beautiful, majestic, elegant, graceful all apply to the Collie, who originated in Scotland. ''Lassie'' was one of the all-time favorite animal movie stars. Once used almost exclusively as a sheepdog, the Collie is now mostly a cherished companion, universally known for devotion to his family.

Grooming Procedure

Getting down to the actual work, start low in the feather on the rear legs with a stiff brush. Use the wire one; some use the nylon. Lift the coat up, leaving just a wisp and brush this wisp with a down and out motion until all matted portions are cleaned out.

Go well into the undercoat but not quite to the skin. When one wisp is done, bring down another from under your hand with the brush and keep repeating until the entire quarter is done. Repeat this for each part of the body until the coat is brushed so all the outer coat or guard hair is standing smoothly and separated well. This may be all you want to do for one day since working too long is very tiring both for you and the dog . . . it is better to do the job in broken doses.

Next, wash the face and feet, making sure you get all the dirt from between the toes and around the nails. Now you are ready to start trimming and stripping. This is an important moment. Stand your dog up and look for his faults, for every dog has them. The idea is to play down the faults and play up the strong points. Trim nails and file them a bit so they are not square on the ends. Do this early for a show dog so if you should cut a quick, it will have time to heal before the dog is shown. Trim excess hair between the toes on the underside of the foot so the toes may lie close and not show a tendency to an open or splay foot. The fringe around the outside of the foot is trimmed, too. The desired effect is like a cat's foot, so use it for a model. The slight feather on the back of the front pasterns and the hair growing on the back of the hock joints are trimmed to neatness.

For a dog with good stifles, keep a straight line from hock to heel, avoid notches, and do not let hair curve out half-way down to give that peculiar, sickle-hocked look. With a dog that is too straight in stifle, trim close at the heel and allow more length as you go up toward the hock joint. Still keep your line straight and even. It is easier to do this if you start from the bottom rather than the top as many do. If the stifle is bent too much, reverse the process. This can improve the looks considerably but, of course, won't do anything for the gait. Brush paws and fronts of legs smooth . . . roughing them up to try to increase appearance of bone rarely helps.

Now we are at the head. So much depends on the dog's type. Some heads need little or no trimming and stripping. Just a careful washing the ears and face, end of nose, teeth if they need it, and around the eyes will do. While the head is still damp from washing, brush the face and keep the hair on the skull, both top and sides, brushed straight back.

Use a fine comb to finish the head. If this hair is allowed to droop naturally, it can give the dog a woebegone expression or cause the skull to look receding or rolling when it is not. There is no sense accentuating the occiput. If the skull is a bit wide or flaring, then by all means strip (NOT cut) some of the fine hair on the sides of the head. There is often a pad of undercoat over the cheekbones and running further back which must be stripped out if the Collie being groomed is to look as clean-headed as possible. Lift the guard hair and strip around the lower jaw and throat to give the appearance of more length. Clippers used judiciously just above where the ruff starts on the throat do wonders if the head looks too deep from the brow down. Lower ear coverts can be thinned out to advantage at times. The top of the skull CAN be smoothed but this is a bit tricky and often done wrong. One must remember the hair lying over a bump is rooted well in front of the bump so you need to strip where the roots of the proper hairs actually are. Leave the guard hair, use a stripping knife to bring out the undercoat.

Try to keep the muzzle smooth and round. If you find "railroad lines", veiny spots, swirls or cowlicks or any other projecting tufts of hair you cannot brush down, singeing the ends with a barber's taper is usually better than cutting or even stripping. Of course, all the whiskers, the coarse, long black or white hairs on the face, need to come off wherever you find them. I like finger scissors for this, but some prefer to use the Duplex Dresser.

Ears are a ticklish problem. Usually some fuzz can come off to good advantage but if the ears are well set, just cleaning them will be sufficient. Some clip or trim them rather closely on the outside and clean most of the hair out of the inside. I like them better just neat, and think the ears look smaller nestled in a medium frame of hair.

Courtesy, Collie Club of America
by Mrs. Fred L. Kem

Rough Collie before grooming.

Same dog is a far more handsome pet after grooming.

The Great Pyrenees

Standard Regarding Coat

Coat—Created to withstand severe weather, with heavy fine white undercoat and long flat thick outer coat of coarser hair, straight or slightly undulating.

Breed Note

The Great Pyrenees is a beautiful, majestic working dog of commanding size and presence. Standing about 30 inches at the shoulder, he is a mountain dog, originating in the Pyrenees between France and Spain. He is an excellent guardian of flocks and has demonstrated outstanding ability as a protector and companion of humans.

In the United States the Great Pyrenees is widely appreciated for his many positive virtues.

Grooming Procedure

Use a pin brush and a Greyhound (brand name) comb to fluff through the hair while drying. While the dog is on the table being dried we rub Clairol Kindness with Extra Hold into the hock hair, and any other place extra body is needed.

Shaping the head is done with thinning shears. We thin the fuzzy hair on the tops of the ears to shape the head. Never cut any hair crosswise—always with the hair. Cut and comb, cut and comb until the ear is smooth. This shaping helps to eliminate the appearance of a high-set ear.

Prominent eyebrows and forehead may be thinned to give a more gentle slope to the head rather than an abrupt stop. This look is often just the result of an overabundance of hair.

To remove whiskers, use a pair of straight manicure scissors with blunt ends. Don't just cut off the whiskers, go to the base of each whisker and cut; dogs, like seals, can move the whiskers back and forth. Place your thumb inside the lip and watch the whisker pop out.

To level a top line, hair may be thinned out of the rump. To begin, comb through the rump hair, lay back the long overcoat, make a few cuts with the thinning shears, comb out and take a look. This is a slow process because of the small amounts of hair removed with each cut. You can even out the entire rump with the cut-comb technique. We have spent as long as an entire week, a little thinning each day before we have it just right. A fast job can give the dog a lumpy look.

The hair on the tail can resemble teased hair if not combed through completely.

Begin at the bone and carefully comb out using short strokes until you can run the comb through freely. Don't forget to turn the tail over, there are two sides. Inches of length and plume can be gained this way.

The base of the tail can be thinned also to help shorten the back. On a dog show day may want to dampen the rump hair, comb through and lay a heavy towel over it until show time.

The ruff should be brushed toward the head. The middle of the back and ruff may be back combed to hold it all together and make a smooth line. Back combing the entire back and smoothing over adds inches to the height. Our dogs are groomed to have offstanding coats rather than appearing slickly brushed.

For the final grooming comb and brush through the entire coat, under the front legs, behind the ears and between the back legs.

Dampen the front legs with a wet wash cloth and grind in baby powder, do the same on foot and pastern—this is done with a soft brush. Let dry, brush briskly, test the hair with fingers to be positive all the powder is out. If you were not stingy with the powder, the legs and feet should be bright white, whiter than after the bath.

Now stand back and look. Is the back line level? Does the rump need flattening; do the shoulders need height? From the rear, is the dog fluffed thoroughly—the shoulders, midsection and hips—to give a full rounded look?

A fine mist of water may be sprayed into the coat and combed through; the moisture makes the hair stand out.

Finally, brush the hair on the legs up to give the impression of greater bone. Comb feathers and hock hair straight out.

Courtesy, Great Pyrenees Club of America and International Great Pyrenees Review by Lorene and Linda Canfield

The Komondor

Standard Regarding Coat

Coat—Characteristic of the breed is the dense, weather-resisting double coat. The puppy coat is relatively soft, but it shows a tendency to fall into cords. In the mature dog, the coat consists of a dense, soft, woolly undercoat, much like the puppy coat, and a coarser outer coat that is wavy or curly. The coarser hairs of the outer coat trap the softer undercoat forming permanent strong cords that are felty to the touch. A grown dog is covered with a heavy coat of these tassel-like cords, which form themselves naturally, and once formed, require no care other than washing. Too curly a coat is not desired. Straight or silky coat is a serious fault. Short, smooth hair on the head and legs is a disfuguration. Failure of the coat to cord by two years of age is a disqualification.

The coat is longest at the rump, loins and tail. It is of medium length on the back, shoulders and chest. Shorter on the cheeks, around the eyes, ears, neck, and on the extremities. It is shortest around the mouth and lower part of the legs up to the hocks.

Breed Note

The Komondor is among the most ancient of working dogs. With his white, corded coat and majestic height (often exceeding 31 inches) he is an imposing sight. He was developed in Hungary over a thousand years ago as a courageous guardian of the flocks.

Grooming Procedure

The rare Komondor, with its corded coat, is one of the most unusual of all breeds. Since the late 1960s there has been a steady increase in show ring activity. Groomers also ask about them. There are basically two extremes of coats in the breed, and instructions for one kind do not help with the other at all. At one extreme is the coat which tends to form itself into narrow cords. At the other extreme is the coat that has a great deal of undercoat and has to be torn into clumps over and over again until it forms into felty mats which stay formed through each washing. Attempts to write about what to do with these latter coats have been made. It is easier to show someone in a few minutes working a dog what cannot be easily expressed in many pages of written instructions.

Courtesy, Middle Atlantic States Komondor Club

The Kuvasz

Standard Regarding Coat

Coat—The Kuvasz has a double coat formed by a guard hair and fine undercoat. The texture of the coat is medium coarse. The coat ranges from quite wavy to straight. Distribution follows a definite pattern over the body regardless of coat type. The head, muzzle, ears and paws are covered with short, smooth hair. The neck has a mane that extends to and covers the chest. Coat on the front of the forelegs up to the elbows and the hind legs below the thighs is short and smooth. The backs of the forelegs are feathered to the pastern with hair two to three inches long. The body and sides of the thighs are covered with a medium length coat. The back of the thighs and the entire tail are covered with hair four to six inches long. It is natural for the Kuvasz to lose most of the long coat during hot weather. Full luxuriant coat comes in seasonally, depending on climate. Summer coat should not be penalized.

Breed Note

The Kuvasz was developed in Hungary as a guard dog and for work with livestock. He is a big dog mea-suring 28 inches at the withers. His white coat, in prime condition, heightens his regal bearing.

Grooming Procedure

Although it is common practice to trim whiskers and eyebrows, the dog's appearance should dictate whether or not this is done. If a dog has an elegant set of whiskers like a cat's and they do the right things to the appearance of his muzzle—leave them on. If the whiskers are like those of an old walrus or make the muzzle look too pointed, take them off. The same holds true for eyebrows. Many people recommend blunt-nose scissors for trimming whiskers, while others prefer bar-ber's shears. With barber's shears take care to aim the points away from the eyes. The best tool of all is an electric clipper but that requires a steady hand. If you have a clipper, practice on your dog several times when there isn't a show coming up for a month before you try it on the eve of your big day.

Some coat-types seem to produce a fringe of very fine hair, like the hair on the back of a Collie or Sheltie ear, about a third or half way down the ear. It isn't much but it can ruin the outline of a nice ear. If your dog has this problem, use the thinning shears liberally right through the fringe combing it out frequently with your "ear comb" until a smooth appearance is achieved. While the Kuvasz hardly ever mats, sometimes nasty little snarls can form behind the ears. Make sure these are all removed before bathing. It is preferable to comb them out but if they are really hard cases, have a few goes at them with the thinning shears and they will comb out much more easily. Don't cut them out if you can possibly help it.

A good pin brush is essential to grooming the Kuvasz. Brush the whole coat in reverse, and remove any mats or loose undercoat. The trousers should be done from the bottom up, one layer at a time, starting right down at the skin. If a dog has exceptionally heavy feathering, use a slicker brush instead of a pin brush. Use a slicker on the front feathering and on the tail. Start doing the tail from the root and work to the tip. Holding the tail straight out, brush the underside down and the topside upwards.

Courtesy, Kuvasz Club of America

The Newfoundland

Standard Regarding Coat

Coat—The Newfoundland has a water-resistant double coat. The outer coat is moderately long and full but not shaggy. It is straight and flat with no curl, although it may have a slight wave. The coat, when rubbed the wrong way, tends to fall back into place. The undercoat, which is soft and dense, is often less dense during summer months or in tropical climates but is always found to some extent on the rump and chest. An open coat is to be seriously faulted. The hair on the head, muzzle, and ears is short and fine, and the legs are feathered all the way down. The tail is covered with long dense hair, but it does not form a flag.

Breed Note

The Newfoundland takes his name from the island of his origin. He is a large dog, standing 28 inches at the shoulder. The breed is at home in water and was once an integral crew member on board numerous fishing ships. The Newfoundland's great strength and natural swimming ability have made him a natural lifeguard. Over the centuries, he has saved countless humans from drowning.

The Newfoundland, Boatswain, inspired the poet Byron to write the following famous epitath.

Near this Spot
are deposited the Remains of one
who possessed Beauty without Vanity
Strength without Insolence
Courage without Ferocity
and all the Virtues of Man without his Vices

This Praise, which would be unmeaning Flattery
if inscribed over human Ashes,
is but a just tribute to the Memory of
BOATSWAIN, a DOG
who was born in Newfoundland May 1803
and died at Newstead Nov. 18, 1808.

Grooming Procedure

In any climate, brushing your Newfoundland not only improves his appearance by controlling mats and shedding but also cleans his coat and skin and reduces odor. Use a wire brush with bristles bent at the end. Work against the grain back to front, then reverse. Mats of dead hair accumulate behind the ears and inside the hind legs. After the permanent coat develops, shedding occurs but twice a year—spring and fall. Newfoundlands living in warm climates need extra care and observation to combat parasites and skin problems. Grooming in these climates is essential. Brushing often means less bathing. When you do give your dog a bath, be sure to remove ALL the soap to avoid skin irritation.

Rinse and rinse again. If toenails are not kept at a moderate length through exercise, they should also be clipped, but learn how to do it properly before trying.

Courtesy, The Newfoundland Club of America

The Old English Sheepdog

Standard Regarding Coat

Coat—Profuse, but not so excessive as to give the impression of the dog being overfat, and of a good hard texture; not straight, but shaggy and free from curl. Quality and texture of coat to be considered above mere profuseness. Softness or flatness of coat to be considered a fault. The undercoat should be a waterproof pile, when not removed by grooming or season.

Breed Note

The nickname for the Old English Sheepdog is the "bobtail". This derives from the absence of that appendage in the breed. Also characteristic of the Old English is his charm and gentleness and all-around good nature. Although his vision may be somewhat limited by the profusion of hair over his eyes, he is compensated by extraordinary senses of hearing and smell. The Old English probably was developed in England's West country where he was used as a livestock drover. Today he is most appreciated as a companion. With his rolling gait and friendly disposition, he is considered a real fun dog.

Grooming Procedure

Probably the primary reason the Old English comes in for professional grooming so often is the fact that the owner invariably does not have the time, the patience, or the inclination to keep the massive coat of the Old English brushed out. Moreover, the heavy undercoat lends itself to excessive matting. It is not at all unusual for the owner to bring the dog in so badly matted that it becomes necessary to "strip" the entire coat off with clippers right down to the skin. The only way professional groomers have found to teach such owners a lesson on proper coat care is to charge a price felt right down to the pocketbook. Oddly enough, this lesson does not always seem to penetrate.

With the exception of stripping the coat, the fundamentals of grooming, as described in Part I, must be applied to the grooming of the Old English (as with all other breeds). If the matted coat is to be saved, a great deal of patience is required. It might call for an all-day grooming session and sometimes it may even be better to spend two or more days on it, so that neither the dog nor the groomer becomes exhausted. In fact, grooming dogs in general often requires a number of "coffee breaks" to pace yourself. Grooming should be more fun than fight.

It is traditional for the topknot to fall over the eyes as with the Lhasa Apso. Use the comb for the finished look. The bottoms of the feet are trimmed to neat roundness.

Another innovation which is catching on in professional grooming is to thin the heavy coat down with the

An ungroomed Old English Sheepdog—a big job for any groomer.

Rather than strip off the whole coat, groomers are using the snap on comb to bring pet coats down to a length the pet owner can easily deal with.

A fully-coated Old English, beautifully groomed is a truly unforgettable sight.

snap-on comb #1 (See Part I), taking off a substantial part of the heavy topcoat. The only scissoring done on the Old English is to give a tidy, even appearance all over the body, the legs, chest, underbelly and rump. Trim the feet level with the grooming surface (table).

Grooming for the Show Ring

How often should the Old English Sheepdog be groomed? The answer to that very frequently asked question is, just enough to keep him clear of mats, but not so much as to lessen the density and fullness of coat. Minimum frequency of required grooming will vary widely depending on the age, texture and condition of the coat. Puppies younger than six or seven months may require only token brushing, to accustom them to the routine; older puppies and very young adults sometimes go through a phase where they mat constantly and need almost daily supervision; and fully mature Sheepdogs, past two or three years old, sometimes thrive on considerably less frequent maintenance. However, as a general rule, all Sheepdogs benefit from a complete grooming once a week.

A thorough brushing will remove a good deal of dirt and grime, but there is no way around the fact that any Sheepdog coat, to be at its healthy best, requires periodic bathing. My own conclusion, after years of doing it the other way, is that soap and water are far superior as cleaning agents to cornstarch or chalk, and a lot less messy. A clean coat will look fuller, it will grow better and be less prone to mat, and is less subject to skin disorders than a dirty one. Depending on the dog's environment and the owner's fortitude, a bath should be given anywhere from once a month to once every three to four months. Some coats tend to soften more than others after bathing, and should be washed several days or a week before a show to allow time for the normal hard texture to return.

The best time to trim the feet and rump, and neaten up the coat in general, is when the dog is freshly bathed and brushed. Scissoring should be done subtly and in moderation, but we have never seen a Sheepdog which did not improve in appearance with a little light shaping. There has always been considerable discussion within the breed on this point, but we have observed that many exhibitors who object to any scissoring by their competitors are pretty good at it themselves, or wish they were.

Brush all the coat on the back and rump towards the rear, and with the scissors or thinning shears, trim the rump into a rounded shape, with no hair extending out past the tail stump. The hair around and just below the rectum should be quite short. Brush out the legs and feet, and trim out the hairs growing between the pads and on the heel of each foot. Then trim each paw into a large but neatly rounded shape, correcting any illusion that excess hair can create of the feet pointing in or out.

119

Remove any overlong wisps of hair that detract from the outline; viewed from front or rear, the legs should appear straight and columnar. Especially in heavier coated dogs, the hair at the point of the shoulder blades and down the shoulders should be slightly trimmed so as to lie almost flat, preventing the dog from appearing heavy-shouldered or short-necked when he is not.

A well groomed Old English Sheepdog not only makes an esthetically pleasing "picture" but will also be a healthier and more acceptable companion. Conversely, if you do not groom your dog regularly you run the risk of seriously damaging his appearance and jeopardizing his health.

Courtesy, Old English Sheepdog Club Of Greater New York

Regular grooming promotes good health in addition to a handsome appearance.

Judith J. Tillinger

The Puli

Standard Regarding Coat

Coat—Characteristic of the breed is the dense, weather-resisting double coat. The outer coat, long and of medium texture, is never silky. It may be straight, wavy, or slightly curly, the more curly coat appearing to be somewhat shorter. The undercoat is soft, woolly, and dense. The coat mats easily, the hair tending to cling together in bunches, giving a somewhat corded appearance even when groomed. The hair is profuse on the head, ears, face, stifles, and tail, and the feet are well haired between the toes. Usually shown combed, but may also be shown uncombed with the coat hanging in tight, even cords.

Breed Note

The Puli's coat, like that of the Komondor, tends to mat and cord. He is much smaller than the always-white Komondor. In color, the Puli may be black, gray or white. Both originated in Hungary. The Puli is not only a superlative sheepdog but a capable hunter and a delightful companion.

Grooming Procedure for the Corded Coat

The striking breed characteristic of the Puli is his unusual, but typical, coat of shaggy hair, the result of hundreds of years of natural development. The shaggy, corded coat is not artificial; it is nature's way of protecting the Puli from the extreme conditions of outdoor living. The shaggy coat consists of a coarse outercoat (which should never be silky), and a very fine, dense, woolly undercoat. The two combine to form cords. The kinds of cords which will result—wide plates, round cords, or strands of different length—depend upon hereditary factors.

Grooming procedures begin during the early puppy stage. The natural divisions of the coat should be respected as much as possible. If you intend to exhibit during the cordless process, continue to brush the coat, at least on the surface, while it is cording, unless the coat is the dense, curly type that was mentioned earlier. NEVER brush this kind of coat while cording; simply wet it down EVERY day. When coats are brushed, they do cord more slowly. Until the puppy coat has reached the length and density where splitting becomes necessary to avoid matting, brush the coat with a soft pin brush.

From eight months to one year, depending on the type of coat, climate, environment and activity, the cording begins. The most important tools for this process are fingers. Never use a comb, coarse or fine, because it not only pulls out too much coat, but it tends to split the coat ends. Carefully separate the strands by tearing each down to the skin. This frees the excess hair (dead undercoat) which will then fall out. It is important not to separate the coat into overly small strands, for such separations are not natural, and always try to follow the natural formations as closely as possible. As the coat grows, these strands or cords will become more pronounced and dense.

The easiest way to tear the cords on a full coated Puli is to wet him down thoroughly in a tub, beginning the tearing procedure while he is damp. This way you can more easily see the natural formations as well as eliminate excessive undercoat which would ordinarily have to be brushed out after each separation. A warm spray of water when finished will remove all the excessive hair. When the Puli is almost dry, check to make certain that you did not miss any needed separations. If it is not practical to wet down the Puli, use a spray bottle of warm water, spraying a section of the coat at a time, then tearing the coat to the skin.

Once the coat has been evenly separated, it is easy to keep and requires care only in accordance with its own speed of growth. With a young Puli, repeat the separation approximately every two weeks. The coat requires the greatest amount of care in the beginning stage. As the Puli nears maturity less care is needed. The fully grown Puli needs only an occasional separation of new growth.

The corded coat is much easier to keep clean and neat because dirt will not penetrate the cord, and the dirt which settles on the surface is very easy to remove. However, the coat must be kept clean while it is cording.

It is extremely important that the ends of the cords be kept open. Even the smallest curl on the end will double back into the cord as the cord continues to grow. If allowed to remain, the ends will look matted, and the Puli will lose his neat appearance. The ends are very easy to check. Simply pick up a handful of cords and examine the ends.

Keep the cords very short on the stomach area of male Pulis because of urine stains. If the stains are allowed to remain in the cords for any length of time, they are difficult to remove. Cutting the stomach cords is also a helpful hint for the male who is being used for stud.

Courtesy, Puli Club of America

Author's Note: In the United States, Pulis may be exhibited brushed or corded. Pets as well as show dogs are often brushed by their owners and groomers. For those wishing to brush their Pulis, the instructions for show grooming Old English Sheepdogs that appear earlier in this chapter will be a helpful guide.

The Longhaired St. Bernard

Standard Regarding Coat

Coat—The longhaired variety completely resembles the shorthaired type except for the coat which is not shorthaired (stockhaarig) but of medium length, plain to slightly wavy, never rolled or curly and not shaggy either. Usually, on the back, especially from the region of the haunches to the rump, the hair is more wavy, a condition, by the way, that is slightly indicated in the shorthaired dogs. The tail is bushy with dense hair of moderate length. Rolled or curly hair on the tail is not desirable. A tail with parted hair, or a flag tail, is faulty. Face and ears are covered with short and soft hair; longer, hair at the base of the ear is permissible. Forelegs only slightly feathered, thighs very bushy.

Breed Note

The St. Bernard originated in Switzerland where he is very popular. The breed is also highly favored in Germany, England, America and numerous other countries. The Saint is a giant of a dog with a powerful appearance; his minimum height is 27 inches. There are two varieties, the Longhaired and Shorthaired, of which the latter is the favorite. In the icy cold of the Alps the Longhaired St. Bernard becomes coated with icicles and restricted in his movements. Although the Saint has many virtues, his fame lies in his great rescue work. He has saved thousands of lives through the centuries by pulling near-frozen travelers buried in the snow, to safety.

Grooming Procedure

Getting a dog ready for a show only requires bathing, cutting whiskers, cleaning ears, trimming nails and a good brushing and combing. Naturally a Shorthaired Saint would require much less work than a Longhaired. In addition on a Longhaired Saint there is the trimming of the hair on the feet and sometimes additional trimming involved.

Courtesy, The St. Bernard Club of America by Joanne Alstede

The Samoyed

Standard Regarding Coat

Coat (Texture & Condition)—The Samoyed is a double-coated dog. The body should be well covered with an undercoat of soft, short, thick, close wool with longer and harsh hair growing through it to form the outer coat, which stands straight out from the body and should be free from curl. The coat should form a ruff around the neck and shoulders, framing the head (more on males than on females). Quality of coat should be weather resistant and considered more than quantity. A droopy coat is undesirable. The coat should glisten with a silver sheen. The female does not usually carry as long a coat as most males and it is softer in texture.

Breed Note

The Samoyed's original habitat was the Yenisei region of Siberia. In this inhospitable environment, he hauled sledges, herded reindeer and was a companion.

The English became enraptured with his beauty and all-around working capabilities. From England the Samoyed eventually became introduced to dog enthusiasts all over the world and today he is one of our most admired purebreds.

Grooming Procedure

Before bathing the Samoyed, comb and brush thoroughly making sure any knots and tangles are removed. Plug ears with cotton and wet dog thoroughly. Using a good, commercial whitening shampoo, work in the shampoo using a squeezing rather than a rubbing motion. Wash, rinse and, if necessary, repeat the entire operation. Towel dry the dog, then blow dry with warm air or air dry, weather permitting. After drying, back brush to make the coat stand up. Use a long pin brush—1″ long pins. Remember to remove cotton and clean inside the ear flaps.

Clean teeth with pumice powder and gauze. Cut hair on paws even with pads.

In addition to the above, for show grooming, do the following:

Cut nails to the quick, trim hocks, trim pastern feathers, trim and shape hair around foot, trim whiskers, chin whiskers and eyebrows. No other trimming is allowed.

Courtesy, Samoyed Club of Long Island
by Rita M. Somers

The Shetland Sheepdog

Standard Regarding Coat

Coat—The coat should be double, the outer coat consisting of long, straight, harsh hair; the undercoat short, furry, and so dense as to give the entire coat its "stand-off" quality. The hair on face, tips of ears and feet should be smooth. Mane and frill should be abundant, and particularly impressive in males. The forelegs well feathered, the hind legs heavily so, but smooth below the hock joint. Hair on tail profuse. Note: Excess hair on ears, feet, and on hocks may be trimmed for the show ring. **Faults**—Coat short or flat, in whole or in part; wavy, curly, soft or silky. Lack of undercoat. Smooth-coated specimens.

Breed Note

The Shetland Sheepdog originated in the Shetland Islands off the northern coast of Scotland, and strongly resembles the rough Collie in miniature. The "Sheltie's" size, beauty, intelligence and gentle nature have made friends for him wherever dog lovers are found.

Grooming Procedure

For a puppy all that is really necessary is that he be clean and brushed. It has become standard practice to trim the whiskers off the face and of course the dog's toenails should be kept trimmed. Excess hair can be removed from around the outline of the dog's feet and from the hocks. However, it is doubtful if any dog ever won or lost because his feet were not trimmed and if in doubt, don't trim too much! Instead of giving the dog an entire bath, just put him in the tub and wash the white parts if they are dirty, or you can use a waterless shampoo. To add extra whiteness to the white parts sprinkle in a little white grooming powder for dogs. If you prefer, you can use plain cornstarch or baby powder as a whitener, taking care to brush it all out again. To make the dog's coat stand away from the body dampen it with a sponge or spray and brush against the grain finishing up by brushing the coat lightly back in the right direction so it fits the body. Be careful to brush it down over the rump as the coat over the rear end may very well be longer and thicker than the coat over the shoulders.

That is really all that is necessary for a Shetland Sheepdog to appear perfectly presentable. There are many complicated grooming techniques employed by many breeders and handlers. If you attend dog shows, you will probably see some of them being attempted by others, but they are not necessary and frequently make little or no difference in the dog's general appearance. It is a matter of personal preference how complicated you make your grooming.

Courtesy, The American Shetland Sheepdog Association

Longhaired (Scissored) Terriers

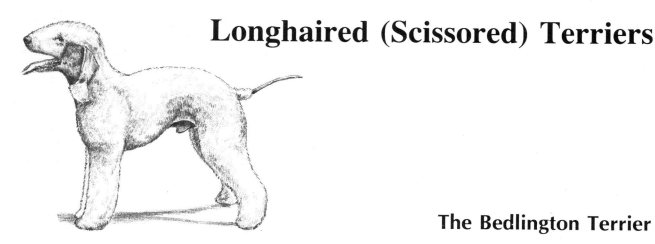

The Bedlington Terrier

Standard Regarding Coat

Coat—A very distinctive mixture of hard and soft hair standing well out from the skin. Crisp to the touch but not wiry, having a tendency to curl, especially on the head and face. When in show trim must not exceed one inch on body; hair on legs is slightly longer.

Breed Note

The Bedlington Terrier was first fostered by miners and other working men in the town of Bedlington, Northumberland England. A courageous foe of all vermin, he was matched against all manner of such creatures and was also used for dog racing. Today the Bedlington is as game as his early ancestors, but is most appreciated as a show dog and an unusual housepet.

Grooming Procedure

The Bedlington Terrier, like the Kerry Blue, is a soft-coated terrier as distinguished from the harsh-coated terriers. Therefore there is no stripping of the coat. Also like the Kerry Blue, there is very little clipping involved on the Bedlington. Most of the work is done with scissors. The only clipping done on the Bedlington is on the head and tail. On the pet, the body may be clipped with a #4 blade.

Head—Using a #10 blade and starting at the corner of the mouth, clip to the outer corner of the eye. The entire underjaw and the underside of the neck is then clipped down to approximately two inches below the Adam's apple to form a deep V. The only other parts of the head to be clipped are the ears.

Ears—The ears are clipped on both sides with the #10 blade. A diamond-shaped tassel is left at the bottom of the ear by stopping the clipping approximately two inches from the end of the ear leather. The exact size of the tassels will depend on the individual dog and what suits it best. It is simple to hold the clippers to form the diamond shape.

Tail—Staying with the #10 blade, clip just the underpart of the tail for its entire length. Then clip the two-thirds of the upper part of the tail furthest from the body to give a "rat-tail" effect. The upper third of the tail should be scissor-blended into the croup.

Scissoring the Bedlington—The Bedlington's body coat is scissored to an even blanket of less than one inch. Professional groomers may use a #4 blade on the body for speed in pet grooming. The tuck-up is trimmed very closely to accentuate the natural arch of the loin. The legs are scissored closely but fuller than the body coat. Unlike most breeds, the Bedlington should be "hare-footed," or longer than the usual "cat-foot." It is, therefore, a mistake to trim a Bedlington's foot round. Some angulation should be showing in the rear legs.

Topknot—The last area for scissoring, the topknot, is most important to the overall picture. The desired effect is a "Roman nose" and to achieve this effect, scissor the topknot evenly from the base of the neck to the tip of the nose. The sides of the face and the topknot should blend together to form about a one-inch frame.

The headpiece if correctly trimmed will give the Bedlington the distinctive, lamblike appearance for which he has become so well-known.

An expertly groomed Bedlington Terrier shows to good advantage
the distinctive lamblike appearance.

A Bedlington prior to trimming and grooming looks like this.

Pet trimming for the Bedlington Terrier

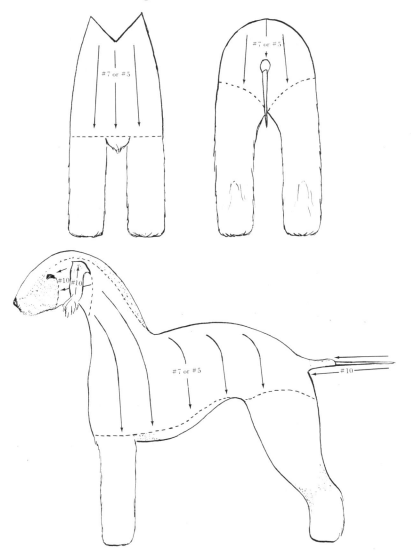

The Kerry Blue Terrier

Standard Regarding Coat

Coat—Soft, dense and wavy. A harsh, wire or bristle coat should be severly penalized. In show trim the body should be well covered but tidy, with the head (except for the whiskers) and ears and cheeks clear.

Breed Note

The Kerry Blue Terrier was developed in Southwest Ireland as the farmer's dog of all work. It was only after being seen on the show bench early in this century that far-sighted fanciers realized his potential as a show dog. Today's Kerry, trimmed and elegant, in his shining, soft, blue coat is one of the most beautiful of the terriers.

Kerry puppies are always born black· and "clear" to their mature color some time before their second birthday.

Grooming Procedure

What follows is not absolute law; it is one version of how to trim a Kerry Blue Terrier. There are other methods and many different opinions on the subject. This explanation is presented simply to help anyone trying to learn the basic principles of grooming a Kerry Blue.

The Feet—Scissor the hair growing between the pads. This keeps a dog from collecting mud and other debris that may irritate his feet.

Comb the leg hair down against the foot and cut off any hair that extends beyond the pad.

The Stomach Area—Place the dog on his back and with clippers fitted with a #10 blade trim his stomach. Trim to about three inches in front of the front edge of the back leg. (This will be about a clipper's width in front of the penis or an area that includes the back three sets of nipples on a bitch.) Trim the hair on the penis with the clipper also, but trim *only* with the grain—or from the body out.

Trimming the Head and Neck—Start with the ears, running the clipper against the growth of the hair on both the outside surface and as much of the underneath surface as you can reach easily (trimming the rest with scissors until tidy). There is a flap of skin on the back edge of the ear. Find this with your fingers and be careful not to cut it with clippers or scissors as it bleeds very profusely.

On the head itself there are three "markers" to trim to—1) the outside corner of the eye; 2) mouth; and 3) the hair follicle (a definite lump) under the chin. Trim against the hair in all areas of the head and neck with the exception of the very flat top of the skull (from the

Show Trimming for the Kerry Blue Terrier

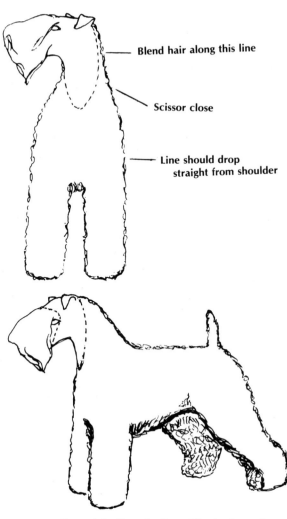

Blend hair along this line

Scissor close

Line should drop straight from shoulder

General Outline of a Kerry Blue in show trim

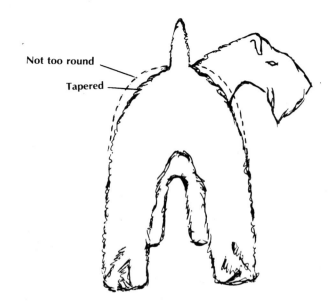

Not too round

Tapered

Pet Trimming for the Kerry Blue Terrier

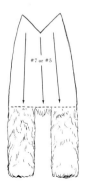

#7 or #5

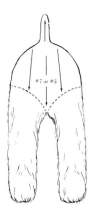

#7 or #5

#10

#7 or #5

brows back to between the ears). Trimming this particular area depends on how curly or straight the hair may be. If it is quite straight, you will have to trim against the growth. Practice can tell you which you like best. Taper the hair to a longer length with a scissor right behind the ears. (When you are more sure of yourself, bring the clipper line about ¾" to 1" past the corner of the mouth—taking the line directly under the chin to the other side.)

Some people use the clipper entirely too far down the throat. This is something again that has to be decided by the individual. A show trim should require more blending with the scissor to make the neck blend into the body. If you trim a V or an oval at the base of the throat, be sure not to carry it too low. This can make your dog appear quite short when coming toward the judge. It also may not give the dog as pleasing a front when viewed from the side.

The Legs—Brush the hair against the grain and then with it, with a wire slicker, with whiskers and body coat. Follow with a metal Poodle comb in the same manner.

After you have combed the hair down, lift the foot and shake the whole leg. Then replace the foot and trim to achieve a tubular or cylindrical effect. This will require a great deal of patience and practice.

The writer prefers to trim the body first, for the legs should make a continuous line down from the body.

The Body—Blend the hair around the clipped areas with scissors. The body coat should be about an inch and a half in length. For a summer or utility trim, use a #5 blade on the clipper for the body. This is marvelous for keeping a litter of puppies looking neat when they pass the three-months mark. Trim the hair on the tail shorter than the rest of the body and be sure the area under the tail is trimmed quite close as well as the rear of the dog.

Looking at your dog from the rear his legs should form an inverted V. Be sure the hips are more tapered than rounded.

The Face—Comb the whiskers forward and with scissors pointing toward the nose cut the hair beside the eyes to make them visible. Trim any *extra long* whiskers to give them a neater appearance.

Courtesy, The United States Kerry Blue Club, by Mrs. Fred W. Rogers, Jr.

The Soft-Coated Wheaten Terrier

Standard Regarding Coat

Coat—Abundant, soft and wavy, of a good clear wheaten color; may be shaded on the ears and muzzle.

The Soft-Coated Wheaten Terrier is a natural dog and should so appear. Dogs that appear to be overly trimmed should be penalized.

Coat on ears may be left natural or relieved of the fringe to accent smallness.

Coat color and texture do not stabilize until about 18–24 months and should be given some latitude in young dogs.

For show purposes the coat may be tidied up merely to present a neat outline but may not be clipped, plucked or stylized.

Breed Note

The Soft-Coated Wheaten Terrier is one of the few coated terriers which is neither wire coated, like the Airedale, nor smooth coated, like the Manchester Terrier. His coat is more like that of the Kerry Blue Terrier, his probable descendant. His coat is quite dark at birth, assuming the typical color by the time the dog is two years old.

Grooming Procedure

There are several important rules essential to grooming Soft-Coated Wheaten Terriers. Here is what every groomer should remember about this charming Irish breed:

1. Thinning shears give best results on the Wheaten coat.
2. Thinning shears are used for both thinning and tipping.
3. Thinning helps coat to lie flat while tipping helps coat to stand up or out.
4. Always begin grooming by determining outline of dog; first clean throat and chest, then tail and rump.
5. Never trim a dirty dog.
6. Dog should show a neat, terrier outline but coat must retain some length. Sharp contrasts must be avoided. Head coat should be blended to present a rectangular outline. Eyes should be indicated, but never fully exposed. Ears should be relieved of fringe, but not taken down to the leather. Enough coat must be left on skull, cheeks and neck to balance the length of body coat. Same holds true for coat on tail and rear quarters.

Ears—Lift ear, using thumbnail as cutting guide and shield to protect edge from nicks. Hold thinning shears pointing upward (same direction as hair lays) and remove all fringe from perimeter, close to edge of ear. Scissor all hair in inside of ear flap.

A small amount of thinning may be done over shoulders to allow coat to lay more smoothly but *must* blend with body coat. When viewed from front there should be gradual widening from withers to a point ⅓ of the way down toward elbow where coat forms a straight line to the ground.

Throat and Chest—Work from corner of throat forward under jaw at least 2″ toward beard. Shorten to approximately ¾″. Work down front of neck and chest tipping and thinning until coat is smooth and relatively flat.

Brisket and Tuck-Up—Create tuck-up in a gentle curving line and remove excess coat from brisket. Use thinning shears to tip coat in this area, shears pointing down and angled under dog toward feet on opposite side. The result is a naturally rounded belly rather than an artificial side curtain.

Tail—Remove the flag from back of tail and some of the side fringes with shears. The underside should be relatively flat and clean, with ample coat left on so as not to look spindly. The tail must blend with body coat.

Rump—With shears, tip and thin bunching hair until outline emerges neat and tidy. Because hair grows in a double cowlick pattern, care must be taken not to remove too much hair leaving the rump bare on this otherwise coated dog. Entire rump must be covered with at least ¾″ to 1″ of coat. Neatly remove hair covering anus. Remove excess "skirt."

Topknot—Starting at the top of the skull, cut hair to approximately 1″. Move forward, allowing hair length to increase as you approach eye to approximately 1″ to 1½″ above eye. Leave remaining fall.

Courtesy, Soft-Coated Wheaten Terrier Club of America

Pet Grooming—Pet grooming the Soft-Coated Wheaten Terrier differs from the guidelines herein only in the trimming of the body coat, which may be done with a #1 Snap-On comb.

Create tuckup in a gentle curving line as pictured and remove excess coat from brisket. Use thinning shears to tip coat in this area, shears pointing down and angled under dog toward feet on opposite side. The result is a naturally rounded belly rather than an artificial side curtain.

Longhaired Toys

The English Toy Spaniel

Standard Regarding Coat

Coat—The coat should be long, silky, soft and wavy, but not curly. There should be a profuse mane, extending well down in the front of the chest. The feather should be well displayed on the ears and feet, and in the latter case so thickly as to give the appearance of being webbed. It is also carried well up the backs of the legs. In the Black and Tan the feather on the ears is very long and profuse, exceeding that of the Blenheim by an inch or more. The feather on the tail (which is cut to the length of about 1½ inches) should be silky, and from 3 to 4 inches in length, constituting a marked "flag" of a square shape, and not carried above the level of the back.

Breed Note

The English Toy Spaniel boasts a long history filled with royal favor. Selective breeding over many years has reduced the English Toy Spaniel down to its present size (nine to 12 pounds). He can be considered a rare breed today, but makes as fine a housepet as he did in the 15th Century.

Grooming Procedure

Grooming the English Toy Spaniel is mostly attending to grooming fundamentals—brushing, bathing, blow drying, ear cleaning and nail trimming—as described in Part I. Beyond the fundamentals, there is a negligible amount of trimming to do.

Thinning shears should be used to smooth out any overgrown, clumpy areas and remove straggly hairs. Excess hair should always be cleaned out with scissors between the foot pads, but not on the tops of the feet. Show dogs require only a little extra attention.

The Japanese Chin

Standard Regarding Coat

Coat—Profuse, long, straight, rather silky. It should be absolutely free from wave or curl, and not lie too flat, but have a tendency to stand out, especially at the neck, so as to give a thick mane or ruff, which with profuse feathering on thighs and tail gives a very showy appearance.

Breed Note

The Japanese Chin probably came to Japan from China as an imperial gift many centuries ago. He is a small toy dog but is extremely hardy and naturally clean, so makes a fine, easily-cared-for pet. Although fairly well-known in Great Britain and Continental Europe, the Japanese Chin is still a rare breed in the United States.

Grooming Procedure

The Japanese Chin is easy to care for as there is no plucking, clipping, or trimming required. The dog should be combed every day using the coarse end of the comb first, following with the fine-toothed section. Brushing cleanses and gives a shine to the hair. The entire body should be massaged daily. This can be done during grooming sessions or while the dog is being held or petted. The general health of a Chin is reflected in the luxuriousness of his coat. Watch carefully for mats behind the ears. These can usually be removed by using the single large tooth at the end of the comb, but if mats are heavy, insert the comb behind the mat to protect the skin and use scissors or a mat splitter to break the mat into sections or remove it entirely.

Courtesy, The Japanese Chin Club of America by Vera E. Schenck

134

The Papillon

Standard Regarding Coat

Coat—Abundant, long, fine, silky, flowing, straight with resilient quality, flat back and sides of body. A profuse frill on chest. There is no undercoat. Hair short and close on skull, muzzle, front of forelegs and from hind feet to hocks. Ears well fringed with the inside covered with silken hair of medium length. Backs of the forelegs are covered with feathers diminishing to the pasterns. Hind legs are covered to the hocks with abundant breeches (culottes). Tail is covered with a long flowing plume. Hair on feet is short but fine tufts may appear over toes and grow beyond them forming a point.

Breed Note

The modern Papillon was developed in France from dwarf spaniels fashionable in Continental Europe during the latter part of the Renaissance. His name is French and is derived from his ear structure, which resembles the outspread wings of a butterfly. It is the ears that distinguish the Papillon from all other dog breeds.

The Papillon today is exclusively a show dog and housepet. He has never really caught the fancy of the American public, but several of the breed have done very well in the show ring.

Grooming Procedure

Grooming a Papillon involves minimal effort. Only the hair on the bottom of the foot is removed being careful not to cut off any toe fringes. The coat is often called a nylon coat as it does not retain soil but is easily maintained by a few minutes of daily brushing. Use a good baby shampoo for washing and blow dry the coat, brushing as you blow it. Special attention should be paid to the ears making sure they are dried well with no water left inside. The ears should be dried inside with a sterile cotton ball.

To maintain a good show coat and ear fringes, the application of a light oil such as cocoanut oil on the fringes and on the body either a light grooming oil, such as Happy Hair or Whispering Mist, is beneficial. Whiskers should not be trimmed off the muzzle as they are needed to protect the eyes. Papillons should always get a dry bath before being shown or for some other special occasion.

Courtesy, Greater Chicagoland Papillon Club
by Beverley C. Berman

The Pekingese

Standard Regarding Coat

Coat, Feather and Condition—Long, with thick undercoat, straight and flat, neither curly nor wavy, rather coarse, but soft; feather on thighs, legs, tail and toes long and profuse. **Mane**—Profuse, extending beyond the shoulder blades forming ruff or frill around the neck.

Breed Note

The Pekingese was discovered in the Imperial Palace of Peking, by English soldiers who plundered royal residence in 1860. Always bred exclusively as a companion, he is by no means timid. He carries himself at all times like the true Mandarin aristocrat. The Pekingese is a great favorite with American dog lovers, ranking consistently among the top twenty most popular breeds.

Grooming Procedure

The first essential is having the necessary tools with which to work. I strongly recommend a good Kent rubber backed brush with Hindes pig bristles, two steel combs with wide teeth so as not to pull the hair, a couple of face cloths and a good quality coat dressing. The dog to be groomed must be scrupulously clean and must have a good coat and fringes.

Dampen the face cloth with warm water and rub it over the coat thoroughly to remove any soil or foreign particles. Brush thoroughly from shoulders forward and up from the sides. Sprinkle a little Johnson's Baby Powder on the ear fringes, the base of the tail and through the fringes on the tail. Work the powder in with the fingertips as one would do giving a scalp massage, then brush thoroughly. With a good atomizer, spray the dog thoroughly. Brush the tail up toward the head and part the tail in the middle with the brush. Again spray the tail and sprinkle a little more baby powder into it, the tips of the ear fringes and the skirts at the base of the tail. Work the powder in well with thumb and forefinger. Then with a wide tooth comb, gingerly comb this out to a "feathery" consistency. Then with absorbent cotton thoroughly moistened in boric acid solution, wipe the eyes and nose wrinkle clean.

Remember to comb the fringes on either side of the forelegs so that they are not matted and are combed straight back. Do not, at any time, let these fringes stick out at the sides. That may give the impression that the dog is out at shoulder, regardless of how sound he may actually be. If the dog's coat tends to be soft and he lacks the proper, stand-off mane, use plain Argo corn starch to give the coat body. Use corn starch just as you'd use baby powder. It is an excellent cleaner.

For show dogs, always provide your Peke an opportunity to shake any powder or dust out of his coat before entering the ring. Put your dog down on the floor or in an exercise pen before going up to the ring, so he can shake as you wish.

Before going into the ring have your atomizer handy and give the dog a quick, light spray. This will hold in any powder that might shake out and also give the dog the same bloom as if he had just had a shampoo with all the hairs standing out and in the proper place.

Courtesy, The Pekingese Club of America
by the late John B. Royce.

The Pomeranian

Standard Regarding Coat

Coat—Double-coated; a short, soft, thick under-coat, with longer, coarse, glistening outer coat consisting of guard hairs which must be harsh to the touch in order to give the proper texture for the coat to form a frill of profuse, standing-off straight hair. The front legs are well feathered and the hindquarters are clad with long hair or feathering from the top of the rump to the hocks.

Breed Note

The Pomeranian is the smallest of the "Northern" breeds, having been bred down from larger Spitz types. One of the most popular Toys, the Pomeranian was known in the United States as early as 1892. He has a loud, sharp bark and is an excellent watchdog. He is also an ideal companion and a consistently successful show dog.

Grooming Procedure

You will need the following:
1. A natural bristle brush, or a "pin" brush with smooth, flexible metal pins set in rubber.

2. A smooth metal comb, rather fine and close at one end, teeth larger and wider apart at other end. Use sparingly to tease apart any mats remaining in coat after brushing.

3. Blunt-tipped scissors for trimming unruly hairs on ears, feet and around anus, for cleanliness.

Brush hair daily to keep it free of tangles and mats, and to remove dust or other debris from the coat. Bathe only when dog is dirty, brushing to remove all mats before bathing. Use any shampoo prepared for humans or pets. (Some are "tear-less" and non-irritating to the eyes.) Protect ears from water by placing a small wad of cotton in each ear and remove later when dog is being dried. Brush dry in front of small hair dryer; one with a stand is preferred as it leaves both hands free to hold and brush the dog.

Trimming—Trimming for neatness is permissible around the feet and up the back of the legs to the first joint; trimming of unruly hairs on the edges of the ears and around the anus is also permitted.

Courtesy, American Pomeranian Club

Longhaired Non-Sporting Dogs

The Bichon Frise

Standard Regarding Coat

Coat—Profuse, silky and loosely curled. There is an undercoat. **Grooming**—Scissored to show the eyes and give a full rounded appearance to the head and body. Feet should have hair trimmed to give a rounded appearance. When properly brushed, there is an overall "powder puff" appearance. Puppies may be shown in short coat, but the minimum show coat for an adult is two inches.

Breed Note

The Bichon Frise developed centuries ago in the Mediterranean and comes to us by way of France. He was officially recognized by AKC in 1973 and included in the Non-Sporting Group. Since then there has been a steady increase in the breed's popularity both as a charming pet and an elegant show dog.

Grooming Procedure

Although there does not appear to be any common ancestry, the Bichon bears a distinct resemblance to the Poodle. In fact when many Poodle owners see the Bichon for the first time they often take it for a Poodle cross breed. This resemblance also extends to the grooming. The Bichon is brushed, bathed and blow-dried in much the same way as the Poodle. The fundamentals of grooming are identical for both.

However, unlike the Poodle, clippers are not used at all on the Bichon but he is scissored throughout. Also unlike the Poodle, there is only one style or pattern for the Bichon Frise. The Bichon is never trimmed in any other style than that described here.

There is an even blanket of hair left on the body with a minimum length of two inches. The legs, of course, are fuller. The feet are trimmed neat, tight and round.

There is no separation between the topknot and ears and there is a full flowing moustache and beard. Only straggly hairs are removed.

When the Bichon is finished he should resemble a white powder-puff accentuated by large, round, dark eyes.

The Chow Chow

Standard Regarding Coat

Coat—Abundant, dense, straight, and off-standing rather coarse in texture with a soft, wooly undercoat. It may be of any clear color, solid throughout, with lighter shadings on ruff, tail, and breechings.

Breed Note

The Chow Chow is an ancient breed of Chinese origin and "Northern" type. He was used as a hunter and guard dog centuries ago and can still perform these tasks today given the opportunity. The breed's name was the result of a slang expression used by English sailors for knick-knacks and miscellaneous items of cargo.

The Chow Chow's beautiful, thick coat may occur in any of a variety of colors. He is an ideal companion for anyone who admires a one-man dog and his fastidious nature appeals to the most meticulous housekeeper.

Grooming Procedure

The basic grooming tool for the Chow Chow is the wire slicker brush for the pet or the pin brush for the show dog. Since the Chow Chow is a longhaired breed which does not require any particular styling (he should be shown as naturally as possible), grooming consists primarily of brushing and combing out the coat.

Strict attention, then, should be paid to the fundamentals of grooming, as described in Part I. If you are grooming a Chow Chow from puppyhood on, it would be most desirable to train the puppy to lie down during grooming sessions, on his side and on his stomach in the positions most comfortable for dog and groomer.

The only trimming really called for is scissoring the Chow Chow's feet, once again using the grooming table as the leveller and scissoring all around the paw for a compact, cat-like effect.

The Keeshond

Standard Regarding Coat

Coat—The body should be abundantly covered with long, straight, harsh hair; standing well out from a thick, downy undercoat. The hair on the legs should be smooth and short, except for a feathering on the front legs and "trousers," as previously described, on the hind legs. The hair on the tail should be profuse, forming a rich plume. Head including muzzle, skull and ears, should be covered with smooth, soft, short hair—velvety in texture on the ears. Coat must not part down the back. **Fault**—Silky, wavy or curly coats. Part in coat down the back.

Breed Note

The Keeshond is the barge dog of Holland where he has been known and admired for hundreds of years. Throughout his history the breed has been kept as a guard and companion. Even today, he maintains his deepest attachments to home and family. Highly intelligent, the Keeshond accepts even the most advanced obedience training well. He is moderately popular at present with a loyal group of admirers looking out for his best interests.

Grooming Procedure

When a Keeshond is presented for grooming and bathing, he is usually in a pretty bad state. Either he is shedding or is badly matted, and requires many hours of work and much patience.

It is most important when grooming the Keeshond to brush and comb out all loose hair, mats and tangles before bathing the dog. If this is not done, all the loose hair in the coat will form huge mats, which will take hours to dry out and which will be almost impossible to remove. Many groomers have made this mistake, and have had to resort to clipping the dog all over much to the consternation of the owners.

The hair must be parted to the skin and brushed in layers by holding back the hair with one hand while brushing with the other. The most suitable brush for removing dead hair is a large slicker. It is necessary to go over the dog several times, as each brushing brings up more loose hair. With a badly neglected coat one will find dead hair packed solid to the skin on the throat and chest, on the back of the neck and around the ears, and in the trousers and over the hips. This dead hair *must* be removed and if it is impossible with the brush then a mat splitter can be used. Never cut out mats with the scissors

140

and *never* use a clipper on a Keeshond. The only exception to the use of the clipper would be around the reproductive organs if the dog was badly matted here and in the ''arm'' pits under the forelegs. Both these areas are very tender and an attempt to remove very large mats with the brush, comb or mat splitter would cause much distress to the dog. Pay particular attention to removing dead hair and mats from the thighs and upper arm areas.

Brush both the underside and the topside of the tail to remove dead hair and comb with a wide-toothed comb. Also brush and comb the front leg feathering. Every area of the dog must be brushed to remove loose hair, and this includes the legs and head, using a soft wire slicker against the lay of the hair on the head. When all loose hair and mats have been removed, comb out the hair on the back of the hocks and trim off all long hair with scissors. Also scissor all surplus hair on the pads of the four feet and on the back of the front pasterns. Cut the nails, and then scissor around the feet to make them appear round and cat-like. Clean the ears and put some cotton in them before bathing.

After the dog has been bathed and rinsed, pour a creme rinse over him, massage it well into the coat, leave on for a few minutes and then thoroughly rinse out. Towel off excess water, remove cotton from ears and dry them inside. Now proceed to dry the dog. The ideal method is by fluff drying, which uses an electric dryer playing a stream of air on the coat and brushing the dog until he is dry. A lot more loose hair will be removed this way as the dog is drying. If the dog is cage-dried, remove him from the cage when partly dry, run the brush over his coat to separate the hairs. This will facilitate quicker drying when you put him back into the crate.

When he is dry it will be necessary to thoroughly brush the dog once more, again layering the coat as much more hair will have been loosened by the bath. When all loose hair has been removed, go over the coat once more with a pin brush, this time brushing against the lay of the hair, starting behind the head and working down the entire body, this will make the coat stand off from the body in the·desired fashion.

When a Keeshond is presented for grooming and is not matted or shedding, he should still be thoroughly brushed before and after bathing, have his nails cut, hocks, pasterns and feet trimmed, ears cleaned and be finished off with a pin brush.

Courtesy, The Keeshond Club of America
by Nan Greenwood

Part III

THE SHORTHAIRED BREEDS

Affenpinscher
Airedale Terrier
Akita
Alaskan Malamute
Australian Cattle Dog
Australian Terrier
Belgian Malinois
Border Terrier
Brussels Griffon
Cairn Terrier
Chesapeake Bay
  Retriever
Curly-Coated Retriever
Dachshund (Wirehaired)
Dandie Dinmont Terrier
Flat-Coated Retriever
Fox Terrier (Wire)
German Shepherd Dog
German Shorthaired
  Pointer
German Wirehaired
  Pointer
Giant Schnauzer
Golden Retriever

Irish Terrier
Labrador Retriever
Lakeland Terrier
Miniature Schnauzer
Norfolk Terrier
Norwegian Elkhound
Norwich Terrier
Saint Bernard
  (Shorthaired)
Saluki
Schipperke
Scottish Terrier
Sealyham Terrier
Siberian Husky
Standard Schnauzer
Welsh Terrier
Welsh Corgi (Cardigan)
Welsh Corgi
  (Pembroke)
West Highland White
  Terrier
Wirehaired Pointing
  Griffon

Shorthaired Sporting Dogs

The German Shorthaired Pointer

Standard Regarding Coat

Coat—The hair should be short and thick and feel tough and hard to the hand; it is somewhat longer on the underside of the tail and the back edge of the haunches. It is softer, thinner and shorter on the ears and the head.

Breed Note

Typical of the continental pointers, the German Shorthair is a medium-sized breed and was developed as an all-around hunter that works relatively close to the gun. Versatility is the breed's strong suit and he has been used on waterfowl, upland game and on fur as well.

His lineage traces to the old Spanish Pointer, various strains of German hunting hounds and the English Foxhound. In view of this, it is easy to understand the reasons for the breed's wide-ranging abilities.

Today the German Shorthair is still held in the highest esteem for his skill in the field. He is also successful in the show ring, in obedience and as a superb companion.

Grooming Procedure

Grooming a German Shorthaired Pointer is relatively simple. Daily brushing keeps the coat gleaming and healthy, by stimulating the natural oils in the skin and removes any loose or dead hair.

Nails should be cut regularly and are best kept short as possible. Before a dog is to be shown, a tiny dab of coat oil on each nail will give a nice shiny finish.

Teeth should be free of tartar and should be scaled if this is needed.

Whiskers and face furnishings on a show dog are trimmed judiciously. Any longish hairs on the abdomen, along the tuck-up, back of the thighs and tail tip should also be trimmed. Ears should be cleaned gently with cotton and a good ear cleaning agent. Bathing is best done a day or two before a show to allow the oil to return to the coat.

Regular attention to teeth, feet and ears will make show grooming a simple matter. A German Shorthaired Pointer so treated will always be in top condition and ready for any event.

*Courtesy, German Shorthaired Pointer Club
of America
by Madeline Schwalm*

144

The German Wirehaired Pointer

Standard Regarding Coat

Coat—The coat is weather-resisting and to some extent water-repellent. The undercoat is dense enough in winter to insulate against the cold but so thin in summer as to be almost invisible. The distinctive outer coat is straight, harsh, wiry and rather flat-lying, from 1½ to 2 inches in length, it is long enough to protect against the punishment of rough cover but not so long as to hide the outline. On the lower legs it is shorter and between the toes of softer texture. On the skull it is naturally short and close fitting, while over the shoulders and around the tail it is very dense and heavy. The tail is nicely coated, particularly on the underside, but devoid of feather. These dogs have bushy eyebrows of strong, straight hair and beards and whiskers of medium length.

A short smooth coat, a soft wooly coat, or an excessively long coat is to be severely penalized.

Breed Note

The German Wirehaired Pointer shows the typical stamp common to all continental pointers. Unlike most, he carries a very thick, wiry, double coat that protects him from the rough cover he was bred to hunt in. The undercoat, which varies in density with the seasons, serves to keep this rugged fellow warm and dry under any conditions.

Not an old breed, the German Wirehair came into being during the second half of the 19th Century. In the natural course of events, type became more even and the breed developed into a distinct entity.

He is an accomplished hunting dog and sportsmen in the United States have been quick to notice the Wirehair's positive combination of assets. The breed is reasonably popular and is appreciated for his companionable personality as for his wise ways in the field.

Grooming Procedure

The Wirehair with a hard, flat coat is very easy to groom. Weekly grooming with a steel comb removes dead undercoat.

Much more time has to be spent on the dog with a heavy, longer coat. The German Wirehaired Pointer Standard calls for a hard, flat outer coat one to one-half inches long.

Between one and two months before showing your dog, strip off the outer coat (NEVER CLIP). Leave only the beard and eyebrows long. Just how soon before the show you should strip your dog will depend upon the rate of growth on the individual dog and can only be determined by experimenting. But, never show your dog newly stripped.

About two weeks before showing your dog, strip

any long hair from skull, top of muzzle and ears. At this time, also remove long hair from throat and sides of neck.

A few days before showing your dog, strip cheeks, underside of tail (scissors may be used here) and flanks. Remove any scraggly hair from body and legs. The hair on the body should be flat-lying and should not hide the body outline. Any long hair between the toes or around the pads of the feet should be trimmed. The dog should not carry any furnishings except on the back of the fore-legs where a *short* fringe may be left.

Remove any scraggly hair from the ears. Shape beard and eyebrows. The hair on the eyebrows should be longest above the inner corner of the eye tapering off and blending into the cheek coat just below the outer corner of the eye. All long hair on top of the muzzle and on the stop (between eyebrows) should be removed. Removal of any hair from between the eyes will make the eyebrows clear and distinct over each eye. Ideally, the coat on the skull and ears should be very short and close fitting and should require very little trimming.

Baths should never be given unless absolutely necessary and never less than two weeks before a show.

Courtesy, German Wirehaired Pointer Club of Illinois

The Chesapeake Bay Retriever

Standard Regarding Coat

Coat—Coat should be thick and short, nowhere over 1½ inches long, with a dense fine woolly undercoat. Hair on face and legs should be very short and straight, with tendency to wave on the shoulders, neck back and loins only. The curly coat or coat with a tendency to curl not permissible.

Breed Note

The Chesapeake Bay Retriever, named for the famous section of Maryland's Eastern shore, was developed as a working gun dog. He was often the choice of market hunters who needed a dog that would bring in hundreds of fallen ducks and geese in a single day. The breed is still greatly valued as a hunting companion, especially where rough weather and other difficult hunting conditions are factors.

The Chessie is known for a strong character and this factor is much appreciated by those who know him. The breed can act as an effective guard dog as well as a stouthearted waterfowl dog.

Grooming Procedure

Chesapeake Bay Retrievers should be shown as naturally as possible. Attempts to improve on nature by trimming, clipping, stripping or combing out the undercoat are wrong and unacceptable. A clean, healthy Chesapeake needs no embellishment. Brush the dog regularly to keep dead hair from accumulating in the coat, but guard and cherish that soft, woolly undercoat. The Chesapeake's undercoat should be thick and dense. The comb should be used only to clean the brush.

A hound glove, *made with natural bristles* is excellent for grooming, smoothing and bringing up the natural gloss on a good coat. Dust and surface oil can be removed with a towel or sponge wrung out in clear water just before going in the ring. Sprays and coat dressings which might serve to alter the natural texture of the coat are undesirable. Trimming off whiskers and eyebrows for show dogs should be optional, for the Chesapeake is a working gun dog and some evidence exists that whiskers help the dog in the field. Nails should be kept short, and if a given dog does not naturally wear them down, trimming nails should be a regular routine.

Courtesy, American Chesapeake Club
by Deborah Reaves

The Curly-Coated Retriever

Standard Regarding Coat

Coat—Should be one mass of crisp curls all over. A slightly more open coat not to be severely penalized, but a saddle back of patch of uncurled hair behind the shoulder should be penalized, and a prominent white patch on breast is undesirable, but a few white hairs allowed in an otherwise good dog. Color, black or liver.

Breed Note

The distinctive Curly-Coated Retriever is the oldest existing retriever breed, having been familiar to British sportsmen before the inception of dog shows. He is also the tallest of all retrievers and is most distinctive by reason of his unique, beautiful coat. The combination of breeds used to develop him is not known, but he undoubtedly shares a common ancestry with the Labrador with a dash of Poodle blood brought in to get the curly coat.

A rarity in North America, the Curly is much appreciated as a gun dog in New Zealand and Australia where he first appeared in 1889.

Grooming Procedure

The Fundamentals of Grooming will serve the Curly-coated Retriever nicely. There is however one exception and that is that the adult coat is never brushed. Brushing, while acceptable for puppy coats, would ruin the important, characteristic curls in the mature animal.

The crisp curls have been described as being similar to Astrakhan and are set and best groomed with a dampened sponge. Some limited use of a comb is also on the agenda and mainly concerns the sides of the head and behind the ears and legs.

The Curly-Coat is yet another breed where condition and superlative muscle tone go a long way toward achieving the desired picture.

The Flat Coated Retriever

Standard Regarding Coat

Coat—Should be dense, of fine quality and texture, as flat as possible.

Breed Note

Typical of the retriever stamp, the Flat-Coated Retriever was developed in England during the 19th Century by judicious crossings of several water dogs types familiar at the time.

It is unfortunate that the breed is so little known compared to the Labrador and Golden Retrievers for he has much to offer the hunter, show person and prospective pet owner. His coat is easy to look after and stands him in good stead in any weather. He is very easy to live with, being anxious to please and quick to learn. And he is also handsome enough to draw admiration wherever he goes.

More recently the breed has been gaining in both numbers and in following and while he is still rare in England and America, his fortunes appear in the ascendancy at the present time.

Grooming Procedure

The Flat Coated Retriever is a very natural dog and requires little in grooming beyond the fundamentals. As with other breeds requiring only minimal grooming attention, preparing the Flat Coat for the show ring includes only the added touch of trimming the facial whiskers, shortening the hairs at the ears and tip of the tail. Also the hair on back of the hocks and pads of the feet should be tidied with scissors.

The Golden Retriever

Standard Regarding Coat

Coat—Dense and water-repellent with good undercoat. Texture not as hard as that of a shorthaired dog, nor silky as that of a setter. Lies flat against the body and may be straight or wavy. Moderate feathering on back of forelegs and heavier feathering on front of neck, back of thighs and underside of tail. Feathering may be lighter than rest of coat.

Breed Note

The Golden Retriever was developed in the North of Scotland by Lord Tweedmouth on his estate, Guisachan, in Invernesshire. The breeding program responsible for the Golden was very carefully documented and there are very few gaps in how the breed came to be over the 55 years the records from Guisachan span.

Today the Golden Retriever is one of our most familiar and best-loved purebreds. He is an ideal companion for young and old, is an able working hunter, has proven himself more than equal to show and obedience competition and can even be seen serving as eyes for blind owners.

In the late 1970s he enjoyed immense popularity and was #6 among all breeds for 1979. Among his numerous admirers is the former President of the United States, Gerald R. Ford.

Grooming Procedure

Our present breed Standard says very little specific about the manner in which a Golden should be groomed for showing, but implies that, as a hunting dog, he is to be presented naturally and specifically states that he should be in hard, working condition. The only references to trimming are under **Head,** stating that removal of whiskers for show purposes is OPTIONAL, and under **Feet,** stating that excess hair MAY be removed to show natural size and contour of the feet. Under **Neck** it requires an untrimmed natural ruff.

The implication that the Golden is to be shown in his natural, normal coat and without barbering or clipping should be obvious. Any trimming or thinning which is felt essential in presenting the dog in a neat and well-groomed manner must be done very discreetly and must never be obvious to the eye or hand.

Most unfortunately, too many exhibitors and handlers have gone far beyond the minimum recognized by the Standard, and the results are to be deplored. The Golden Retriever's coat is completely different from that of a Setter or Spaniel, and should NEVER be subjected to the type of grooming used on these breeds, such as (but not limited to) the use of electric clippers on ears, throat and head.

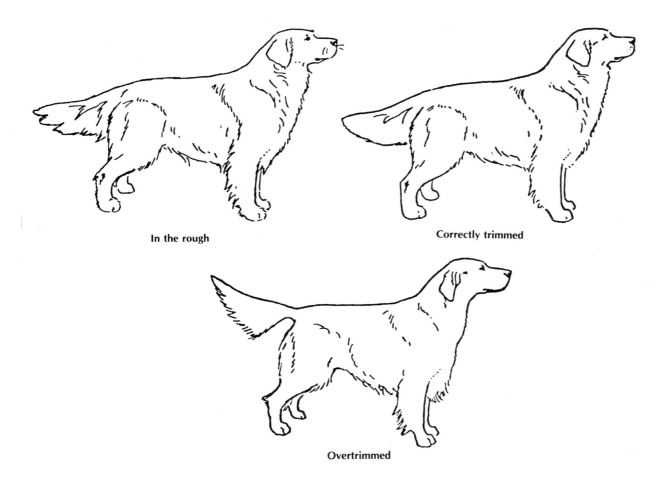

In the rough

Correctly trimmed

Overtrimmed

Trimming The Head

Drawing A—A nice sort of Golden "in the rough." This dog has very noticeable whiskers and will have a neater appearance with some tidying done. Some dogs with fine, unobtrusive whiskers could well be left alone, just brushed neatly and in clean condition.

Drawing B—Here our Golden has had a few minutes spent removing feelers, and some scraggly hairs on ears and lipline neatened. But the effect is natural and soft.

Drawing C—Overtrimmed. The removal of too much hair gives a harsh, foreign look to the Golden's head. Use of clippers and scissors changes texture and color of the coat by removing the darker, finer tips of the hairs and revealing the lighter color base and under-coat.

DO NOT—repeat, DO NOT clip the ruff. Electric clippers have no place in the Golden's grooming bag! The ruff must be left natural, with no bare throat, no bald cheeks, no shaved neck. The framing of ears and ruff gives the Golden's head much of its distinctive quality and kindly expression, and is a definite feature of the breed. Don't spoil it.

When practicing trimming, use a dog not being shown for your practice—or experiment well ahead of show dates until you've got the knack of producing a neat, natural dog who doesn't show any signs of having been trimmed!

Courtesy, The Golden Retriever Club of America

The Labrador Retriever

Standard Regarding Coat

Coat—The coat is another very distinctive feature; it should be short, very dense and without wave, and should give a fairly hard feeling to the hand.

Breed Note

The Labrador is the focus of global popularity. Go to Australia, South Africa, France, Scandinavia and many other places. There you will find Labradors and those that admire them above all other dogs.

It's not hard to understand why the breed is so universally loved. He has excellent temperament, pleasing appearance, is highly intelligent and makes a wonderful companion.

Newfoundland is really the breed's place of origin and he probably got his name by his close association with Labrador. Here he was used as a retriever and came to the notice of English sportsmen who took him back to Britain.

His success in England was proverbial as a gun dog, a show dog and even as a police dog and guide dog for the blind. He continues to be one of England's most highly regarded breeds.

In America he is second only to the Cocker Spaniel in popularity among the Sporting breeds. The Lab has even made inroads on the Eastern shore of Maryland, the home of his cousin the Chesapeake.

Admirably suited to retrieving, the Labrador combines courage, stamina and no-nonsense, functional conformation in a package that many consider all that could be asked for in a Sporting dog.

Grooming Procedure

The Labrador Retriever's grooming requirements are very simple and mainly concern themselves with the fundamentals discussed in Part I of this book.

The grooming tool of choice is a natural bristle brush or a hound glove and this is used vigorously all over the body. There is almost no trimming required for a Labrador, with optional removal of whiskers being about the sole particular.

This is a completely natural breed that looks best when in good weight, neither too fat nor too thin. He should be in good hard flesh displaying excellent muscle tone and a bright, dense coat. Of course, this is more a matter for the owner than the groomer and little can be done with a fat, sloppy Lab. With this breed good looks and good grooming come mostly from within.

The Wirehaired Pointing Griffon

Standard Regarding Coat

Coat—Hard, dry, stiff, never curly, the undercoat downy.

Breed Note

The Wirehaired Pointing Griffon was developed during the last quarter of the 19th Century by E.K. Korthals, a Dutch sportsman. As Korthals traveled extensively, breeding activity took place in Holland, France and Germany. The Griffon is a particularly versatile gun dog—equally adaptable to fur and feather. He is not as fast afield as other sporting breeds, but makes an excellent personal shooting dog. Sadly, he has never really caught the fancy of the American public.

Grooming Procedure

The Wirehaired Pointing Griffon is very much a natural dog. His shaggy, tousled appearance is typical and correct. Regular brushing with removal of the longest hairs is best to always keep him looking as he should.

The reader may refer to the instructions for grooming and trimming the German Wirehaired Pointer as a general guide for working with the Griffon. He should remember, though, to preserve the Griffon's natural look. It is wrong to trim as closely as is advised for the former breed. In addition, the fundamentals of grooming for all breeds apply here to keeping the Griffon clean, healthy and well-looked-after.

153

Shorthaired Hounds

The Wirehaired Dachshund

Standard Regarding Coat

Coat—With the exception of jaw, eyebrows, and ears, the whole body is covered with a perfectly uniform tight, short, thick, rough, hard coat, but with finer, shorter hairs (undercoat) everywhere distributed between the coarser hairs, resembling the coat of the German Wirehaired Pointer. There should be a beard on the chin. The eyebrows are bushy. On the ears the hair is shorter than on the body, almost smooth, but in any case conforming to the rest of the coat. The general arrangement of the hair should be such that the wirehaired Dachshund, when seen from a distance should resemble a smooth-haired. Any sort of soft hair in the coat is faulty, whether short or long, or wherever found on the body; the same is true of long, curly, or wavy hair, or hair that sticks out irregularly in all directions; a flag tail is also objectionable.

Breed Note

The Wirehaired Dachshund is the youngest of the three varieties of this familiar breed. German sportsmen seeking a dog that could better cope with punishing cover than those they had, crossed Smooth Dachshunds with various harsh-coated terriers and then bred for the Dachshund features after the desirable coat charactertistics were fixed.

Seldom seen outside the showring, the Wire combines all the personality traits ordinarily seen in Dachsies with his own unique appearance. The result is a loving, faithful companion with a distinctive look that turns heads and draws admiration everywhere.

Grooming Procedure

In grooming the Wirehaired Dachshund, you are attempting to enhance proper body shape and emphasize the wire characteristics. There are basically two methods of grooming the Wirehaired Dachshund—plucking and stripping, or a combination of both. Plucking consists of using the thumb and index finger to pull out the longer hairs. Stripping is done with a "stripping knife." There are many types of stripping knives available; you must find the one which is most comfortable for you to use. Stripping is done by placing the knife against the coat, catching a *small amount* of hair against the blade with your thumb and pulling the longer hairs out of the coat. With either method, small amounts of hair should be taken at a time, and the hair should be pulled in the direction of coat growth with quick, pulling motions. Never pluck or strip the hair against the direction of coat growth.

When you plan to remove a great deal of coat ("take down"), you should do the major work eight to 12 weeks before the dog is to be shown, and then do the fine work on the coat during the last two weeks before the show. The rate of coat growth differs from dog to dog, so you might have to experiment to determine the best time schedule for your dog.

Once you get the coat in show condition, you can maintain it by stripping or plucking the longer hairs on a weekly basis. This removes any dead hair and allows for constant new growth of hair. This method is called rotation or "rolling" the coat.

Head—The head should be stripped or plucked from just behind the eyebrows, over the top of the skull and down into the neck area; between the eyes; and the cheek area from the outer corner of the eye to the corner of the lip. Stray hairs at the inner corner of the eye should be removed and the eyebrows should be longer at the inside corner of the eye tapering to the outside corner of the eye where they are flush with the skull structure. The eyebrows should be short enough to allow the eyes to be readily seen.

Since the overall head structure should be uniformly tapered, it may be necessary to thin out the beard to achieve this look. It is also possible to remove some of the coat from the center of the underjaw to allow the beard to lay closer against the muzzle.

Ears—Remove all the longer hairs from the outside and underside of the ear. Usually this hair has to be removed only once or twice; it does not tend to grow back. The hair on the inside of the ear where the ear joins the cheek should be scissored very close to the skin to allow the ear to lay flat against the cheek.

Neck—The longer hairs on the neck should be stripped or plucked under the chin and down the throat to the breast bone, along the sides of the neck; and on the back of the neck, blending into the shoulder area.

Body—The body coat is kept a little longer than the head and neck—about ½ to ¾ inch long. Stripping or plucking should be done from the neck area along the topline and sides back to the tail. The underside of the body should be plucked or stripped to conform to the rest of the body. Do not leave great length of coat here as it will look like a skirt. If the dog does not have a deep chest, groom the coat on the underside of the body so the chest hair is slightly longer, and taper it up into the loin.

Tail—The tail should be plucked or stripped to give an even, tapered look. Since the underside of the tail may be sensitive, you may wish to use thinning shears on this area. When using any type of scissor always cut with the growth of the hair, never against it. Be sure to cut the hairs around the anus for a neat appearance which conforms to the rest of the grooming.

Legs—The hair on the legs should conform to the body coat, but may be just a little longer. Judicious plucking or stripping of the longer hairs should be done to enhance the full, wire coat growth.

Feet—Use straight scissors to trim the hair on the bottom of the feet even with the pads. With the foot placed securely on a flat surface, use a straight scissor to trim the hair around the foot. The desired effect is a round, compact foot.

Pet Grooming the Wirehaired Dachshund

You can achieve the same results in the appearance of the dog by using a clipper; however, in most instances, you will not be able to maintain harsh coat texture with this method. Clippering is a time-saving method of keeping the dog neat and generally conforming to the desired look of the Wirehair.

Follow the same pattern of grooming as outlined before, using the following blades:

Head, Underside of Neck, and Ears: #10

Back of Neck, Body, and Tail: #5 (leaves the hair ½ inch long) or #7 (leaves the hair ¼ inch long)

Eyebrows and Beard: Scissor these to the desired shape and length.

Courtesy, National Miniature Dachshund Club, Dachshund Club of America by Jeanne A. Rice

The Norwegian Elkhound

Standard Regarding Coat

Coat—Thick, hard, weather-resisting and smooth-lying; made up of soft, dense, woolly undercoat and coarse, straight covering hairs. Short and even on head, ears, and front of legs; longest on back of neck, buttocks and underside of tail. The coat is not altered by trimming, clipping or artificial treatment. Trimming of whiskers is optional.

Breed Note

The Norwegian Elkhound is one of the most ancient purebreds, going back to the Stone Age. The Elkhound hunted big game with the Vikings and was the esteemed companion of these legendary nomads. He is today almost unchanged from the original form.

The Norwegian Elkhound is also a working dog and has been used extensively as a sled dog. He was used by the Norwegian army to transport goods and supplies.

This Nordic hunting dog enjoys the great outdoors, but he also enjoys the family hearth.

Grooming Procedure

The Norwegian Elkhound requires very little grooming beyond the fundamentals in Part I. Brushing is really the only grooming necessary. The brush used is a hound's glove. Clipping is not acceptable with the breed.

Courtesy, Norwegian Elkhound Association of America

The Saluki

Standard Regarding Coat

Coat—Smooth and of a soft silky texture, slight feather on the legs, feather at the back of the thighs and sometimes with slight woolly feather on the thigh and shoulder.

Breed Note

The Saluki emerged in the Middle East many centuries ago and was a favorite coursing hound of desert tribes and Egyptian nobility. Built for speed, he was adept at catching antelope and gazelle. Early in the twentieth century, the Saluki, together with the Afghan Hound began appearing in Europe and America. While the Saluki has never attained great popularity, he is much appreciated for his beauty, dignity and ease of management.

Grooming Procedure

The Saluki, is one of the shorthaired breeds, which does not require anything beyond the fundamental grooming. A natural bristle brush, applied daily over the entire body, would remove any dead hairs and keep the coat smooth and glossy.

The Saluki should be shown in his natural state. Nothing should be done in the way of clipping, stripping or trimming.

Courtesy, Chicagoland Saluki Club
by Nancy L. Culotta

Shorthaired Working Dogs

The Akita

Standard Regarding Coat

Coat—Double-coated. Undercoat thick, soft, dense and shorter than outer coat. Outer coat straight, harsh and standing somewhat off body. Hair on head, legs and ears short. Length of hair at withers and rump approximately two inches, which is slightly longer than on rest of body, except tail, where coat is longest and most profuse. **Fault**—any indication of ruff or feathering.

Breed Note

The Akita is the national dog of Japan. He is a working dog and was bred in the mountains of Northern Japan as a hunter and retriever of waterfowl.

A solid, compact dog standing 26 to 28 inches at the withers, the Akita gives the impression of tremendous power. The breed came to general notice after World War II and is now known throughout the world for his unflinching devotion to his family.

Grooming Procedure

A well-groomed Akita is a dignified, noble-looking animal. His size and obvious strength embody the dignity the breed is known and admired for. His short, thick, lustrous double coat softens the rugged outline of muscle and bone. A well-groomed Akita, such as those which grace the annual Rose Bowl Parade in Pasadena each year, invoke proper expressions of admiration. But an uncared for Akita is a pitiful sight.

Grooming the Akita Puppy

When an Akita is still in his puppy stage, his daily and weekly grooming should begin. A daily scrubbing with a bath towel will keep him clean, and a brushing will accustom him to being groomed, so that he looks forward to each session. Keep the inside of his ears clean with a cotton swab. The Akita puppy should be taught early to allow the groomer to handle him and to welcome the feel of the brush and comb and the attention of his groomer.

Combing The Akita

Daily or twice weekly combing followed by a brushing will remove all of the dog's dead hair, brighten his coat and improve his overall appearance. Combing from his head back, followed by brushing, is a natural flow and will soon be welcomed by an Akita. Take care not to pull against or break the skin. An Akita is not clipped or sheared. The breed's double coat is thick and dense, and the outercoat is harsh but not wiry. The undercoat is soft to the touch. This double coat keeps the Akita warm in cold weather and, after combing out, cool in warm weather. Properly fed, an Akita will not have any skin problems.

The Akita's feet should always be well trimmed. The breed's cat foot requires that the toenails be trimmed, and the hair around the feet kept even with the toes. The feathers between the dog's foot pads may be trimmed, but not too closely, as they are there to serve him in colder climates as protection from snow.

The Akita's brushing pattern may be from the rear forward, against the natural pattern so as to collect all loose hairs, stimulate the skin and provide vitality and sparkle. The rear legs may be brushed upward, the hindquarters up then outward. The shoulders and neck against the pattern upward and forward. The tail against the pattern for its entire length. Combing, followed by brushing is the recommended sequence for daily grooming.

After all loose hairs have been removed, and the coat invigorated, brushing with a stiff brush alone, in a pattern from front to rear will settle the coat and provide the finished look.

For the show ring, a last-minute touch-up with a hairbrush may be necessary. This will impart to the coat the sheen that impresses judges and draws admiration from the ringside.

Whiskers

Those adorable cat's whiskers an Akita has may be left as is, unless the dog is entered in a show. For show dogs the whiskers should be cut off with small sharp scissors two or three days before a show.

Courtesy of Raritan River Akita Club
by Louis Fallon

The Alaskan Malamute

Standard Regarding Coat

Coat—The Malamute should have a thick, coarse guard coat, not long and soft. The undercoat is dense, from 1 to 2 inches in depth, oily and woolly. The coarse guard coat stands out, and there is thick fur around the neck. The guard coat varies in length, as does the undercoat; however, in general, the coat is moderately short to medium along the sides of the body with the length of the coat increasing somewhat around the shoulders and neck, down the back and over the rump, as well as in the breeching and plume. Malamutes usually have shorter and less dense coats when shed out during the summer months.

Breed Note

The Alaskan Malamute was the sledge dog of the Mahlemuts, a highly skilled tribe of Innuit hunters and fishermen. The breed's story is deeply interwoven with Alaskan history since the coming of the white man. Indeed, the Alaskan Malamute helped make Alaska fit for habitation by the settlers. His feats are legendary and formed the basis for the novels of Jack London and J.O. Curwood.

The Alaskan Malamute is noted for his exceptional strength and hardiness, transporting men and supplies over vast expanses of snow and ice. He has an extraordinary sense of direction and can find the trail even when covered with heavy snow. In the worst blizzard he can find the only habitable place in the entire icy waste.

Among his other attributes the Alaskan Malamute is extremely loyal and intelligent; he is a clean dog and makes an excellent family companion.

Grooming Procedure

As might be expected, there is very little in the way of grooming for the Alaskan Malamute. According to Maxwell Riddle and Eva Seeley, authors of *The Complete Alaskan Malamute:*

> There are almost as many ideas about grooming as about feeding. Commercial grooming tools, if used incorrectly, can injure the oil pockets in the skin of Arctic, double-coated dogs. There are several ways to handle the shedding dog. One which we use at Chinook Kennels is to wet a newspaper and massage and rub the coat with it. We use a bristle hand brush dampened in oil of lanolin for daily grooming.

The Alaskan Malamute may be bathed in accordance with the directions as described in Part I, but after the dog is dried, oil of lanolin should be brushed into the coat.

The Australian Cattle Dog

Standard Regarding Coat

Coat—The weather resisting outer coat is moderately short, straight and of medium texture, with short dense undercoat. Behind the quarters the coat is longer, forming a mild breeching. The tail is furnished sufficiently to form a good brush. The head, forelegs, hindlegs from hock to ground, are coated with short hair.

Breed Note

The Australian Cattle Dog was admitted to AKC registry in May 1980 and was shown in the United States for the first time in September of that year.

The breed came into being to meet the specific needs of cattle raisers in Australia. European stock dogs did not adapt well to Australian terrain and weather. As a result, various crossings were tried to develop a dog that could work cattle well in the rugged Australian grazing lands.

The Dingo, a feral canine form native to Australia, figured prominently in the development of the Australian Cattle Dog. The Dingo was crossed with blue merle Smooth Collies as a base. Later, a Dalmatian cross was done to instill a natural love of horses and to increase the dogs' protective instinct. Finally, the Kelpie (a native sheepdog) was brought in to restore a bit of the herding instinct that the Dalmatian cross diminished.

The end result of all these crosses is a medium-sized, handsome dog of unusual color and markings. He is rugged and strong, yet an intelligent, personable companion.

Grooming Procedure

Natural is the word that best describes the Australian Cattle Dog. His grooming needs, therefore, can be completely satisfied by following instructions for the Fundamentals of Grooming, discussed in Chapter 1.

The Belgian Malinois

Standard Regarding Coat

Coat—Comparatively short, straight, with dense undercoat. Very short hair on the head, ears and lower legs. The hair is somewhat longer around the neck where it forms a collarette, and on the tail and the back of the thighs.

Breed Note

The Belgian Malinois originates from Belgium and is an elegant dog with a short, fawn colored coat. He is a big dog, measuring 24 to 26 inches at the withers. Like his cousins, the Belgian Sheepdog and the Belgian Tervuren, the Belgian Malinois is essentially a guard dog and a shepherd.

Grooming Procedure

Since grooming the Belgian Malinois is practically identical with grooming of Belgian Tervuren and since the American Belgian Tervuren Club was kind enough to contribute material to this book, we refer groomers and Malinois fanciers to the section on the Tervuren, in Part II. The Malinois coat is, of course, shorter than the Tervuren's and correspondingly easier to maintain.

The German Shepherd Dog

Standard Regarding Coat

Coat—The ideal dog has a double coat of medium length. The outer coat should be dense as possible, hair straight, harsh and lying close to the body. A slightly wavy outer coat, often of wiry texture, is permissible. The head, including the inner ear and foreface, and the legs and paws are covered with short hair, and the neck with longer and thicker hair. The rear of the forelegs and hind legs has somewhat longer hair extending to the pastern and hock, respectively. Faults in coat include soft, silky, too long outer coat, woolly, curly, and open coat.

Breed Note

One of the most familiar of all purebreds, the German Shepherd Dog is known and admired by dog enthusiasts from every corner of the earth. The love of the breed has overcome the barriers of space, time and language and today the Shepherd's admirers form an international brotherhood of fanciers.

When Germany became an industrialized nation during the 19th Century, there was less need for a stock dog than before and the native shepherd's dog was in danger of dying out. Farsighted fanciers caught the imagination of the government and the public as to the potential for police or military work inherent in the Shepherd. That their efforts were successful has been proven many times over in the ensuing years.

The breed has served with distinction as a war dog, a civilian police dog, a guide for the blind and, as tradition dictates, a stock dog. He is also justly famous as a protector and a canine customs agent often detecting the activities of drug smugglers. Today the German Shepherd Dog is kept as a companion, a show dog, a top notch obedience dog and one of the most truly useful, versatile and handsome of the world's dogs.

Grooming Procedure

A German Shepherd should be thoroughly groomed regularly in order to maintain coat and skin health and to enhance the dog's appearance. The ears should be cleaned weekly with either medicated ear powder or any of the liquid ear cleaners. Nails should be clipped monthly if needed, using guillotine nail clippers.

Brush the coat with either a stiff brush or, if the coat is shedding heavily, a matting comb or English rake should be used to remove dead hair.

Use a good shampoo to wash the dog, wetting the coat thoroughly with warm water. You can use either a small brush or your hands to work the shampoo into the dog's coat. Care should be taken not to get shampoo into the dog's eyes or ears. Rinse the coat off with warm water, making sure to get all of the soap out.

Before using a dryer, towel the dog dry. After the dog is completely dry, brush him out again using either a stiff bristle brush or a large pin brush.

If you are planning to show your dog, it would be better to wash him at least two days before the show, allowing the natural oils to return to his coat.

Courtesy, The German Shepherd Dog Club of Long Island by Louis Sullo

The Shorthaired St. Bernard

Standard Regarding Coat

Coat—Very dense, short-haired (stockhaarig), lying smooth, tough, without however feeling rough to the touch. The thighs are slightly bushy. The tail at the root has longer and denser hair which gradually becomes shorter toward the tip. The tail appears bushy, not forming a flag.

Breed Note

The Shorthaired St. Bernard differs from the Longhaired variety only in the length of the coat. The Shorthair is the older of the two. The Longhair was developed from crossings with Newfoundlands, but it was subsequently learned that the long hair was a handicap in deep snow and ice.

Grooming Procedure

To get a dog ready for a show all that is necessary is bathing, cutting whiskers, cleaning ears, eyes and trimming nails. Naturally a Shorthaired Saint would require much less work than a Longhaired specimen.

Courtesy, The St. Bernard Club of America

The Siberian Husky

Standard Regarding Coat

Coat—The coat of the Siberian Husky is double and medium in length, giving a well-furred appearance, but is never so long as to obscure the clean-cut outline of the dog. The undercoat is soft and dense and of sufficient length to support the outer coat. The guard hairs of the outer coat are straight and somewhat smooth-lying, never harsh nor standing straight off from the body. It should be noted that the absence of the undercoat during the shedding season is normal. Trimming of the whiskers and fur between the toes and around the feet to present a neater appearance is permissible. Trimming of the fur on any other part of the dog is not to be condoned and should be severely penalized.

Breed Note

Currently the most popular of all Northern breeds, the Siberian Husky is the medium-sized member of the sled dog family. He was developed by the Chukchi people as a draft dog that could travel long distances with light loads. Many times the survival of these Siberian nomads depended on the dogs.

After the turn of the century, when the white man discovered the breed, his value as a working and racing dog earned great celebrity. A monument to the memorable lead dog, Balto in New York City's Central Park was erected as a tribute to the dogs and drivers who got urgently-needed diptheria serum to the City of Nome, Alaska during the epidemic of 1925.

Today the Siberian Husky enjoys great popularity as a delightful companion, show dog and top drawer race competitor.

Grooming Procedure

The Siberian Husky is a comparitively easy dog to care for, and is naturally clean. Freedom from body odor is another factor in his favor. He is presented in the show ring well-groomed but requires no clipping or trimming. At least once a year the Siberian Husky sheds his coat, and it is then, armed with a comb and a bushel basket, that one realizes the amazing density and profusion of the typical Siberian Husky coat. Some people feel that this periodic problem is easier to cope with than the constant shedding and renewal of many smooth-coated breeds.

Courtesy, Siberian Husky Club of America

The Cardigan Welsh Corgi

Standard Regarding Coat

Coat—Medium length but dense. Slightly harsh texture, but neither wiry nor silky. Weather-resistant. An overly short coat or a long and silky and/or curly coat are faults. Normal grooming and trimming of whiskers is permitted. Any trimming that alters the natural length of the coat is not permitted and is a serious fault. A distinctly long coat is a disqualification.

Breed Note

The Cardigan Welsh Corgi is an extremely ancient canine form. Indeed, the exact time the breed came into being cannot be accurately ascertained. Just as the time of the breed's development is obscure, so is his background. He is, however, related to Dachshunds and other low-stationed hound types.

For purposes of certain, instant identification, the Cardigan Corgi has a long, almost foxlike, tail while the better-known Pembroke has no tail at all. While certain colors are common to both breeds, Cardigans can also be black and white, blue merle or brindle.

This natural breed is highly intelligent and successfully combines good looks with a marked ability to learn befitting a working dog.

Grooming Procedure

For the show ring the only extra attention the breed requires is a bit of trimming to tidy the hair around and between the foot pads and on the back of the rear pasterns. Some people like to trim the feelers on the dog's face. Beyond this, normal attention to the fundamentals of grooming will suffice to keep a Cardigan presentable at any time.

The Pembroke Welsh Corgi

Standard Regarding Coat

Coat—Medium length; short, thick, weather-resistant undercoat with a coarser, longer outer coat. Overall length varies, with slightly thicker and longer ruff around neck, chest and on the shoulders. The body coat lies flat. Hair is slightly longer on back of forelegs and underparts, and somewhat fuller and longer on rear of hindquarters. The coat is preferably straight, but some waviness is permitted. This breed has a shedding coat, and seasonal lack of undercoat should not be too severely penalized, providing the hair is glossy, healthy, and well groomed. A wiry, tightly marcelled coat is very faulty, as is an overly short, smooth and thin coat.

Very Serious Faults—

Fluffies—A coat of extreme length with exaggerated feathering on ears, chest, legs and feet, underparts and hindquarters. Trimming such a coat does not make it any more acceptable.

The Corgi should be shown in its natural condition, with no trimming permitted except to tidy the feet, and, if desired, remove the whiskers.

Breed Note

Although he is not as old as the Cardigan Welsh Corgi, the Pembroke is no newcomer to the family of dog breeds. The Pembroke has been familiar on the farms of South Wales for centuries serving as a watchdog and drover. The breed was relatively obscure, even after the establishment of dog shows until 1933 when the then future King George VI of England presented his daughters, Elizabeth and Margaret with a Pembroke puppy. This brought the Pembroke to general notice and now he is admired by dog lovers all over the world.

Highly intelligent, very trainable and an easy dog to look at and live with, the Pembroke Welsh Corgi combines numerous positive virtues that have endeared him to legions of faithful friends.

Grooming Procedure

Pembroke Welsh Corgis require no special grooming techniques for everyday living. Occasional combing and brushing will keep the normal coat in good condition. During times of seasonal shedding, the coat should be thoroughly combed to remove the dead hair.

Before a show, a Pembroke Welsh Corgi should have the white parts washed and thoroughly rinsed, the body wiped with a damp towel to remove surface grime, and the hair about the feet trimmed. Some exhibitors trim the whiskers, but this is optional. Under no circumstances should the coat be trimmed anywhere. Nor is it wise to give a Corgi a complete bath unless absolutely necessary.

Courtesy, Pembroke Welsh Corgi Club of America
by Mrs. Wallace Harper

Hard Coats, Long Legs

IT WILL SIMPLIFY GROOMING IN-structions for hardcoated terriers if we divide them into long-legged and the short-legged categories. Understand that within categories long-legged and short-legged Terriers are all groomed in similar fashion, with the exception of the head. Following is a list of the hard coated terrier breeds divided into long-legged and short-legged classifications:

Long-Legged Terriers	Short-Legged Terriers
Airedale Terrier	Australian Terrier
Border Terrier	Cairn Terrier
*Giant Schnauzer	Dandie Dinmont Terrier
Wire Fox Terrier	Norfolk Terrier
Irish Terrier	Norwich Terrier
Lakeland Terrier	Scottish Terrier
Miniature Schnauzer	Sealyham Terrier
*Standard Schnauzer	West Highland White
Welsh Terrier	Terrier

*Standard and Giant Schnauzers are not classified in the Terrier Group (they are Working Dogs) but for grooming purposes they are fundamentally the same as the Miniature Schnauzer.

The Miniature Schnauzer and Scottish Terrier are our models for the long-legged and short-legged terriers respectively. Once again, with the exception of the head, all the long-legged and short-legged Terriers are groomed, within categories, in very similar fashion. So, once you have grasped the basics of Schnauzer grooming, you will be able to groom other similar terriers easily.

Obviously, the same applies to the short-legged terriers. Particular attention should be paid to the differences in the headpieces which give the terrier breeds their distinctive characteristics.

All the terrier pets may be clipped. Hardcoated terriers which are to be shown must be hand-stripped. But clipped or stripped, pet or show, all terrier grooming, like grooming any breed, should strive to conform to the Standards of the respective breeds.

The Miniature Schnauzer

Standard Regarding Coat

Coat—Double, with hard, wiry outer coat and close undercoat. Head, neck and body coat must be plucked. When in show condition the body coat should be of sufficient length to determine texture. Close covering on neck, ears, and skull. Furnishings are fairly thick but not silky. **Faults:** Coat too soft or too smooth and slick in appearance.

Breed Note

The Miniature Schnauzer was developed in Germany as a stable dog and ratter. The American Kennel Club classifies the Miniature Schnauzer in the Terrier Group, and, indeed he is the most popular of all the terriers. A reflection of that high popularity is the breed's current ranking of eighth among all breeds in AKC registrations.

Grooming Procedure

After fundamental grooming operations have been completed (brushing, bathing, blow-drying, ear cleaning, and nail trimming), the *pet grooming* of the Miniature Schnauzer proceeds as follows:

Body—First clip the body coat, using the #8½ blade. This blade will leave the coat approximately ¼ inch long. Starting at the base of the skull, move down the backbone to the base of the tail. Clipping smoothly and always moving in the direction in which the coat grows clip the entire body coat down to just above the elbow on the front legs and to the point of tuckup on the hindlegs. Unlike the other terriers, whose legs are untouched by clippers, the Schnauzer's hindlegs are clipped in a semi-circular fashion, extending down from the tuckup to the hock joint but leaving a fringe of hair on the forepart of the hindleg. There is no precise measurement for how much fringe should be left on, but it should extend approximately one inch from the stifle. The forelegs are left full, untouched by clippers.

Tail—Continuing with the same #8½ blade, clip the tail (top, sides and undersides) leaving an open, slightly tapered effect.

Head—The last area for clipping is the headpiece, which includes the skull, the face, the throat and the ears. The ears require separate treatment. Changing to the #10 blade, start at the top of the skull or crown (just above the eyebrows) down to the base of the crown. Clip the entire crown. Then, using parallel strokes, clip from the corner of the eye to the base of the ear and from the corner of the mouth to the line of the throat, on both sides.

Ears—The ears are clipped front and back with the #15 blade. Since the ears are too soft to hold up for the

Pet Trimming for the Miniature Schnauzer

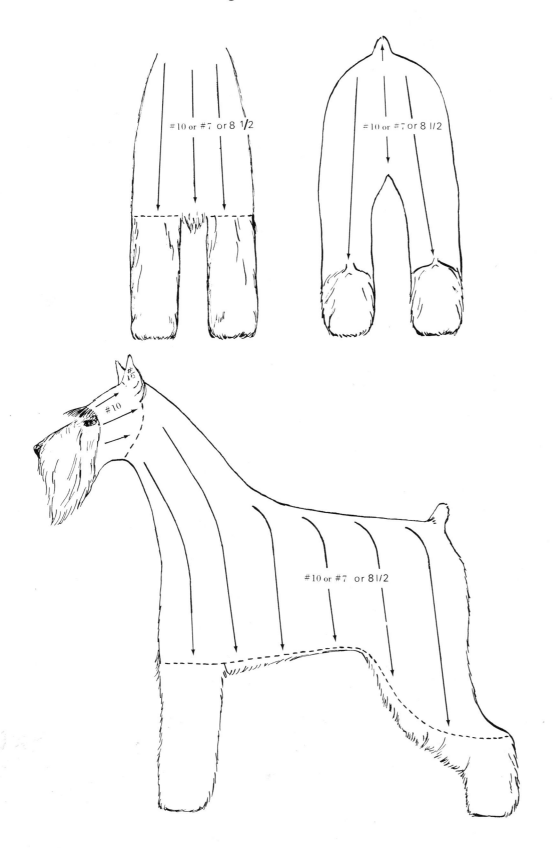

A pet Miniature Schnauzer before grooming and trimming.

Clipping the back.

Blending neck and shoulder with the clipper.

The brush being used is a soft wire slicker

Blending over the ribs.

Blending the hindquarters.

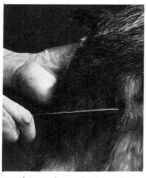

Combing through furnishings will reveal any mats present.

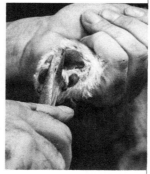

Excess hair is cleaned from between pads with scissors.

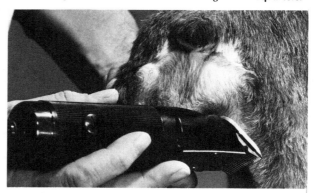

Cleaning between the hindlegs.

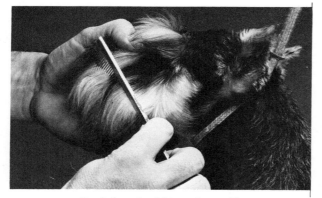

Comb face furnishings thoroughly before doing any head trimming.

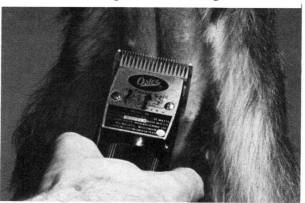

Cleaning hair from groin.

Clipping sides of backskull.

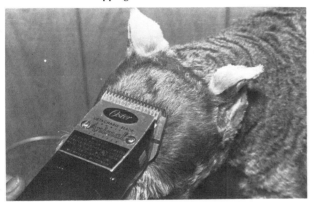

Clipping top of backskull.

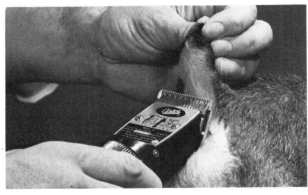

Clipping underside of tail with the grain.

Clipping underside of neck.

clipper, each ear must be held firmly with the free hand while being clipped. The clipping follows the grain outwards from the center of the ear to the edge. Do not clip the edges themselves, since this must only be scissored.

SCISSORING THE SCHNAUZER

Since scissoring the headpiece (including the ears) is essential to the correct expression of the Miniature Schnauzer, the headpiece is left for last. Before the head, the groomer should concentrate first on all other scissoring work.

Inasmuch as the entire body coat has been clipped closely, there is no need for any scissoring on the body.

Front Legs—Comb the furnishings so that they stand out from the legs. With the scissors pointing straight down, trim in a circular fashion, to achieve the cylindrical effect. Trim in a straight line, from the point of the elbow to the bottom of the leg. Make sure no stray hairs extend from the elbow or elsewhere. The hair on the feet should be trimmed in a full circle, appearing round, never pointed. The two center toenails on the front feet should be hardly visible, no more than ⅛″.

Hindlegs—The main difference in trimming the front legs and the hindlegs is blending the furnishings left on the stifle with the furnishings on the hock, following the contour of the leg. Another important area to be considered is the overall appearance of the hindlegs which when finished, should resemble two columns joined together by an arch. This effect calls for very clean, straight lines.

Foot Pads—Trim hair straight across. All knots and mats between the pads and toes should be removed, preferably with clippers using a #15 blade.

Chest—Thinning shears (double or single serrated) are best for blending the forechest into the legs. It is important that no part of the forechest appear to have a hollow look down to the brisket.

Underbelly—Starting in front from just below the elbow, taper the underbelly furnishings slightly upward and back to the rear of the last rib (the tuckup).

Head—The last (but most important) trimming on the Miniature Schnauzer is the head, where we now concentrate first on the eyebrows and beard so important to a typical look. Since divided eyebrows are customary, the first step is to scissor the hair between the eyes (at the stop) thus forming the division. The cleaner and closer the scissoring the better the division will be accentuated. Next scissor the eyebrows to form a separated visor. Comb the eyebrows forward. Then scissor the eyebrows at the stop straight forward on a line parallel with the center of the nose. Comb the eyebrows forward again and place the scissors at the outside corner of the eye at the widest part of the skull. Point the scissors toward the center of the nose and scissor diagonally,

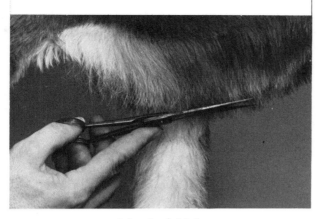

Scissoring brisket.

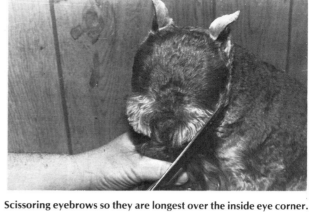

Scissoring eyebrows so they are longest over the inside eye corner.

Clipping front of ear.

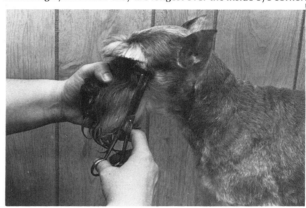

Blend shorter hair into eyebrows.

Clipping back of ear.

Finished head

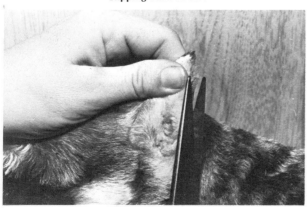

Trimming edges of ears with scissors.

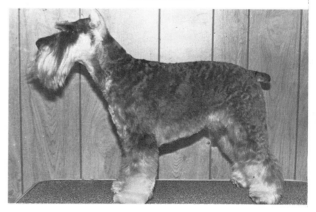

"Johannes" in his finished pet trim. *Courtesy, Michael Millar.*

174

straight across, meeting the point of the first straight cut, thus forming two inverted V's.

Beard—Comb the beard forward. To achieve the right look, shape the beard to form a rectangle by trimming on a line from the widest part of the skull to where the beard will fit within a rectangle. Do not cut any hair under the eyes. For the rest, comb and trim the beard to remove any uneven, straggly hairs.

Ears—The last step for scissoring on the headpiece is the ears. We have already clipped the ears, and now must remove the fuzzy hairs remaining on the edges. Holding the earflaps firmly with your fingers, scissor very slowly and carefully the outer edges until all fuzziness is removed. Use the middle part of the scissors for better control.

STRIPPING AND PLUCKING

Stripping and plucking a terrier's coat is mandatory for exhibition in the show ring. These hand operations assure maintenance of the natural texture of the coat, whereas clipping will cause the coat to lose both color and texture. Stripping and plucking the coat is the main difference between preparing terriers and other wire-haired breeds for show or clipping them as pets. The technique described here is basically the same for all breeds whose wire coats call for this special attention.

While the terms stripping and plucking are often used interchangeably, a fine distinction can be made between the two by describing stripping as that which is done with the aid of a stripping knife and plucking as that which is done with the fingers, or finger plucking.

The particular method used depends on a variety of factors: Condition of the individual's coat, length of time to a show (or shows) and the personal preference of the person doing the grooming are some examples. Some professional handlers and experienced amateurs prefer to finger pluck the entire coat. All this hand work is time consuming and costly. It also requires constant attention for proper maintenance. These are the main reasons why pet owners and most professional groomers do not trouble to learn these trimming methods.

Stripping/Plucking—Stripping the coat should commence when the coat has "blown," i.e., when the coat has passed its prime. When a dog has "blown its coat" it simply means that the topcoat has completed its growth cycle and must be removed before the new coat can come in. This dead hair should then be pulled out if the coat is to maintain proper condition.

Techniques of Stripping—Note, in the accompanying photos, how the stripping knife is held. Using your thumb to trap a *small* amount of hair against the knife, pluck the hair out firmly, in the direction of the lie of the coat. Do not twist the wrist or pull upward as this will cause the hair to be broken off. The object is to pull the hair out straight by the root. This is stripping the coat.

The basic stripping method and technique is the same for all the hard coated terriers. An oversimplified way of explaining the difference between the pet and show grooming of the Schnauzer is to simply substitute stripping the dog for show where clipping has been used for the pet. Scissoring of the Schnauzer remains the same for pet or show dogs.

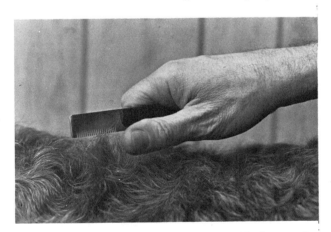

Stripping consists of pulling out dead hairs with the use of a specially designed tool. Holding the tool, or stripping knife, with four fingers, the groomer pushes a few hairs against the blade with the thumb.

When the small hank of hair is in place, the thumb presses it down against the knife blade prior to pulling it out.

The hair is pulled out in the direction of coat growth.

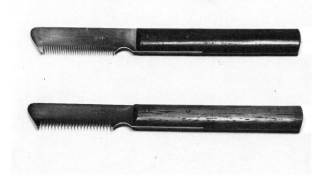

Stripping knives are available in numerous styles and degrees of fineness. Experiment whenever possible to find one you like best.

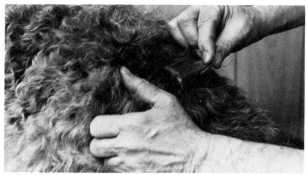

Plucking differs from stripping in that the hairs are removed by finger and thumb rather than with a knife.

A good-quality natural bristle brush is essential equipment in any terrier grooming situation.

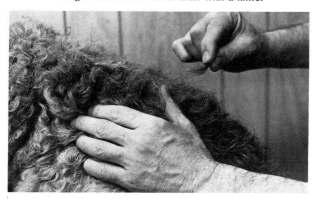

As with stripping, the groomer removes only a few hairs at a time and always with the lie of the coat.

A hound glove, when properly used puts a beautiful sheen on a terrier's coat and helps keep the jacket tight and in good condition.

French white chalk rubbed into the coat will help better grip the hairs to be removed.

The terrier palm pad is an indepensible grooming article for all harsh-coated breeds. It is excellent for use on all areas of the body and is particularly good when working on head and leg furnishings.

The Standard Schnauzer

Standard Regarding Coat

Coat—Tight, hard, wiry and as thick as possible, composed of a soft, close undercoat and a harsh outer coat which, when seen against the grain, stands up off the back, lying neither smooth nor flat. The outer coat (body coat) is trimmed (by plucking) only to accent the body outline. When in show condition, the outer coat's proper length is approximately 1½ inches, except on the ears, head, neck, chest, belly and under the tail where it may be closely trimmed to give the desired typical appearance of the breed.

On the muzzle and over the eyes the coat lengthens to form luxuriant beard and eyebrows; the hair on the legs is longer than that on the body. These "furnishings" should be of harsh texture and should not be so profuse so as to detract from the neat appearance or working abilities of the dog. *Faults*—Soft, smooth, curly, wavy or shaggy; too long or too short; too sparse or lacking undercoat; excessive furnishings; lack of furnishings.

Breed Note

The Standard Schnauzer, like the smaller Miniature Schnauzer and the larger Giant Schnauzer, comes originally from Germany. The Standard is an intelligent, reliable working dog. Today he is used mainly as a watchdog and bodyguard, but he has also served man as a ratter, a yard dog, a war and police dog and as a companion among other roles. The distinctive characteristics of all three varieties of Schnauzer are the long, bushy eyebrows, the rectangular beard, the erect, cropped ears and docked tail.

"ROLLING" COATS

"Rolling" a coat is the constant stripping-off of dead hairs to keep the coat in year-round show condition (without ever stripping down to the skin). The dog thus carries a coat that always consists of about one quarter hairs preparing to "blow," one quarter hairs at a good show length, one quarter hairs approaching show length, and one quarter hairs just emerging at the skin.

The coat can be taken out with either your fingers (which are best anyway when you get down to the fine touches at show time) or a stripping comb. If you can find one, Hauptner makes a stripping comb that is great for rolling a coat—it's a big wooden-handled jacknife, and the blade has big, coarse teeth that can only grab long hairs.

Starting with a naturally hard but long and bushy coat, it will take at least three months to get a nice coat by rolling. That's because hair follicles out of which coat is taken today will be holding a nice, show-length coat in 2½ to 3 months. Where another quarter to third of the coat is taken out next month, there will be a good coat in 3½ to 4 months. So it will be two to three months from the starting point before the last of the original coat is removed. After that, if you keep up the good work, you'll be able to just keep "rolling" along.

How Often Do You Work a Rolling Coat?

The idea is to have a complete changeover of coat every three to four months, which means that a quarter to a third of the coat will be removed every month. Since the coat should look immaculate for shows, weekly sessions will probably be necessary while the dog is being shown. Between times, it may be possible to get away with monthly trimming sessions.

Warning Notes

Although somewhat more hair is taken off on the head, neck and probably shoulders, thighs and rump, the body coat should be of a uniform length throughout. To do this, you must go over the dog removing equal amounts of hair all over each time you work on him.

If you get sloppy and neglect the dog for two or three months, the coat will be ruined and you will have to start over from scratch.

HOW TO STRIP BY SECTIONS

A Blown Coat

A blown coat is one that is loose, tending sometimes to fall out of its own accord, and is ready to strip out. See page 175.

Scheduling

Scheduling depends to some extent on the individual dog, on the weather, and (one often feels) on the "coat pixies." Some dogs always tend to grow coat at the same rate every time they are stripped. Others, who were perhaps in beautiful coat ten weeks after last being stripped, turn up next looking naked (or perhaps almost "blown") ten weeks after stripping. That is due, of course, to those awful "coat pixies."

As a general rule, begin a sectioned stripping eight to ten weeks before the dog is to be shown. Time the interval between sections so the head is done about five weeks before the show(s).

If illness or laziness or some such problem strikes and you must wait more than 14 days between doing two sections, at least strip a band an inch or so into the next section so there will not be an abrupt difference in coat length between those sections in the finished product. Remember that in salt and peppers, color and shading change with coat length, so sectioning differences will be more noticeable.

Most coats last for about three months before getting too long to be showable. A coat may or may not be loose enough at this time to be easily stripped. If, for any reason, it should be necessary to rush the timing, a good warm bath may loosen the coat enough to permit stripping.

Be sure to mark a calendar with the dates you start stripping various areas and the date each dog appears to be in perfect coat. By doing so, you'll know when to start next time.

Stripping

In stripping, always pull in the direction in which the hair is growing (usually toward the rear or toward the ground). Hold the skin taut so the hair comes out quickly and without pulling the skin up with it. On most of the body you can grab a large fold of loose skin, but in doing the head you will have to hold an ear or hold the eyebrows firmly onto the bridge of the nose to keep the skin taut. Grip the hair between the blade of the stripping comb and your thumb, and pull straight. DON'T twist your wrist, or you'll cut the hair off instead of pulling it out. You may find it easier in some places (head, ears, side of neck) to use just rubber finger stalls.

Clipped Areas

How close to clip on cheeks and throat depends on your dog. A very cheeky, coarse-headed dog would be clipped much shorter (and closer to the show date) than a fine-boned, narrow-skulled dog. Leave ¼" or so of hair behind the eyes and angle to within ½ to 1" of the corner of the mouth. This leaves you some hair to blend in with thinning shears.

Clip the belly from the navel to the rear. Use a fine-toothed blade so you don't accidentally clip off a nipple. On males, be sure to closely trim the sheath, but it is best to neatly, *and carefully,* scissor hair on the testicles.

Use a #8½ or #10 blade, with a clipper, scissors or thinning shears to trim the rear. If you use a clipper, do the work a week or two in advance of the first show.

Blending Furnishings

The "blended" areas are points at which the short hair of the body gradually tapers into the longer hair of the legs. Shorten the tuft at the elbow severely and neatly scissor backs of hindlegs.

Face and Eyebrows

Comb eyebrows forward so they fall naturally. Then, looking at the dog head-on (just like you're looking at the pictures), brace your scissors against the backskull and cut off the corner hairs that protrude past the outside eye corner. Then recomb the remaining eyebrows and cut on an angle, your imaginary line running from the outside corner of his eye to the *opposite* corner of his nose. For dogs with light eyes, more eyebrow should be kept.

DON'T leave long hairs sticking out from the sides of the dog's head in a puff so he looks like he has the mumps. Trim these hairs off so the head looks long and rectangular. DON'T cut in under the eyes, or you'll get a "Figure 8" look instead of a rectangle.

Feet

Turn foot upside down, comb hair in direction of arrows, and scissor around edges and across back of large pad. Then set foot down on table (with the dog standing on it) and do final scissoring. Remember, the foot is to look neat and relatively small, with the toes tight together. It is NOT supposed to look like a big, fat snowshoe.

CHALKING

Why

Chalking not only helps whiten the leg furnishings and whiskers (and chest and rump, if needed), but also separates each hair and helps the furnishing stand out in thick columns instead of twirling into clumps and just "lying there." Chalk *must* be brushed out thoroughly, since a dog can be excused from the ring if the judge sees puffs of chalk dust obscuring its legs from view. Do be careful.

How

Foam the dog's legs and whiskers up with a waterless shampoo, towel them to just damp, and apply a dab of hair conditioner to your palms and rub it into each leg and the face (Wella Kolestral or Alberto VO5 for blue or white hair are good for this). Then scrub in the powdered chalk by hand or with a nail or shaving brush. The hair should have been damp-dried so that the chalk absorbs the rest of the dampness and all areas are now almost completely dry. You can now walk the dog around a little to shake out some of the heaviest of the chalk, put him in a crate for a while or let him stay on the grooming table until he is completely dry. Then use a medium-bristle brush to brush out the rest and pat his legs and whiskers with both hands to remove surplus powder to make sure no more clouds come out. Then it's time to comb the leg furnishings into neat columns. A thin film of Wella Kolestral applied to the leg furnishings will keep them from collapsing in the ring.

CLIPPING A PET

The pattern and finish work should be the same on stripped show dog and clipped pet. There is no excuse for "doughnut moustaches" or "Scottie side fringes" or "umbrella eyebrows."

A freshly clipped coat, to look neat, is shorter than a good length of stripped show coat because a longer blade (#5 or #7) leaves most coats looking like a pack of giant moths ate their way through it.

Try doing the nails and feet first, before they get covered with cut hair. On a dog that's not used to the clippers, do the body next, to get him used to the sound and vibration before going on to the head.

Clip *with* the grain of the hair—it helps prevent skin irritation ("clipper burn"). Don't try to go the whole length of the dog with one stroke: take short overlapping strokes, to create a smooth finished product.

A blade will not clip if its teeth are clogged with hair, so keep a nail brush handy for keeping the blade's teeth clear.

Courtesy, Standard Schnauzer Club of America

The Giant Schnauzer

Standard Regarding Coat

Coat—Hard, wiry, very dense; composed of a soft undercoat and a harsh outer coat which, when seen against the grain, stands slightly up off the back, lying neither smooth nor flat. Coarse hair on top of head; harsh beard and eyebrows, the Schnauzer hallmark.

Breed Note

The Giant Schnauzer is, of course, the largest of the three Schnauzer varieties, standing about 28 inches high at the shoulder. The Swiss share a part in his breeding, and during the Second World War the German army used him as an auxiliary to the armed forces. The Giant Schnauzer is said to have no equal as a guard dog.

Grooming Procedure

A Giant Schnauzer in fresh show coat standing majestically at attention is a sight to behold and one that takes the breath away. On the other hand, a "Giant" that is unkempt, ungroomed, and with long, matted hair should not be taken into public view, and is a disgrace to its owner, other "Giant" fanciers, and unfair to the dog itself.

All Giant Schnauzers that are shown should be hand stripped. That is, the hair should be pulled out of the body by hand, with the aid of a stripping knife. This method of removing the hair is not painful to the dog, provided it is done when the hair is long and the coat has blown. It is the most effective grooming method and assures that the hard, wiry coat described in the breed Standard will be preserved. Hand stripping has been used by fanciers of all three Schnauzer sizes for many years; however, most people are not familiar with this grooming technique because most pet groomers will usually not hand-strip hard-coated breeds. The preference is for the use of clippers, which is much easier, faster and far less costly. However, the continued use of clippers on the Schnauzer coat causes it to become soft and to lose the texture desired. On salt and pepper coats, continued use of clippers will turn the coat silver in color and the salt and pepper effect disappears entirely.

In order to properly groom the "Giant," several tools are essential. The basic tools are a steel comb (with coarse and medium teeth), a fine-toothed steel comb for eyebrows, a medium stripping knife, a pair of barber's shears, a pair of thinning shears, blunt-end scissors (for hair between the pads) and a pair of toenail clippers. Of course, there are very many more tools that one could obtain to help with the grooming job; however, these are the bare minimum for the job at hand. For those who wish to use clippers on parts of the dog, such as the under belly, which is very tender and should not be stripped, an Oster clipper with #10 blade would be ideal.

Many "Giant" fanciers have no desire to show their dogs and are anxious to keep the dog in trim without the necessity of hand-stripping. We do not recommend clippering since the method tends to soften the coat as previously stated. However, for those who will clipper their "Giants," please get a good quality clipper such as the Oster. These clippers cost much more than ordinary clippers but are constructed to do this job and are the best that we have been able to find.

A #5 Oster blade is the plucking-length blade. Use this blade on the body if you like the coat fairly long. The #7 blade is semi-plucking length and the #10 blade will leave a very short coat. Each individual must evaluate his preference, taking into consideration the time of year and whether the dog is outside much of the time or is kept inside. We recommend that the #5 be used and the job done more often. Regardless of which blade is used on the body, it is recommended that the #10 blade be used on the head, ears and underbody. Always remember that the blade should be used to cut the hair with the grain; otherwise you will be cutting too close. Let your blade do the work as it was intended.

Courtesy, The Giant Schnauzer Club Of America
by Bonnie and Robert Barker

The Airedale Terrier

Standard Regarding Coat

Coat—Should be hard, dense and wiry, lying straight and close, covering the dog well over the body and legs. Some of the hardest are crinkling or just slightly waved. At the base of the hard very stiff hair should be a shorter growth of softer hair termed the undercoat.

Breed Note

The Airedale comes from the green dales of Yorkshire and is the largest of the terriers, standing 23 inches at the shoulder. He came about as a result of crossing small terriers with Otterhounds. The result is a game terrier with a peerless nose and an affinity for water. He has been successfully hunted on big game, but can still act like an overgrown puppy at home and will play all day if allowed. The Airedale makes a superb watchdog and guard and an ideal companion for children of any age.

Grooming Procedure

Those interested in trimming a pet, and desiring the quick and easy method would be wise to invest in a pair of electric ''small animal clippers.'' By this method you can keep your pet neat and trim at all times, with a minimum of effort; however, the following should be heeded:

1. This applies to pets only. Never clip an Airedale you expect to take into the show ring.
2. A clipped coat grows in soft and curly.
3. If clipped too close to the skin it may cause an irritation. On areas which appear to have been clipped too closely, such as under the throat, or around the ears, apply a good salve, or baby oil.
4. A stripped coat is all new hair, but when clipped the dead hair, and all undercoat are left on the dog, thus frequent combing and brushing with the wire center brush are advocated, to remove the dead hair and improve the texture of the coat.

People who admire the beautiful harsh Airedale coat, attained by ''plucking,'' shudder at the mere mention of touching clippers to the breed. The fact remains that it is being done, and to the great satisfaction of many pet owners. An Airedale is one of the easiest breeds to clip, terrier or otherwise, and a trimmed Airedale is a much happier dog and more welcome member of the family circle.

Most small animal clippers come with extra blade sets, but in the event you purchase clippers with just one blade (or head) either #5 or #7 will do the job. A #5 leaves hair ½" long, and #7 leaves hair ¼" long. With the #5 head, run the clipper with the lay of the hair, except where shorter hair is desired, such as throat, ears, sides of head and tuck-up, and in these areas run the clipper against the "grain."

Chest hair is not clipped, but combed forward and trimmed diagonally toward the tuck-up. Tuck-up is clipped short.

Use either a finer blade (#10) or run the #5 against the lay of the hair, for trimming the sides of head and ears. Run clipper over edge of ears, pressing against forefinger to bevel the edges. Cut ragged hairs on edges and inside ears with scissors. Strip eyebrows to a semblance of show trim, i.e., longer over the inner corners of the eyes, and shorter over the outer corners, blending in length with hair on skull. Comb face hair forward and strip, or cut, the too-long hair at top to make top of head look level.

Note, the most important thing in trimming, by hand or clipper, is a smooth flow of lines from one part of the dog into another—no abrupt changes in length of hair, just try to blend one area with another.

Trim fringe away from dog's feet, trim out long hair between pads, cut nails, give dog a bath—and presto—the job is done! He may have acted like he hated every minute of it, but will now strut around quite proudly, looking like the whole thing was really his idea in the first place.

Courtesy, The Airedale Terrier Club of America

The Border Terrier

Standard Regarding Coat

Coat—A short and dense undercoat covered with a very wiry and somewhat broken top coat which should lie closely, but it must not show any tendency to curl or wave. With such a coat a Border should be able to be exhibited almost in his natural state, nothing more in the way of trimming being needed than a tidying-up of the head, neck and feet.

Breed Note

The Border Terrier comes from the Cheviot Hills between England and Scotland—hence the name.

One of the smaller terriers, he is not handsome but makes up for any lack of looks by his strength and courage. He was bred to hunt all manner of vermin and this he does extremely well given the opportunity.

Grooming Procedure

The Border Terrier is a breed of no exaggerations and any attempt to pretty this working terrier to make it look like any other breed is doing it a great disservice. There are a few points that may help prepare a Border for the show ring and that should be done well before a show, not the day before or at the show itself.

The breed must have a hard, weather-resisting coat, soft undercoat and hard outer coat. Only the loose undercoat should be removed with a slicker for the Border is required to have a double coat. Few professional groomers use the thumb-and-finger method of removing the dead outercoat for it takes time and patience but this is the preferred way providing the dog has the proper coat. A soft coat is undesirable and it takes hours on end to trim such a coat by hand. Assuming that one cannot or will not use the thumb-and-finger method and uses a stripping knife, it must be a very DULL knife, otherwise the hair is cut and the dog shows a mottled appearance.

The head is wedge-shaped and should appear as broad as possible between the ears. The skull should be clean, wisps of hair at the top of the ears, any fringes on the ears (they should appear as short and clean as possible) and the very edges of the ears not cut with scissors but pulled by hand. Inside the ears the hair can be removed—a very few at a time. Eyebrows should be removed (the Border is not a Schnauzer) and the "eyebrow pencil line" at the outer corners of the eyes should show thus excess hair on sides of head and cheeks should be removed. The hair on the stop will sometimes grow in a fan shape in front of the eyes. This should be removed but do not take off anything from in front of the cheeks. A Border is not "bearded" but a few short whiskers are natural to the breed. It should not resemble an Airedale or other breed with heavy face furnishings. A moustache is natural to the breed.

There should not be a lot of hair left on the chest and between the front legs and no attempt should be made to try to make a Border Terrier short-coupled or square. The Border should be narrow in shoulder, about a rib longer than a Fox Terrier to enable him to maneuver underground, narrow in loin—no barrel ribs—but a deep body, presenting a ''racy'' appearance.

The tail should be thick at the base then taper to the end. Long, thin tails are undesirable. They should be undocked and as naturally short as possible. Long fringes will grow on the under side of the tail and these should be removed. Most people use scissors here but, depending on the amount of hair, the stripping knife or thumb and finger makes a cleaner job. There is some undercoat at the base of the tail which can come out and the tail stripped when the rest of the coat is done.

Belly hairs are a touchy subject with some dogs and not with others and all depends on the individual as to whether to remove these hairs as well as those sparse ones inside the thighs with fingers or scissors. Underneath the tail should be clean and if the dog has a good turn of stifle which many lack, this should show to advantage.

Courtesy, Border Terrier Club of America
by, Marjorie L. Van der Veer

The Wire Fox Terrier

Standard Regarding Coat

Coat—This variety of the breed should resemble the smooth sort in every respect except the coat, which should be broken. The harder and more wiry the texture of the coat is, the better. On no account should the dog look or feel woolly; and there should be no silky hair about the poll or elsewhere. The coat should not be too long, so as to give the dog a shaggy appearance, but, at the same time, it should show a marked and distinct difference all over from the smooth species.

Breed Note

The Wire Fox Terrier is the coated version of the classic terrier. The only difference between the modern Wire and Smooth is the coat.

Originally bred to bolt the fox after the hounds had run it to ground, the Fox Terrier was an integral part of the traditional, mounted hunt. Today's Wire is the epitome of elegance and style. He is known and appreciated where ever dog fanciers gather, and is also a wonderful pet as clever and lively as he is handsome.

Grooming Procedure

The Wire Fox Terrier is groomed almost exactly like the Miniature Schnauzer. The differences are slight.

Whereas with the Schnauzer the accent is on the broadness of the face, giving the Schnauzer the "macho" look, with the Wire Fox the face is elongated by showing more muzzle and less beard. The length of the face is then accentuated by combing the beard straight forward, overlapping the chin.

The only other difference with the Schnauzer is that the Wire Fox (like all the other long-legged Terriers) carries somewhat more hair on the hindlegs.

186

Pet Trimming for the Wire Fox Terrier

This chart can also be referred to (with minor modifications) for trimming Airedale, Irish, Lakeland and Welsh Terriers.

The Irish Terrier

Standard Regarding Coat

Coat—Should be dense and wiry in texture, rich in quality, having a broken appearance, but still lying fairly close to the body, the hairs growing so closely and strongly together that when parted with the fingers the skin is hardly visible; free of softness or silkiness, and not so long as to alter the outline of the body, particularly in the hindquarters. On the sides of the body the coat is never as harsh as on the back and quarters, but it should be plentiful, and of good texture. At the base of the stiff outer coat there should be a growth of finer and softer hair, lighter in color, termed the undercoat. Single coats, which are without any undercoat, and wavy coats are undesirable; the curly and the kinky coats are most objectionable.

Breed Note

The Irish Terrier is nicknamed the "Daredevil," and this sobriquet tells a great deal about his personality. He is utterly fearless, loyal to his family and naturally protective. The Irish is also ready for fun at any time—a wonderful family dog.

The Irish Terrier closely resembles his cousins, the Wire Fox and Welsh Terriers. The main distinctions are the Irishman's glowing red coat, racier body outline and medium size.

Grooming Procedure

Preparing an Irish Terrier for the show ring is not complicated once the principles of terrier trimming and basic characteristics of the breed's coat are clearly understood.

The first principle is that the coat should be stripped or plucked, either by hand, which is best, or with a dull stripping knife. By studying a few hairs closely it is easy to see the reason for this. The hairs are darker red and wiry at the tip, narrowing and lightening in color as they approach the skin. If they are cut, both the coveted rich red color and wiry texture are lost.

Stripping is readily learned with practice. Basically it is a matter of pulling out the long, dead hairs, leaving room for the new hairs to grow in, red and wiry. The technique is to grasp a small tuft of hair between thumb and forefinger, or thumb and a dull stripping blade, and give a quick jerk in the same direction as the hair lies—not against the grain.

Simply stated, the method for preparing an Irish Terrier coat for show is this:

Depending on the individual coat's growth rate, strip very close, except beard, eyebrows, and leg hair, approximately 11 to 12 weeks before you intend to show the dog. Again depending on the dog's coat growth, strip out the undercoat (the short, soft coat) approximately four to five weeks later. Two or three weeks before the show, re-strip the ears, head and neck, being careful to blend well into the longer hair on the body.

It should be noted here that this is only the ground work for the finished show specimen. A great deal of attention still has to be given to such details as expression, feet and nails, furnishings, teeth, ears, and general neatening up of scraggly hairs on the belly, insides of hind-legs, and around the base of the tail.

To achieve proper expression, great care should be taken in trimming the head. The skull should be trimmed close but the furnishing left longer on the muzzle to fill in the foreface. The beard should be left long enough toward the front of the jaw to add length to the head, but not so long as to unbalance the overall picture.

Cheeks and throat should be trimmed very close to give a clean appearance to the head and neck. Hair on the cheeks grows very fast and should not be allowed to "get away."

Furnishings tend to become lighter colored and softer if dead hair is not weeded out regularly. Daily combing of whiskers and leg furnishings usually is sufficient to keep them in good condition. If, however, the dog has unusually hard, sparse leg hair and whiskers, application of baby oil tends to speed growth to keep the hairs from breaking off.

Daily brushing is necessary to keep an Irish Terrier's coat clean and lubricated by the natural oils present in his coat and skin. A natural bristle brush or hound glove is used for this work. Always brush with the lay of the hair, never against it. Application of baby oil on the brush or glove before brushing is also recommended for a very harsh coat, but only until about two weeks before the dog is to be shown.

It cannot be overemphasized that conditioning and grooming are daily tasks. It is impossible to short-cut the job and expect to get the same results as with daily attention.

Courtesy, Irish Terrier Club of America

Authors Note: As with all the other terriers, clipping of the *pet* Irish Terrier may be executed with the #8½ blade on the body coat.

The Lakeland Terrier

Standard Regarding Coat

Coat—Two-ply or double, the outer coat is hard and wiry in texture, the undercoat soft. Furnishings on muzzle and legs are plentiful as opposed to profuse.

Breed Note

The Lakeland Terrier is a small, extremely game working terrier from the lake districts of Northern England, where he was bred and raised many years before dog shows came into being.

He is one of the most successful terriers in the show ring today in spite of small numbers. The Lakeland also makes a very playful, affectionate house pet for any size home.

Grooming Procedure

Grooming the Lakeland is substantially similar to grooming the other terriers of similar stamp. The major difference concerns the head as the Lakeland does not carry divided eyebrows. His foreface is fashioned in a "fall" starting just above the eyes and in this respect he resembles the Kerry Blue. The Lakeland, Kerry Blue, Soft-Coated Wheaten and Sealyham are the only Terriers of their particular stamp which are groomed with a face fall rather than divided eyebrows.

The Welsh Terrier

Standard Regarding Coat

Coat—The coat should be wiry, hard, very close and abundant.

Breed Note

The Welsh Terrier is yet another terrier breed that evolved from the same background as the Airedale, Irish and Fox Terriers. Well-known as a sensible companion, he has a full measure of terrier spirit, without being argumentative.

A genuinely handsome breed, the Welsh Terrier's richly colored, black and tan coat, his unique, wise expression and his obvious terrier stamp draw admiring attention wherever he goes.

Grooming Procedure

A well-groomed Terrier will always look very proud and alert, and it is wise to start a Welsh Terrier puppy early on a routine of regular grooming. He will soon look forward to his grooming sessions and the physical contact between you and your dog will be a pleasure for both of you.

Nature provided the Welsh Terrier with a double coat. The top or guard coat is rough and wiry—the undercoat is fairly soft. This is to protect his hide in a natural environment while hunting small game and vermin in rough cover. In the absence of exposure to the natural environment, fingers or special trimming tools must take the place of briars and brambles to pull out the Welshie's dead coat.

You may decide to have your dog professionally stripped several times a year, or you may wish to do it yourself. Should you wish to strip your Welsh Terrier yourself, we suggest that you consult the breeder from whom you bought him. The breeder will be able to give you valuable tips for the proper procedure. If you decide to have him professionally stripped, make certain that the operator truly knows how to properly strip a Terrier. Under no circumstances let an operator use a clipper or razor tool if stripping is what you want. Any tool that merely cuts the coat leaves in the dead shanks, thus ruining the color and texture. The proper tool, other than one's fingers, is a blunt, dull, serrated-edged tool. It looks something like a kitchen paring knife, but it definitely must not have a sharp edge. With the correct tools, or with your fingers, you can do a fairly presentable job of grooming.

Courtesy, Welsh Terrier Club of America

The Short-Legged Terriers

The Australian Terrier

Standard Regarding Coat

Coat—Outer coat harsh and straight, and about two and one half inches all over the body. Undercoat short and soft. The topknot, which covers only the top of the skull, is of finer texture and lighter color than the body coat.

Breed Note

The Australian Terrier offers an ideal illustration of how breeds develop to suit local conditions. When Britons emigrating to Australia found the dogs from home lacked some qualities needed in this new wilderness, they set about to create a new breed better suited to this rugged life. Crossings of various terrier breeds eventually gave rise to the "Aussie," a small, working terrier that is easy to look after, very trainable and fine companion for city or country.

Grooming Procedure

Little trimming is required to prepare the Australian Terrier for the show ring. Therefore, for the sake of cleanliness and neatness, "pet" owners may follow the few basic principles herein. Bathe rarely, and allow at least four or more days for the coat to regain its harsh

texture. Allow a mature, healthy dog to run briskly in the rain whenever possible and follow immediately with a thorough drying, using a clean, rough towel. Brush and comb frequently. Allow no parting; groom straight from neck to stern (tail) to emphasize level backline, and downwards on rump and shoulders. Always encourage topknot upward. Use outward stroke toward shoulders from under chest to cultivate a fullness or ruff, and downwards from under chin to strengthen apron effect. Brush down on muzzle. Cut feelers in proportion to length of coat; this is optional.

Pluck with fingers long hairs around ears and between eyes. Use scissors to tidy the hindparts and feet, up to first joint of legs and external genitalia. Keep hair short on underside of tail and remove dead, untidy hairs from tip. If more detailed grooming is desired, use a rather blunt, small stripping knife to clean up face to enhance expression, and trim back of neck for greater emphasis on its length and to contrast fullness of ruff. Keep clean the characteristic black, leathery space which extends on bridge of muzzle in a V-shape. The Australian Terrier requires a minimum of grooming and sheds only very lightly. Small, it requires little conscious effort for its welfare.

Courtesy, Australian Terrier Club of America

Judith J. Tillinger

The Cairn Terrier

Standard Regarding Coat

Coat—Hard and weather-resistant. Must be double-coated with profuse harsh outer coat and short, soft, close, furry undercoat. **Faults**—Open coats, blousy coats, too short or dead coats, lack of sufficient undercoat, lack of head furnishings, lack of hard hair on the legs. Silkiness or curliness. A slight wave permissible.

Breed Note

The Cairn Terrier comes to us from the Isle of Skye and most closely resembles the old Scotch Terrier found in the background of all the terriers of Scotland. His name is derived from the ever-present "cairns" or stoneheaps of the region which are a natural refuge for the vermin he was used to hunt.

The Cairn is an intelligent, devoted little dog and is widely appreciated as an excellent housepet.

Grooming Procedure

The following hints on grooming a Cairn Terrier for the show ring are not to be considered complete instructions. They are meant as helpful suggestions for improving the appearance of a dog. Practice and observing correctly groomed dogs will gradually point out additional touches necessary to present your own dog in full bloom.

An actual grooming demonstration is undoubtedly the best way to obtain pointers for increasing your own skill. However, you will need to do some work on your dog beforehand if you plan to show.

To encourage good coat condition, brush the body coat forward. You will notice many hairs that are much longer than the rest. Pluck these by hand, a few at a time; comb the hair down to see the result and then forward and repeat. Do not take off too much at a time as you may leave "holes." This operation serves a two-fold purpose—it smooths and "neatens" the dog's appearance, and at the same time by pulling the long hairs, you will be bringing up new coat to support the old as it begins to blow. Pay particular attention to the head furnishings as the hair will probably be too long. The face frame needs to be thinned and shaped to the desired appearance.

Elbows and shoulders should be cleaned of any long hair that might float out as the dog moves creating the illusion that the dog is out at the elbows.

All the straggly hairs should be plucked from the

tail, leaving it thicker at the base and tapering to a point at the end. It should look like a "fat carrot" turned upside down.

The Cairn Terrier is a "head breed," meaning a good head is of prime importance to the total picture. Much can be done by careful trimming to achieve the desired, alert expression and generally enhance the head. Pluck all the hair from about the top third of the ears. The trimmed portion of the ear should look like velvet, if done properly. Do not leave long hair in front of the ear. Pluck a few of these at a time but do not remove so much hair that the ear opening is clearly visible. Brush the face furnishing forward and again pluck out the longest ones. If the hair falls over the end of the nose, these furnishings are too long.

Here you will have a decision to make—whether you have time enough to pull the excess long furnishings or whether you should pull some and cut some with the Duplex Dresser or thinning shears. Plucking is always preferred, but sometimes the razor or thinning shears is necessary because of the time element if a dog is being shown.

Next comb the whiskers forward and with the thinning shears trim the whiskers just beyond the end of the nose. Long, droopy whiskers detract from the appearance of the dog. This operation should be done four to five weeks before the show so that they will have a chance to grow a bit before the show so as not to look trimmed.

If there are long wispy hairs on the legs, remove these with fingers. They only detract from the dog, standing or moving.

Trim long hairs from between the foot pads with blunt-tipped scissors. Next, shape the feet with the scissors, remembering the hind feet should be smaller than the front. Do not scissor on top of the foot, just around the edge of the nails and at the back of the foot. Also, be sure the nails have been clipped and filed back as short as possible.

Having completed this tidying, comb out the dog thoroughly and have someone lead it so you can see it going, coming and from the side. Is the topline level? Is there more coat on the front of the body than on the back? Does the dog have excess furnishings behind the tail? Do the feet look trim and in proportion to the dog's size? If they appear small, do not trim them quite as close. Could you, by thinning the neck and shoulder a bit more, improve this area? These are a few of the places where improvement in appearance can usually be made.

Courtesy, The Cairn Terrier Club of America

The Dandie Dinmont Terrier

Standard Regarding Coat

Coat—This is a very important point; the hair should be about 2 inches long; that from skull to root of tail, a mixture of hardish and soft hair, which gives a sort of crisp feel to the hand. The hair should not be wiry; the coat is what is termed piley or penciled. The hair on the under part of the body is lighter in color and softer than on the top. The skin on the belly accords with the color of dog.

Breed Note

The Dandie Dinmont Terrier, from Scotland's border, acquired his name from a character in *Guy Mannering*, one of Sir Walter Scott's Waverly novels. The character, Dandie Dinmont, was a rugged farmer and the dogs and their work were described in some detail in this 1814 work.

The Dandie has many unusal characteristics, particularly for a terrier: long body, pendant ears, domed forehead and large, round eyes. The Dandie's very short legs, long, curved body, and distinctive topknot all contribute to his singular appearance.

Withal, the Dandie can be an amusing, delightful pet.

Grooming Procedure

Before beginning to groom a Dandie, a picture of the finished product—what you are striving for—should be in your mind's eye. The picture sharpens in time by reading and rereading the breed Standard and observing in pictures and the flesh as many Dandie Dinmont Terriers as possible. Once you begin grooming, work toward bringing out the flowing lines and curves of the body, tail, and the sweep of the topknot while maintaining a proper balance—all described in the Standard. The breed should always retain a natural, unbarbered look when groomed, for which the following instructions strive.

A certain understanding of the Dandie coat is also necessary before starting to groom. The ideal body coat of a mature dog is 1½ to 2 inches long and a mixture of one third soft to two thirds hard hair which gives a crisp feel to the hand. The hard hair is glossy with a fairly firm texture, but not wiry. The color is a band on the end of the hair shaft only. This is one of the reasons for the necessity of pulling the coat out to shorten it as cutting eliminates the color. The soft coat is creamy white and linty in texture. Here, too, there sometimes will be a small band of color on the end of new growth. It is the band of color on the sufficiently long, hard hair interspersed with the soft coat which gives the desired penciled effect called for in the Standard. While following the diagram provided for stripping, observe the dog's natural hair growth pattern to see if it coincides with the lines shown in Diagram. Each dog can vary slightly and the stripping lines may be changed a bit to be tailored to the individual dog.

Stripping the Body Coat—When the body hair has reached a length of more than two inches it is time to strip the old coat. Each Dandie has its own individual coat condition. Some have a more profuse, soft coat than others, and some Dandies when stripped always have new growth coming in while others do not. Because of this, instructions for stripping will vary with each Dandie to a certain degree, but the groomer should work toward producing the ideal coat in all cases.

Chest—Groom by breaking off chest hair below line B-B to two inches long. Blend the area at B-B into the body coat with a combination of shortening and plucking.

Front Legs—Comb hair straight out from the leg and even off to two inches in length on all sides. Now comb hair down on legs and, when standing in front of the dog, pluck as needed so that the leg appears straight from the shoulder downward. Groom the same smooth transition from body coat to furnishings as described for the chest. With scissors, trim hair from between pads and around bottom edges of feet. Now view leg from all angles and remove any excess hair marring a clean outline. Observe the dog moving and make any corrections necessary. The area to watch is the junction of leg and body—front, side and behind.

Rear Legs—Below Line D-D break off hair to about two inches in length, again blending into the body coat. The inside of the legs should be trimmed to make them appear straight. Move the dog to see that there is no flopping hair. Trim the rear feet the same as the front.

Tail—Remove long hairs extending past tip of tail. From there proceed to shape underside to the proper shape by plucking. Hair at the longest point is two inches, tapering smoothly to the tip. This will probably need doing periodically as the tail hair grows quickly and is usually profuse. Plucking a little and often keeps the hair rolling and prevents thinning the flag too much with any one grooming.

Under the Tail—Pluck (or trim short with thinning shears if you desire) the hair at the rear end of the dog. Pluck to blend back of hip smoothly from stern to thigh.

Grooming the Head

Top of Muzzle—For a show dog, shorten by plucking, or for a pet use thinning shears, in a strip almost as wide as the black part of the nose just to the stop (between the inside corners of the eyes). This should be done well ahead of a show so there will be no bare skin.

Eyes—The fringe of hair remaining at the inner corner of the eye after the muzzle is groomed should be plucked. Pluck out eyelashes on upper lid. (If untended these will grow to an extreme length.) If hair grows on the black rim under the eye, it should be plucked away. Avoid pulling too wide a rim which would distort the desired round appearance of the eye.

Ears—Pluck long hair on the outside of the ear leather. Leave hair on and above the fold line of the ear

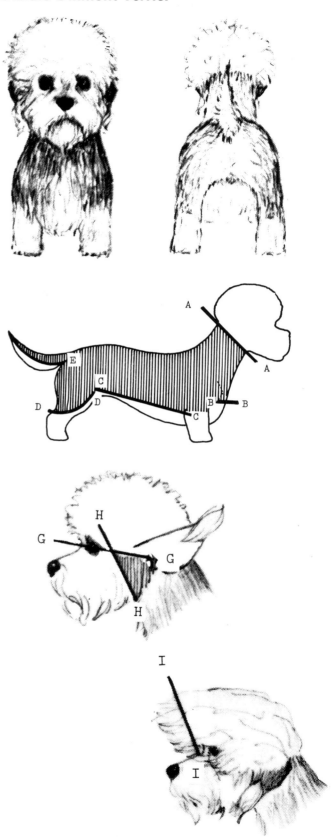

Show Trimming for the Dandie Dinmont Terrier

to become part of the topknot. Also leave a feather of hair at the tip of the ear. The feather should cover two inches of the ear tip starting with a modified point at the top and ending about one inch below the ear. The bottom of the feather should be shaped to come to a distinct point. Clean off the inside of the ear flap in the same manner as the outside, leaving the same feather, and pluck the hair from the ear canal. A small amount of powder may be used as an aid in gripping the hair. It is important to keep the ear canal free of hair to avoid conditions which may lead to infection.

Cheek—Refer to Diagram herein. Line G-G is from the outside corner of the eye to the ear canal. Line H-H is from a point about ¾″ back from the outside corner of the eye extending to the point of the jawbone. The hair above Line G-G is part of the topknot. The shaded area enclosed by Lines G-G and H-H should be sparingly plucked to blend smoothly from the length of the neck hair into the length of the longer muzzle hair.

Topknot—To begin, brush entire topknot lightly forward and by either pulling, breaking or a combination of both, even off across the front to softly frame the eyes in a bonnet effect. Line I-I begins one inch down the muzzle from the stop and tips outward toward the end of the nose. Now brush out or have the dog shake and continue shaping sides and back to resemble a large football mum. The guideline for shaping the back of the topknot as viewed from the side is a continuation of the back edge of the ear. Usually the hair on the ear in the area of the backside of the fold will extend in a tuft beyond the back edge and should be shortened. Viewed

from the front the outline of the topknot again follows the flow of the ear's back edge. Continuing, remove any hair from the front which obscures the eyes expression. The length of the dog's topknot must be in balance with the total dog.

In preparation for a show, to help the topknot stand up, a good quality chalk powder may be applied to a dampened topknot and thoroughly brushed out. A talcum preparation (sold at pet shops for this purpose) on a dry topknot gives somewhat the same effect for at-home grooming without the drying effects of chalk.

Grooming the Pet Dandie—Many pet owners are not interested in the precise grooming and stripping techniques necessary for show presentation. The family pet can be maintained in good coat and looking like a Dandie with a few modifications in technique. The previous grooming instructions had the pet owner in mind just as much as the exhibitor. In shaping the furnishings (legs, chest hair, topknot, etc.) the pet owner may use thinning shears or scissors if breaking off or pulling the hair is too time-consuming. The body coat however should never be cut or clipped. Periodically pulling out the longest hairs, both hard and soft, will keep the dog from becoming too shaggy without resorting to clippers. Regular vigorous brushing will also help remove any long dead coat. Few, if any grooming shops will strip a Terrier. If a pet has been clipped in the past he can be brought back to the proper color and texture. Hard brushing and pulling the shaggy hairs eventually will pay off.

Courtesy, Dandie Dinmont Terrier Club of America

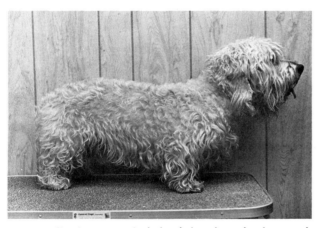

A pet Dandie Dinmont Terrier before being trimmed and groomed.

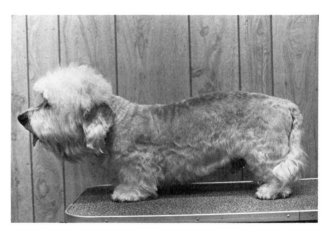

The same dog after a good grooming session.

The Norfolk and Norwich Terriers

Standard Regarding Coat

NORFOLK TERRIER

Coat—Hard, wiry and straight, lying close to the body. It is longer and rougher on the neck and shoulders, in full coat forming almost a mane. Hair on the head, ears and muzzle, short and smooth, except for slight eyebrows and slight whiskers.

NORWICH TERRIER

Coat—As hard and wiry as possible, lying close to the body, with a definite undercoat. Top coat absolutely straight; in full coat forming almost a mane on shoulders and neck. Hair on head, ears and muzzle, except for slight eyebrows and whiskers, is absolutely short and smooth. These dogs should be shown with as nearly a natural coat as possible. A minimum of tidying is permissible but excessive trimming, shaping and clipping shall be heavily penalized by the judge. **Faults**—Silky or curly coat.

Breed Note

The Norwich and Norfolk Terriers are very closely related and at one time were classified as one breed, differing only in ear carriage. Both breeds come from that part of England known as East Anglia and share a colorful, interesting history. Bred as hunt terriers, they also make admirable ratters and first-class indoor and outdoor companions.

In recent years both the Norfolk and Norwich Terriers have become much in demand both as pets, working terriers and show dogs. The breeds' rugged good looks and almost no-maintenance coats are plusses in their favor.

Grooming Procedure

Perhaps the most important statement for anyone grooming a Norwich and Norfolk for show is that they should be shown with as nearly a natural coat as possible; trimming is heavily penalized; never use scissors; brushing is better than bathing; never a rinse or dye. With a good coat, stripping is seldom needed, as regular brushing removes the dead hair, and a bit of plucking on and around the ears and tail will take care of the rest.

The characteristic coat requires no trimming. Lying close to his body, it is a protection against any type of cover and against all kinds of weather. It should be hard, straight and wiry, forming almost a mane where it grows from his thick, protective hide at the neck and shoulders. All shades of red, grizzle, wheaten and black and tan are acceptable.

Courtesy, The Norwich and Norfolk Terrier Club
by Marcella Congdon

The Scottish Terrier

Standard Regarding Coat

Coat—Rather short, about 2 inches, dense undercoat with outer coat intensely hard and wiry.

Breed Note

The Scottish Terrier is probably one of the world's most familiar purebreds. His legion of faithful friends can be found wherever dogs are appreciated.

Originally bred to hunt a wide variety of small game the Scottie still retains his proverbial terrier fire today and at the same time, makes a delightful companion. He is distinguished by his erect ears, thick eyebrows and whiskers and darkly piercing expression.

Grooming Procedure

There is outstanding material on grooming by very knowledgeable people, and what follows should be considered an extension of this expert material—not the total answer to Scottie grooming. These notes are meant to give you another method of grooming the Scot. With this addition to your grooming techniques you'll be able to choose the best grooming program for any given Scot. Remember no two dogs are alike, since the rate of hair growth differs from dog to dog.

Start by being sure your dog is brushed out completely. Use the slicker or palm brush.

We like stripping the entire dog in one session. We find that by taking the entire coat down and then working the coat as it comes in, we have a tighter, better balanced coat.

The method of stripping the coat is relatively easy.

Pour some Foo Foo or other grooming powder into the Scot's withers. This helps loosen the hair to be plucked and assists getting the hair out without breaking or cutting it.

Start pulling with index finger and thumb, using a rubber finger cot on each if you feel you need them. Hand plucking is absolutely the best trimming method. Bear in mind that unlike your own skin, a dog's skin is loose on his body—it stretches. Hold his skin firmly, stretching it in the opposite direction to the way you are pulling. This is done by placing the left hand just above the area to be pulled and holding the skin with just enough pressure to avoid discomfort to the dog during stripping. When you strip, be sure to pull straight as the hair grows, especially if you are using a stripping knife. When you twist your wrist you cut or break the hair. This ia a major reason for curly or wavy coats, a common fault made by all. The coat should be straight and hard. Stretching the skin lifts the hair to be pulled, making the hair easier to see and remove. Now that we've described the stripping method, pull the hair in Diagram A; use the grooming powder whenever necessary.

By pulling from the withers back, you will find that the hairs from occiput to withers come out relatively easily.

Continue stripping from the withers to the rump and then up the tail, down over the rump to where the hair forms a cowlick. When you finish stripping the anal region, clean the straggly hairs with scissors.

After the body and the rump have been stripped out, the occiput is the next area for attention. Strip from the occiput to the withers, including the neck. The hair on the back of the ears is usually soft, so dab some grooming powder in this area to make pulling easier.

Take a good look at your prospective show dog at this point. If you're satisfied, you are making the same mistake most people make. The top coat will grow in the be tight and hard, but the bottom half of your Scot looks like he's wearing a hula skirt. Too many Scots are shown in the ring with profuse furnishings or a definite line separating top coat from bottom furnishings. Most of these furnishings are dead. If you think the furnishings won't grow back, think again. They will. If you are trying to cover a fault, you may very well be accentuating it. The proper amount of hair in the right place will minimize a fault and give your Scot the appearance of being able to do the job for which he was bred. You should always be able to see daylight under any Scottish Terrier. So with this in mind, take out *all* the dead furnishings and ONLY THE DEAD FURNISHINGS!

Now blend the top coat, (or body coat), into the furnishings so that as the new coat grows, there will be a complete picture with all the hair in the right place. Remember, furnishings should grow from the elbows down the leg, not from the shoulders down. From the bottom of the belly or lower rib area down, not from the top of the back down, and from the bend in the thigh down, not from the buttocks down. Take a good look at the top winners for reference. These dogs carry just enough furnishings, all healthy and in the right places, to be most flattering to themselves.

Always brush the head and throat area in the direction you want to pull. Begin by brushing the dog's eyebrows and face furnishings forward. Now brush from behind the eyebrows to the ears, toward the back of the skull. If you have evaluated the dog's head, you know where the hair should be longest and shortest. A combination technique works for this writer. First handstrip the head and throat, then with the electric clipper or hand clipper even up the entire area. To this day, the best results are always attained "by the *old timers'* method"—finger and thumb. Few people do this today.

With the neck completed, return to the head. Clean out the hair in the stop between the eyebrows. Pull as much as you can as the entire neck and head will be finished off with the clippers.

Show trimming for the Scottish Terrier

A dog whose coat is completely grown out is said to be "in the rough."

In working on a Scottish Terrier, follow the direction of the arrows for trimming and grooming.

Work in the direction of the arrows for grooming and trimming on the hindquarters.

Show trimming for the Scottish Terrier

the coat grows in, it is essential to properly *blend* the body at smoothly into the side furnishings and legs as shown by the ows. At this time it is also important to strip closely on the backs of the ears.

The arrows in this sketch show trimming and grooming details for the Scottish Terrier's head. Take care to trim to the individual dog, minimizing faults and accentuating strong points.

A Scottish Terrier, correctly trimmed and properly conditioned, is a strikingly handsome animal. The groomer who can do a Scot properly is indeed a skillful operator.

The ears, eyebrows and face furnishings are now finished, taking them in that order. Clean off the tips of the ears with an Oster electric clipper, using a #15 head or a 000 Oster hand clipper. Clip only the top half of the ear with the lay of the hair or toward the tip. Sprinkle some grooming powder into the ear tufts, front and back. With a magnet stripper, clean out the dead hair, shaping it to fall inside of and along the back of the ear. If the dog's ears are large, leave a little extra hair to give them the appearance of being smaller. Be sure to pull the hair behind the ear—don't clip it. Clipping this hair will cause the growth to be curly and you'll be unhappy with the appearance. At this point, you've stripped most of the head and your Scot has bushy eyebrows and a wild-looking muzzle.'

The eyebrows are combed forward, and starting from the outer corner of the eye, the longest hairs are pulled out with magnet stripper. Pull toward yourself and remember that the shortest hairs at the outside corner of the eye and the longest on the inside toward the bridge of the nose. Eyebrows should not be too thick, but just heavy enough to cover the dog's eyes. The eyebrows should not be Fox Terrier short or as long as those of a Skye Terrier. If your Scot has the correct small, dark almond-shaped eye, well set under the brow, you are very fortunate and can trim the brows fairly thin and short. But most Scots need a little more brow and a bit more hair over the eyes. If brows stick straight up then apply some Vaseline or similar hair dressing to make them lie even with the skull. If they are still bushy then lower them from the top. Don't attempt to get the brows right in just one session. It takes many sessions of pulling one or two hairs at a time to get the brows perfect.

Now comb the face furnishings forward. With your finger and thumb start taking out all the long, straggly hairs, especially the dead ones. A little grooming powder, and then combing, will help you locate the dead furnishings for they will float just after combing. There's nothing worse than long, ''billy goat'' beards. Firstly, they usually fall apart the moment the dog shakes his head. Long furnishings make the dog's head appear longer, but they should also be alive and healthy. Furnishings on the face and body are right when some are in prime condition, some are coming in and some are ready to pull.

Now all the stripped areas on the head are finished with an Oster electric clipper using a #8 ½ blade or an Oster 000 hand clipper. Clip the entire backskull and cheeks in the direction of coat growth. Clip the underside of the neck from the top of the breastbone up to the mole under the lower jaw and then up the line where the throat and neck hairs meet to behind the back of the ear.

The finishing work is done with a pair of single-edge thinning shears. Clean the hairs where they meet along the neck and throat. With the dog's head in your hand and facing the dog, use the thinning shears to shape that ¾ inches you left from the corner of the eye to the corner of the lip. Make straight, clean cuts along that same imaginary line to give the impression of greater length.

Don't try to fine-trim the dog now, for the head will have to be trimmed repeatedly while the body coat grows to the right length. With straight-edge scissors, make a single, diagonal cut from the outer corner of the eye to the bridge of the nose to even up the eyebrows.

Trimming the ears is relatively easy. With your finger and thumb, slide down the outer edge of the ear lobe. This makes the hairs stand away from the edge. Scissor as close to the edge of the lobe as possible, always cutting up to the tip of the ear, never towards the skull.

If you make a mistake, don't fret, "it will grow back." We learn by our mistakes and lastly, remember the key word to grooming Scottish Terriers is . . . BALANCE.

Courtesy, The Scottish Terrier Club of America by Tom Natalini

Clipping The Pet Scottish Terrier

Clipping the pet Scottish Terrier is very much like clipping any pet terrier. In fact, if you follow the basic steps of clipping the pet Schnauzer (as outlined previously) or adapt all the instructions in this section for trimming the show dog, the result will be a pleasingly-groomed Scottie pet.

Body—Clipped with #8 ½ blade.
Tail—Same blade, corresponding to body.
Head—Change to #10 blade and follow closely outline of head as shown in the accompanying diagram.
Ears—The Scottish Terrier's ears are distinctively trimmed. While the back of the ear is clipped entirely, the front side is clipped only halfway down on the inner edge and tufts of hair are left on the head directly in front of the ears. These tufts are then carefully tidied with scissors. The size of the finished tuft depends on the size of the ear—large ear = large tuft, smaller ear = smaller tuft.

Pet trimming for the Scottish Terrier

The Sealyham Terrier

Standard Regarding Coat

Coat—Weather-resisting, comprised of soft, dense undercoat and hard, wiry top coat. Silky or curly coat bad fault.

Breed Note

The Sealyham Terrier is the creation of Captain John Edwardes who wanted a small, game terrier to control vermin on his estate, Sealyham in Haverfordwest, Wales. Although the combination of breeds in the Sealy's background is not certain, the Dandie Dinmont and Pembroke Corgi played a large part. Subsequent crossings with the Bull Terrier produced the white coat of the Sealy and increased gameness. He is a fine watch dog and makes an excellent family pet.

Grooming Procedure

The Sealyham Terrier most closely resembles his probable ancestor, the Dandie Dinmont, and is quite similar to the Scottie. In trimming these shortlegged Terriers, it is important to direct their trimming with the objective of achieving a solid, squat appearance. Moreover they have long, natural skirts.

The major features that mark the appearance of their headpieces are the broad faces, the fall and the full beards.

The Sealy headpiece differs from the Westie and Scottie in that the Sealy has dropped ears which are clipped (for pet) or stripped (for show) completely, front and back. In addition, unlike the Scottie, the eyebrows are undivided.

A nicely trimmed Sealyham head.

Pet Trimming for the Sealyham Terrier

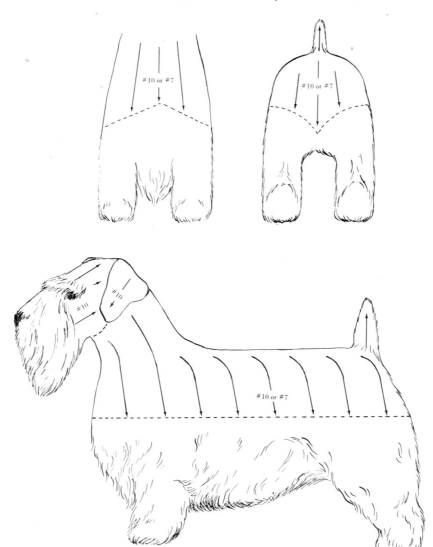

A pet Sealyham before grooming.

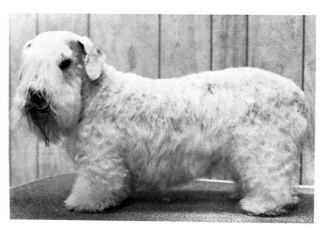

The same dog after grooming is completed.

204

The West Highland White Terrier

Standard Regarding Coat

Coat—Very important and seldom seen to perfection; must be double coated. The outer coat consists of straight hard hair, about 2 inches long, with shorter coat on neck and shoulders, properly blended. **Faults**—Any silkiness or tendency to curl is a serious fault, as is an open or single coat.

Breed Note

The West Highland White Terrier shares a common origin with the Cairn Terrier and became a distinct breed when the white coat became a trait sought after by breeders and other terrier enthusiasts.

Over the years Westie type became more distinct from the Cairn and today's Highlander is a larger dog with a more compact body than his near relation. The West Highland White is much sought-after today as a wonderful pet for the person who wants an active, fun-loving companion—a universally popular terrier breed.

Grooming Procedure

The neatly trimmed, well-groomed West Highland White Terriers that attract the prospective owner don't always just "come that way," nor do they remain neat and stylish without some attention and a bit of effort.

Trimming and grooming a Westie, whether for show or everyday neatness is important to the dog's well-being and a source of personal pride to the owner. Once you know what to do, and how to do it, you can keep a Westie neat and well-groomed looking with surprisingly little time and effort.

All Westies should carry a double coat composed of short, thick, cottony hair next to the skin, termed undercoat. Over this grows the top coat—long, coarse hair that can reach two or three inches in length. Most of your work will be with the top coat which grows and reaches full bloom and then dies and must be pulled out. When a dog has "blown its coat" it simply means the long hairs have lost that bright, alive look and should be pulled out, allowing room for new growth. This pulling out is called "plucking" or "stripping." With a judicious bit of trimming here and there it is easy to keep a Westie coat looking neat and trim. It is also possible, with proper working of the top coat, to "keep it rolling" which means holding the proper length while stripping out sufficient hair to permit new coat to grow whereby the overall coat includes three distinct growths, one old, one new and the other in-between.

205

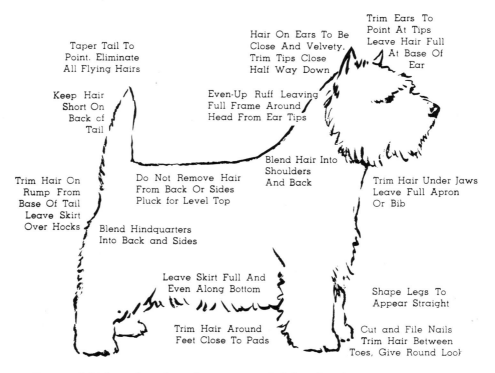

General Trimming for the West Highland White Terrier

The following suggestions and diagrams are obviously not intended for those with years of experience. They are offered as a guide to help the new Westie owner or groomer acquire some of that know-how.

Try to keep a clear picture in your mind of how a Westie should look from typical, well groomed animals you have seen either in the flesh or pictures, then try to keep it looking that way. Most experienced Westie people will be glad to show and help you develop the skill.

Trim hair closely inside ears, about half way down from tips. Cut hair on tips of ears close and even, at angle in drawing shown to blend into ruff. Trim hair on back of ears about one inch from tips leaving velvety hair. Leave hair long around base of ears. The idea is to make ears look small and set wide apart.

Comb eyebrows forward and trim on slant. Separate eyebrows slightly with trimming knife and let eyes show. Comb ruff forward and out, then trim both sides even with thinning shears. Leave ruff full but don't over-balance the head with respect to rest of body.

Use thumb and forefinger, or the stripping knife here. Take it easy; the key word is BLEND. Trim lightly on top of neck, starting behind ears and blending into body hair on neck and shoulders. If hair is very thick on sides of neck and shoulders, you may have to use thinning shears here. Taper into shoulders and body.

Clean hair on neck under head down to point of the breastbone, leaving a bib, or apron of long hair there. Clean on each side of bib to point of shoulder. When using thinning shears always cut with the lay of the hair—not across. Take a snip or two, comb out and check before each cut.

If hair on neck and back is loose enough to be pulled out easily with the thumb and forefinger, pull it and wait for a new growth to come in. Use your stripping knife to even up the top coat to give the back a straight, level look. If there is a dip in the topline, leave hair full or if there is a hump, trim close to even up.

Shape the tail to look like an inverted carrot and to appear as short as possible. Trim hair on the back of the tail so that it is almost a flat triangle from the tip, blending into the hips. Remove long hair on rump from base of tail to about half-way to the hocks, leaving a skirt between the legs.

Comb hair on legs up then down and study to see where you need to trim to give them that straight, full look when viewed from any direction. Even up feather so that when dog is moving the hair at elbows does not fly out. Trim very lightly. Leg hair grows very slowly.

Now cut the hair around the feet close to the pads to give feet a round, full look. This is best done with the dog's weight on the foot. You can make him stand by

Trim ruff from ear tips to frame of face.

Trim hair under chin to point of breastbone

Shape legs to look straight. Even feather on elbows.

Shorten hair behind ears and blend into shoulders

Trim hair on rump from base of tail. Leave skirt over hocks.

Blend hair from the back of the neck to flow smoothly into the shoulders.

Hair on underside of neck is trimmed close, blending into a full apron on the breastbone.

Comb topknot and ruff forward and upward and study the effect before doing any head trimming.

Even up face frame with thinning shears.

Comb hair on legs up, then down to show what needs to be trimmed. Dense furnishings are more important than long ones on the legs.

Strip or pluck any hair on the body loose enough to come out easily. Work for a straight topline.

Trim edges of ears at angle shown and clear tips of any long hairs. Blend into ruff.

The tail should approximate an inverted carrot and the hair over the rump trimmed to neatness and gradually blended into a skirt over the hocks.

Trim outside of feet to appear round and clean out all hairs growing between pads.

207

Pet trimming for the West Highland White Terrier

A pet West Highland White before grooming.

After grooming the dog offers visual proof of the breed's enormous charm.

raising the opposite foot during the trimming. Also trim the hair between the toes.

Conditioning and Cleaning

It shouldn't be necessary to bathe a Westie very often. In fact, it is better not to do so if you can avoid it. Regular brushing and grooming should keep him clean and neat. A stiff bristle brush or a hound glove used on the coat a couple of times a week will work wonders in keeping coat looking flat and white.

Chalking

While AKC rules require that there be no physical evidence of chalk in a dog's coat in the show ring, it is permissible to use chalk as a cleaning agent. However, it is imperative that there be no loose chalk in or on the dog's coat that will rub off on the judge's hand or come out when the dog is patted.

Before applying chalk, mix a pan of very soapy water and, with a sponge, wash the face, legs and feet and belly furnishings thoroughly. Rub the soapy sponge with the lay of the coat to get it clean but keeping coat as flat as possible. Now take a bath towel and rub as much moisture out of coat as possible, rubbing one way from neck to tail. The legs and head may be dried as usual. While coat is still just slightly damp apply chalk liberally to the face and head furnishings, back, belly, tail and legs. Cake or block chalk is preferable although powdered chalk may be used.

Comb and brush coat down as flat as possible and then pin a towel on the dog to keep things in place. Use large safety pins to do this, one under the neck, one just back of the front legs and one under the flanks. This will allow for movement but won't permit coat to "fly" or stand up.

Leave blanket on dog until coat is thoroughly dry . . . even overnight before day of show. Next morning remove towel and with dog on tack box or grooming table pat or slap with both hands every bit of the dog's body that might have chalk on it. This patting will loosen chalk that just won't be brushed out. This should be repeated several times until your patting won't raise the slightest chalk cloud.

The dog is now ready for the final brushing and combing. Sometimes a little non-greasy hair conditioner rubbed into the coat and furnishings will help to keep things in place.

Preparing for a Show

If you plan on showing your dog and have to take the top coat down completely, this should be done at least three months before the show, starting with the hair on the neck. Two or three weeks later take off the back coat from shoulder to tail. During these operations do not remove belly hair, feathers or whiskers. This hair grows slowly and if removed will take from five to six months to re-grow. Some coats grow back more quickly but you can always take off a bit here and there . . . you can't put it on! You should work on your dog's coat at no less than weekly intervals to bring it to full bloom and trim.

Careful trimming and plucking should be done a couple of weeks before the show so the coat can even itself out. A couple of days before the show a final bit of tidying up should suffice. If your dog needs bathing, now is the time to do it so as to allow natural oils to return to the coat. On the night before the show sponge the dog all over and rub him almost dry before working chalk into every part of his coat. Brush and comb lightly to get the hair to lay flat, then pin a towel around him to keep things in place, and put him in a crate.

An hour or so before show time pat the coat thoroughly on two or three occasions until all chalk is loosened and can be removed . . . completely, that is. (Your dog can be disqualified under the rules if chalk is apparent under normal conditions of handling.) Now brush, comb, and groom until every hair is in place. Be at ringside when your class is called. Get your arm band, enter the ring, take your place in line . . . and pray!

Courtesy, West Highland White Terrier Club of America

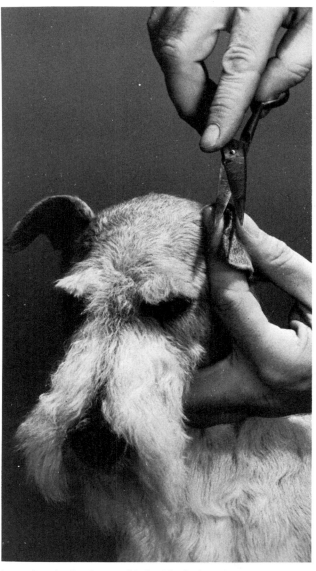

The Wire Fox Terrier has been dubbed the "Classic Terrier" by fanciers, and indeed he is the prototype for all the long-legged terriers of that stamp. Any groomer who can trim a Wire's head should be capable of handling the heads of all terriers.

TERRIER HEADS

Trimming the hardcoated terrier breeds is virtually the same for all, with the exception of the headpieces. Although head type and conformation vary from breed to breed, even if all terriers were groomed exactly alike they would still look different. It is the trimming that brings out the most typical features of each breed.

What follows, then, is a closer examination and more detailed explanation of the headpieces of the various hard coated terrier breeds.

Hard coated Terrier heads all fit into certain categories based on individual conformation.

They may be classified as rectangular, cylindrical or round, as follows:

Rectangular	Cylindrical	Round
Airedale	Fox (Wire)	Cairn
Australian	Irish	Dandie Dinmont
Border	Welsh	Norfolk
Lakeland		Norwich
Miniature Schnauzer		West Highland White
Scottish		
Sealyham		

Some readers might argue that a given breed is in the wrong category. If so, we have no quarrel. You may put the particular breed you disagree about in the category of your choice, as long as you do justice to the breed's characteristics and expression. A Schnauzer should look like a Schnauzer and a Wire Fox like a Wire Fox, etc.

The Miniature Schnauzer head, then, together with all rectangular heads, should have this *rectangular* configuration

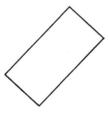

The Wire Fox Terrier head, together with other cylindrical heads, should have this *cylindrical* configuration

And finally the West Highland White, with other round heads, should have this *round* configuration

If we add the terrier eyebrows to these configurations, we come up with something like this:

Rectangular *Cylindrical* *Round*

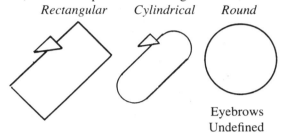

Eyebrows
Undefined

Now we add the typical terrier beard to these configurations

Rectangular *Cylindrical* *Round*

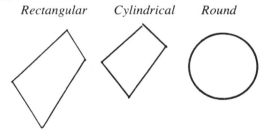

The sum total of the above configurations would be roughly equivalent to the following:

Rectangular *Cylindrical* *Round*

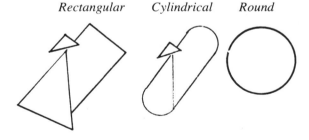

All that remains to be known is that the rectangular heads have more separation between the eyebrows than the cylindrical heads, while the round heads like the Westie's, have little, if any, separation of the eyebrows.

Finally, four terrier breeds are trimmed with a face fall rather than divided eyebrows, namely, the Kerry Blue, Lakeland, Soft-Coated Wheaten and Sealyham. Although one occasionally encounters a Lakeland or Sealyham with divided eyebrows, Kerries and Wheatens are *never* trimmed this way.

Shorthaired Toy Dogs

The Affenpinscher

Standard Regarding Coat

Coat—A very important factor. It is short and dense in certain parts and shaggy and longer in others, but should be hard and wiry. It is longer and more loose and shaggy on the legs and around the eyes, nose and chin, giving the typical monkey-like appearance from whence comes his name.

Breed Note

The Affenpinscher is a German Toy dog, and his name means *Monkey Terrier*. And, in spite of his diminutive size, he is very much a terrier in character. He is very devoted to the family and is an alert watchdog and tireless playmate.

His unique expression is decidely comic, which may have helped give him his unusual name. One interesting point about the Affenpinscher is even though his own background is obscure, he is in the background of the Miniature Schnauzer, one of our most popular purebreds.

Grooming Procedure

There are three things that can and should be taken care of a week before the show. Proper attention to the nails, the teeth, and to the ears are small improvements which add to the overall picture of the dog.

Check the dog's nails; if they have been worn down by exercise then no trimming is needed. Generally, dogs who are house pets need their nails cut. There are several types of nail clippers on the market; use the one easiest for you to handle. If your dog has a tendency to put on the *you're killing me* act, it is better to hold the dog in your lap and firmly grasp the paw in your hand—otherwise, you can put the dog on your grooming table. Experienced groomers quickly learn how much nail they can cut so that they don't cut into the quick and cause the nail to bleed. A small penlight flashlight held behind the nail will show where the blood vessel is located—this is a handy hint to remember if you don't have experience. A metal file (which most pet supply stores should have) can be used to round the sharp edges after trimming. Nails should be kept trim because long nails not only make the paws look longer than they are but also change the shape of the foot and have a tendency to spread the toes. Nails shouldn't be trimmed too close to the day of the show. Trimming the nails can alter the gait and if you've accidentally trimmed too close the dog may limp. We also suggest that you keep Quick Stop (or another coagulant) on hand. Should you cut into the quick, this can be applied to stop bleeding.

Along with the nails, trim the hair on the bottoms of the feet. A dog who exercises on concrete often wears away excessive hair. If he doesn't, this hair should be trimmed to pad level with a blunt-tip scissors. The blunt-tip prevents accidentally cutting the pad. Excessive hair can also spoil the shape of the foot.

The ears should be checked regularly and excess hair in the external ear canal should be plucked out. Accumulated wax can be removed with a fresh mixture of half hydrogen peroxide (antiseptic strength) and half glycerine. Your vet can best show you how to properly clean ears without injuring the dog. If you notice your dog repeatedly scratching at his ears or shaking his head frequently, it would be best to have your vet check his ears as there may be an infection present.

General appearance is one of, if not the most important single point in the Affenpinscher. A clean, glossy, sweet-smelling coat does much to enhance a show dog's appearance.

A bath should be given only as necessary. Some dogs can go quite a long time between baths with the use of waterless coat cleaners. However, a dirty, dull coat requires a regular bath.

If your adult Affenpinscher has a very hard coat, a good brushing against the way the coat grows is probably all that is needed to keep the coat in shape. Regular brushing will remove dead hair. A natural bristle brush is used.

If your dog carries a great deal of coat it often becomes necessary to strip out dead coat. A coat should be prepared three months before you plan to show your dog. Hair on the face and legs should not be plucked. Grasp a small amount of hair between the thumb and forefinger and pull out in a rolling motion. This will remove the dead hairs from the coat. Your purpose in stripping is to remove the dead hair not to cut off the ends of live hair—so don't use a clipper or scissors! Baseball resin (available in sporting goods shops) can be rubbed on your finger and thumb so you can get a better grip on the coat. During the show season you can maintain the coat by plucking small amounts of coat every few weeks. If you're presently showing your dog and want to get the coat in better shape, use the maintenance plucking method instead.

The Affenpinscher is a distinctive breed; in grooming him one should try to keep him as natural appearing as possible. In any case, he should not be made to look like any other breed.

Ears

Use thinning shears on the outer edge of the ears, evening the hair to the edge. If the ears are rather small the inner edge may be trimmed in like manner. A blunt tipped scissor may be used for the job if you're careful.

Face

Very little trimming should be done on the face. Occasionally it may be necessary to use the blunt-tipped scissors to trim hair on the bridge of the nose. Trimming is done to accentuate the eyes.

Feet

While clipping the nails, remove excess hair between the pads with a blunt-tip scissor. Next, trim the hair around the feet fairly close to the nails. If done neatly it makes the feet appear smaller yet natural.

Tail

The tail hair should be trimmed evenly to resemble a well-bristled paint brush.

Rump

Thinning shears may be used to tidy up excessive or straggly hairs around the anus and tail.

Feathers

Feathers on the legs and abdomen sometimes need a little touch of trimming with the thinning shears just to tidy up straggly hairs. DON'T overdo it or you'll ruin the dog's appearance.

Courtesy, Affenpinscher Club of America

The Brussels Griffon

Standard Regarding Coat

Coat—There are two distinct types of coat—rough and smooth. The rough coat should be wiry and dense, the harder and more wiry the better. On no account should the dog look or feel woolly, and there should be no silky hair anywhere. The coat should not be so long as to give a shaggy appearance, but should still be distinctly different all over from the smooth coat. The head should be covered with wiry hair slightly longer around the eyes, nose, cheeks, and chin, thus forming a fringe. The smooth coat is similar to that of the Boston Terrier or Bulldog, with no trace of wire hair.

Breed Note

The Brussels Griffon is one of the most interesting and different of all Toy breeds. The modern version of the breed is a refinement of a Belgian street dog crossed with the Affenpinscher. Over the years various other breeds were brought in for various features. The successful crosses were maintained and the failures discontinued. In due course the terrier-like charmer with the almost human expression, as we know it, came into being.

While the Brussels Griffon is a rarity among dogs, he has fared very well in the show world. Some have even become top winners in all-breed competition. These have indeed been great good will ambassadors for their breed.

It is of interest that the breed occurs in two coat types—rough and smooth. Both are equally delightful companions and while the rough is the more familiar, the smooth is much easier to groom.

Grooming Procedure

Beyond the need for the fundamentals of grooming (brushing, bathing, drying, ear cleaning, nail trimming) the Brussels Griffon coat calls for hand stripping, since it is a harsh coated breed. Like all the other harsh coated breeds, the Brussels Griffon's coat will lose its natural texture and the color will fade, if clippers are used.

A natural bristle brush or hound glove is best for routine grooming and regular brushing will reduce the need for frequent bathing. Since regular brushing helps keep the coat free of dead hairs, the need for combing is considerably lessened. In fact, over-combing may take out too much live undercoat.

For the stripping/plucking technique, we refer the reader to the section on Stripping/Plucking in Part III. Owners of smooth Griffons, or *Brabancons,* should refer to the grooming instructions for the Pug.

214

The Shorthaired Non-Sporting Dog

The Schipperke

Standard Regarding Coat

Coat—Abundant and slightly harsh to the touch, short on the ears and on the front of legs and on the hocks, fairly short on body, but longer around neck beginning back of ears, and forming a ruff and a cape; a jabot extending down between the front legs, also longer on rear where it forms a culotte, the points turning inward. Undercoat dense and short on body, very dense around neck, making ruff stand out. Culotte should be as long as the ruff.

Breed Note

The Flemish provinces of Belgium gave the Schipperke birth. Here he was popular as a watchdog, ratter, barge dog and family companion. In recent years these dogs have been given the nickname "Schips" as a diminutive of the Flemish for "Little Captain"—the real meaning of his name.

The Schipperke is quite distinctive and resembles no other breed closely. His unique silhouette is helped by the depth and distribution of his coat and his characteristic tail-lessness. The coat is always solid black.

He makes a delightful pet, is extremely bright, quick to learn and eager to please.

Grooming Procedure

The Schipperke requires only minimal grooming to look well. In fact, his grooming needs beyond the fundamentals are negligible. With the Schipperke any noticeable trimming is penalized in the show ring where the breed should be presented in a natural state.

Part IV

THE SMOOTHHAIRED BREEDS

American Foxhound
American Staffordshire
  Terrier
Basenji
Basset Hound
Beagle
Black and Tan
  Coonhound
Bloodhound
Boston Terrier
Boxer
Bulldog
Bullmastiff
Bull Terrier
Collie (Smooth)
Dalmatian
Dachshund (Smooth)
Doberman Pinscher
English Foxhound
Fox Terrier (Smooth)

French Bulldog
Great Dane
Greyhound
Harrier
Ibizan Hound
Italian Greyhound
Manchester Terrier
  (Toy)
Manchester Terrier
Mastiff
Miniature Pinscher
Pointer
Pug
Rhodesian Ridgeback
Rottweiler
Staffordshire Bull
  Terrier
Vizsla
Weimaraner
Whippet

Because smoothhaired breeds do not become matted, tangled, or knotted, they are that much easier to groom. In fact, in the majority of cases the fundamentals of grooming are mostly required (Brushing, Bathing, Drying, Ear Cleaning and Nail Trimming). No blow-drying is needed on smoothcoats. Towel and cage drying will do. The most important element in the grooming of the smoothcoats is to brush regularly with a natural bristle brush or a hound glove (with natural bristles), to keep the coat smooth and sleek. Where indicated on certain breeds, a rubber curry comb should be used.

Likewise, with most smoothhaired breeds there is little trimming or styling required and they are best presented "au naturel."

Smoothhaired Sporting Dogs

The Pointer

Standard Regarding Coat

Coat—Short, dense, smooth with a sheen.

Breed Note

A Sporting dog of classic beauty and flowing, elegant lines, the Pointer was known in England as far back as the 17th Century. It is even possible that he existed before that time although there is no definite proof.

The Pointer is named for the manner in which he signals the presence of game to the hunter and many paintings and sculptures have paid tribute to the timeless beauty of the Pointer "on point."

Today the Pointer is still the hard-charging, enthusiastic hunting dog, being rather a specialist on upland birds. He is also highly successful in the show ring where his great beauty has frequently carried him into the winners' circle.

Grooming Procedure

Since there is no written information on grooming a Pointer, I will describe what I do to prepare my dogs for the ring.
1. Bathe dog with a whitener shampoo.
2. Clip nails and grind if necessary.
3. With clippers, (#10 blade) clean hair off the underbelly and tuck up. Also clean the pastern. If dog is lacking in stop, use clippers there.
4. With a fine stripping knife clean stop, use on cheeks to show chiseling, and from occiput down to the withers to clean neck. The underside of the tail is also cleaned with the same knife.
5. With thinning shears, clean muzzle, neck area and rear.
6. With scissors, round off tail, clean pastern area and cut off whiskers.

Courtesy, American Pointer Club
Marjorie Martorella, President

The Vizsla

Standard Regarding Coat

Coat—Short, smooth, dense, and close-lying, without woolly undercoat.

Breed Note

The Vizsla is the Hungarian development of the continental pointer and strongly resembles other breeds of that stamp. An old breed, the Vizsla's ancestors probably came into Hungary during the Magyar invasion over a thousand years ago. The breed developed into its present form over the ensuing centuries to suit the specific hunting conditions of its native land.

The Vizsla has a reputation as a versatile gun dog and works on waterfowl and hare as expertly as on upland birds. Since being introduced to the United States the breed's rate of growth has been steady and today he enjoys moderate popularity as a pet, personal shooting dog and show dog.

Grooming Procedure

The Vizsla being groomed for the show ring will have his whiskers and odd hairs over eyes and cheeks trimmed close. Thereafter, his face is smooth all over, as is his beautiful golden-rust coat. He should be bathed so his coat is shiny and silken-soft. His ears are cleaned in preparation for the judge's examination and for sensible hygiene. His toenails are cut short so they look neat and do not touch the ground. Hair between the toes is trimmed so it does not show when the judge lifts the foot to look at the pads. The end tufts on the docked tail can be trimmed and gently rounded to give a finished look.

His teeth can be brushed and/or scaled if needed. Since his skin in sensitive and very much like our own, we use the same soap or shampoo on our Vizsla as we do for ourselves. Since the Vizsla has very short hair, about ¼ inch, grooming is really a very simple procedure.

*Courtesy, Vizsla Club of Southern California
by Jean Heliker*

The Weimaraner

Standard Regarding Coat

Coat—Short, smooth and sleek, solid color, in shades of mouse-gray to silver-gray, usually blending to lighter shades on the head and ears. A small white marking on the chest is permitted, but should be penalized on any other portion of the body. White spots resulting from injury should not be penalized. A distinctly long coat is a disqualification. A distinctly blue or black coat is a disqualification.

Breed Note

The Weimaraner's land of origin is not at all clear although he is thought to have originated from the town of Weimar in Germany. Whatever his origin there is no doubt about his abilities as a hunter and retriever.

The Weimaraner is an unusual looking dog, with his magnificent head, keen intelligent look, and silver-gray coat. He has attained a large following in the United States.

Grooming Procedure

This sleek, smooth-coated dog requires little grooming beyond the fundamentals. Regular brushing with a natural bristle brush will keep that smooth, sleek coat healthy and shining. Frequent baths are unnecessary and, in fact, unadvisable. It is a good idea after bathing your Weimaraner to massage the coat with the palms of your hands, as this will help restore the natural oils in the skin and hair follicles.

Smoothhaired Hounds

The Basenji

Standard Regarding Coat

Coat—Short and silky. Skin very pliant.

Breed Note

The Basenji, sometimes known as the Congo Dog, came originally from Central Africa. During the nineteenth century, an attempt was made to bring the Basenji to England. The first imports did not survive but later attempts proved successful in America as well as England. Today, the Basenji enjoys moderate popularity. There is enough breeding conducted to preclude extinction, but not the runaway demand so potentially harmful to any breed.

The Basenji was used by natives for hunting and tracking game. He is very agile and graceful and a great jumper, so much so that he has often been compared to a fawn. His distinguishing characteristics are erect ears, a curled tail and wrinkles on his forehead. He is also famous as the "Barkless Dog" though he is not mute and communicates through a series of yodels, chortles and yelps.

Grooming Procedure

Because Basenjis clean themselves like cats, whatever is applied to the dog's coat must be non-toxic. This is a vitally important consideration for anyone who expects to groom Basenjis.

As a house pet, a Basenji usually needs very little grooming—an occasional bath with a gentle dog shampoo, at least weekly brushing with a hound glove or soft-bristle brush, and nails clipped as needed. In colder weather, more frequent brushing may be necessary to remove soft undercoat that detracts from the normal glossy, stiff Basenji coat.

For Show

Head—For a smooth appearance, whiskers on the muzzle and eyebrows are cut even with surrounding hair. Hairs around the lips are also cut.

Hair in the ear, at the base, is cut short following the contour of the inner ear. Long hair on other parts of the ear is trimmed to blend with the short hair on and in the ear. Long hair on the edge of the ear is trimmed.

Body—To accentuate the tuck-up, waist hair is cut coat length in the loin area. Long hairs on the chest are cut off to further accentuate the tuck-up. Stack the dog and work from the judge's view—complete side view.

Then, using the thinning shears as a comb, comb the hair on the hindquarters to remove some of the undercoat. Then a little thinning, with the shears, may be necessary to blend the hindquarter hair with the smooth hair on the leg *and* to accentuate the angulation. Lastly, with the dog stacked—feet placed well back—cut wild, long hairs. The hindquarter angulation should be well defined.

Tail—Again using the thinning shears as a comb, holding the tail uncurled, comb the hair on the tail on all sides. Then let the tail return to its natural position. With the tail in its natural position, thin the hair coat length from the base of the tail to the tip on the outside part of the tail. The outer portion of the tail hair should be smooth and cut close to the skin.

Nails—All toenails should be trimmed to the quick.

Coat—A good all-over brushing with a hound glove or brush to smooth and shine the coat complete the grooming for the show ring.

Courtesy Loretta Kelley

The Basset Hound

Standard Regarding Coat

Coat—The coat is hard, smooth, and short, with sufficient density to be of use in all weather. The skin is loose and elastic. A distinctly long coat is a disqualification.

Breed Note

The Basset Hound originated in France, but seems to have really flourished in the United States.

He is a good hunter, with highly developed trailing hound instincts, but he is not very fast. His best hunting traits are his patience and quiet vigilance. He is slow but sure.

In the right home, the Basset Hound is one of the most delightful pets, with his friendly eyes, charming expression and sweet disposition.

Grooming Procedure

A clean dog, with ears cleaned inside and out; whiskers cut back to skin level; excess hair trimmed on the pads; toenails trimmed so that you cannot hear the dog's footsteps; judicious trimming (to evenness) of the "britches" if called for—this is grooming the Basset. Do NOT remove the feathering on the tail; the Standard calls for it to be there.

Trimming toenails is a must, whether or not the dog is headed for the show ring. Maintaining clean ears is also a must; uncleaned Basset ears are a great source of bad odor and become a health problem.

Courtesy, The Basset Hound Club of America
by Beverly Stockfelt

The Beagle

Standard Regarding Coat

Coat—A close, hard hound coat of medium length. **Defects**—A short, thin coat, or of a soft quality.

Breed Note

The Beagle is said to be one of the most ancient English hunting hounds and was the favorite of English kings and sporting gentry. He looks like and actually is, a small Foxhound. Beagles have been used successfully on hare, wild rabbit, squirrel and quail, as well as fox. In the United States, the Beagle is the basis of a sport involving countless thousands of outdoorsmen.

The Beagle has become a great pet, probably because in addition to his hunting abilities, he is a very affectionate dog, very playful and merry, and adapts extremely well to family life, but is happiest as an outdoor dog doing the breed's work. So popular has the Beagle become in the United States that he ranks consistently among the top ten in popularity.

Grooming Procedure

As with most smoothhair breeds, grooming the Beagle consists of simply attending to the fundamentals of grooming as described in Part I of this book. And grooming for the show ring only requires the additional trimming of whiskers around the muzzle and trimming any long, straggly hairs elsewhere on the body.

The Black and Tan Coonhound

Standard Regarding Coat

Coat—The coat should be short but dense to withstand rough going.

Breed Note

The Black and Tan Coonhound has an English background but was developed in the American Southeast. He is similar to the Bloodhound in his hunting instincts and he can hunt entirely by scent, with his nose to the ground. As soon as he has treed his quarry, he will bark to give notice. Not only is he a specialist hunting coon, but he is equally good with deer, bear and other game.

Grooming Procedure

First, there is a decided difference in coat texture in dogs kept outside, as opposed to those in the house. Most hounds do so well in extremes of weather, they are to be considered outside dogs.

In early spring preparation for shows—use a serrated edge (thinning shear; hack-saw blade/rake) and comb through the entire coat. New hair comes in—rusty, in spring—especially along the neck cowlick. If you try to remove this color, you will be removing hair which later will turn black and fill in, so don't! After raking

through the entire body, head and tail, cut the hair on the underside of the pads level with the pad. Cutting between toes just before a show can throw the dog's gait off. Next a good brush (then shampoo). Repeat, brush—shampoo. This loosens the hair again. Rinse thoroughly. Rinse again. Ordinary cider vinegar leaves the hair squeaky clean, and you can apply a nice smelling rinse to the coat later. No need for a dryer—just allow the dog, after towel drying, to rest in a crate, or move freely in an area that is at room temperature. Do not chill him. Before he is allowed to dry, do the final show preparations. The night before the show cut or grind the nails but try not to cut the quicks. Clean the teeth especially the canines using "Kontrol," a dentifrice for tobacco stains, to remove food coloration. Scale the tartar if necessary. The dog's mouth will smell sweeter, and the dog will generally hold still for this. The toothbrush rubbed on the teeth and gums is a pleasurable sensation.

You cannot pay enough attention to the Coonhound's long ears! Apply some rubbing alcohol into the ear and massage the base gently. Remove excess alcohol with a cotton-wrapped finger. When you bathe the dog, wash the ears well, on the inside surface area too. Trim off all whiskers on head and muzzle and shape the tail tip to a "V." With thinning shears, straighten neck cowlicks. A well-fed and kept hound will carry a naturally glossy coat. Bathing sometimes washes away some natural oils, so a light hair dressing rubbed first into palms of both hands, and then on the dog's sides and topline; over skull and down ears and legs lightly and down feet is a helpful measure.

After sleeping, some hounds' eyes can show a buildup of matter. Clean the eyes with sterile water, or any eye drop rinse. Wipe clean with cotton, or clean, soft pad.

Hounds, being black, get dusty on the way to a show. Wipe dust off the coat with "Show-Coat" pads or flannel pads cut, folded and placed in a clean jar. Just pour some part of a bottle of "Show-Coat" liquid over the pads. They last several shows and are easily disposable.

The hound glove is a helpful grooming tool but any hand massage or brush, used even occasionally, will reduce shedding and keep coat and skin healthy. It is also worthwhile to bathe a hound before every show.

Courtesy, The American Black & Tan Coonhound Club
by Jacqueline Iden

The Bloodhound

The Bloodhound is one of only two breeds whose Standard makes no mention of the coat.

Breed Note

The Bloodhound is the quintessential trailing hound and was developed many centuries ago in England. He is famous for his phenomenal sense of smell and is universally regarded as the supreme man trailer. He has been called "a dog behind a nose."

Yet, the hard-charging Bloodhound, so dedicated to his calling, is a very gentle, mild-mannered dog in the home.

Grooming Procedure

The Bloodhound is a "natural" breed—not much grooming is required. This is often taken to mean, by lazy owners, that *no* grooming is necessary. However, the appearance of *any* dog is enhanced by basic good grooming, and judges prefer *clean* dogs.

1. Bathe your Bloodhound! They have sensitive skins, so please use a quality dog shampoo. Use a "dark coat" for the blacker dogs, and a protein shampoo for reds or livers. Use a soft nylon bristle brush to work the shampoo in, paying special attention to the ends of their long ears (often very dirty). A very thorough warm rinse, then another water rinse. Towel very well, and dry.

2. Brush your Bloodhound! Depending on the thickness of the hound's coat (they are double-coated as a rule with short, hardish, guard hairs and a downy undercoat), use a Warner's slicker or a Quik Shed 'n' Blade. After the initial, coat loosening brush, use a rubber "brush" that painlessly and effectively removes dead hairs anywhere! Brush the ears, the face, the legs, and all the body *very* well. By now, the coat should gleam, and the hound ready for the small amount of touch-up grooming necessary.

3. Nails and ears. Cut and file your hound's nails—long nails are responsible for many a bad appearing foot. If you own an electric nail grinder, accustom your hound to it and use it! Next, gently clean the wax from your hound's ears, using a Q-Tip and R-7 (or similar lotion). Judges look inside ears, too!

Head—Remove whiskers with blunt scissors or #10 blade. Check profile, and if hound's peak is not showing well, use double-serrated thinning shears, carefully, to accentuate the peak. Be sure ends of ears are free of dirt—comb with a fine flea comb or card with fine stripping knife. Lastly, a bit of Vaseline on the nose makes it look moist and shiny.

Feet—Check inside pads for long hair—if any is present, your hound could slip. Scissor it out, or use a

#10 blade to remove. Check pasterns—if the hair is longish, you can use the #10 blade with the hair to accentuate a good pastern.

Belly—The Standard calls for a ''deep keel'' so hair is usually untrimmed on the belly, but any long, offensive hairs, especially under the loins, should be evened with scissors.

Rear—The cullottes should be removed with thinning shears to show rear angulation.

Stern—The tip of the stern is carefully rounded with scissors or thinning shears. The brush is combed down and accentuated.

Final Touches—A lanolin coat spray may be used to further shine the coat. Nails may be oiled to shine. Check teeth for tartar and remove! A diaper makes a super shine cloth—as does velvet.

Courtesy, American Bloodhound Club
by Phyllis Natanek

The Smooth Dachshund

Standard Regarding Coat

Hair—Short, thick, smooth and shining; no bald patches. Special faults are: Too fine or thin hair, leathery ears, bald patches, too coarse or too thick hair in general.

Breed Note

The Smooth Dachshund is identical to the Longhaired and Wirehaired varieties in every respect except for his short, sleek coat. He is by far the most popular of the three Dachshund varieties.

Grooming Procedure

The Smooth Dachshund has a short, thick, shiny coat. Very little grooming is required in order to show this variety.

Head—Use straight shears with rounded tips to cut whiskers on the muzzle, over the eyes, on the cheeks, and underside of the jaw. These should be cut very close to the skin.

Neck—If the dog has a particularly thick coat, you may have to scissor the stray hairs on the sides of the neck where the coat growth from the back of the neck joins the growth from the front. You may also have to trim the wispy hairs which may protrude at the point of the breastbone. This may be done with either straight scissors or thinning shears, but cut slowly and carefully so that you do not leave a bare spot or sharp line.

Tail—If the hair on the underside of the tail is thick and unkempt-looking, trim with scissors or thinning shears to give a sleek, tapered look.

Feet—Trim any hair that protrudes on the underside of the feet so that the hair is even with the pads.

A light spray of coat oil, or a small amount of baby oil rubbed on your hands and then applied lightly to the coat, will add a lustrous sheen to the finished product.

Pet Grooming the Smooth Dachshund

The Smooth Dachshund that is not being shown requires practically no grooming to be the ideal house pet. He should be bathed occasionally and brushed often to keep the skin healthy and the coat glowing.

Courtesy, National Miniature Dachsund Club by Jeanne A. Rice

The American Foxhound

Standard Regarding Coat

Coat—A close, hard, hound coat of medium length.
Defects—A short, thin coat or of a soft quality.

Breed Note

The American Foxhound is the result of blending many British and Continental European strains. This was done to obtain a hound that was especially well-suited to hunting conditions in the United States. Mostly a product of the Southeast and South Central states, the American Foxhound is bred in various types for various forms of hunting. While the breed is worked in packs, they are used in other ways as well. In recent years, a number of American Foxhounds have made very fine wins in strong all-breed dog show competition, and while the breed is not numerous compared to most others, the bulk of working Foxhounds are rarely seen by any but those who use them for their intended purpose.

Grooming Procedure

In addition to attending to the fundamentals the only extra fine point of grooming the American Foxhound for showing is the use of the natural bristle brush to remove dandruff from the coat and then the use of the hound glove for that extra shine. All long, uneven or straggly hairs can be scissored off.

The English Foxhound

Standard Regarding Coat

Coat—Not regarded as very important, so long as the former is a good "hound color," and the latter is short, dense, hard, and glossy. Hound colors are black, tan, and white, or any combination of these three, also the various "pies" compounded of white and the color of the hare and badger, or yellow, or tan.

Breed Note

The English Foxhound is the classic hound of the mounted hunt. For pursuing the fox he has no peer. In England the sporting set and the landed gentry followed the hounds for great distances in the chase. Many famous paintings attest to this. He is tireless and can run a trail from morning to night with unbounded energy.

Grooming Procedure

The English Foxhound is groomed exactly like the American Foxhound. This consists simply of attention to the fundamentals plus the extra little attentions for showing (use of the hound glove and trimming of straggly hairs).

The Greyhound

Standard Regarding Coat

Coat—Short, smooth and firm in texture.

Breed Note

The Greyhound is one of the most ancient of the family of purebred dogs. Likenesses of the breed were found in Egyptian relics dating back almost three thousand years before the birth of Christ. In all his long, proud history the elegant Greyhound was the prototype coursing dog. He was raced for sport, hunting, for food and was always the pride of the people around him.

The Greyhound's classic, understated beauty and symmetry have captured the imagination of artists down through the centuries and from around the world. Paintings, sculpture, tapestry and other media have all transmitted the timeless beauty of the breed.

When he is not showing his incredible speed of foot, the Greyhound will, if given the opportunity, show what a splendid companion he can be—quiet, dignified and completely loyal to his family.

Grooming Procedure

The Greyhound's short, sleek coat presents a negligible amount of grooming attention for home or show ring. Good, hard condition, regular attention to basic hygiene—inside and out—and trimming the odd straggly hair that shows itself as well as the hair at the sides of the neck and backs of thighs will cover most of it. Brushing and hand massage are said to be important in helping achieve prime condition by stimulating the oil glands and thus promoting a bright, shiny coat. For the show ring, chalk, corn starch or a similar product is often used to clean dogs with extensive white markings.

Day-to-day maintenance involves vigorous, daily brushing with a natural bristle brush to remove old, dead hair, stimulate the new coat and generally brighten the whole jacket all around.

The Harrier

Like that of the Bloodhound, the Harrier Standard does not make any mention of coat.

Breed Note

The Harrier, as we know it, originated in England. He is really a smaller version of the Foxhound and has a superb sense of smell combined with tremendous speed and seemingly unlimited vitality. He can run down a hare without even stopping for breath.

The Harrier is distinguished by a compact body, perfect balance and a smooth coat. He has been followed on foot and on horseback and is known among hound men for the good sport he provides.

Grooming Procedure

The Harrier, like most other smoothhaired scent hounds, requires very little effort to look presentable. For the show ring one need only remove whiskers and long hair from the face and muzzle and, with thinning shears, neaten the long hair on the back of thighs and rump.

The Ibizan Hound

Standard Regarding Coat

Coat—*Short:* Shortest on head and ears and longest at back of thighs and under tail. *Wire-haired:* Can be from one to three inches in length with a possible generous mustache, more hair on back, back of thighs and tail. Both types of coat are always hard in texture. Neither coat is preferable to the other.

Breed Note

The Ibizan Hound, of Egyptian origin, was first imported to the United States in 1956. This is one of the latest breeds to be recognized by AKC, becoming eligible for exhibition as recently as 1979.

The Ibizan Hound can be smooth coated or wire-haired and has a typical sighthound stamp. This ancient breed goes back to the time of the Pharaohs, numerous ancient artifacts having been discovered to establish the Ibizan's claim to antiquity. A life-size statue of Anubis, the deity of the dead, was found in the tomb of Tutankhamen. It looks exactly like the Ibizan Hound we see today!

The Ibizan Hound is a regal looking, elegant dog with an excellent temperament and makes a marvelous companion.

Grooming Procedure

Like most smoothhaired breeds, the smooth Ibizan Hound requires little grooming beyond the fundamentals. A good brushing with a hound glove or natural bristle brush, an occasional bath, trimming nails and cleaning ears, will keep the Ibizan Hound perfectly well-groomed. The wirehaired variety is groomed in almost the same fashion.

The Rhodesian Ridgeback

Standard Regarding Coat

Coat—Should be short and dense, sleek and glossy in appearance, but neither woolly nor silky.

Breed Note

The Rhodesian Ridgeback illustrates how a breed can be brought into being to fit a specific need.

Soon after European settlers arrived in South Africa in the 16th and 17th Centuries, they realized the need for a dog that was better suited to the conditions of their pioneer life than those they brought from home. When European immigration to South Africa closed for almost all of the 18th Century, native dogs came strongly into play in the genetic jigsaw.

A native type, much favored by the Hottentots, bred freely with white settlers' dogs and the melding of genes eventually led to a dog that was an excellent guard, superb big game hunter and ideal family dog for his special surroundings.

The characteristic ridge is his alone in the entire purebred family and it identifies a distinctive breed that is naturally handsome, highly intelligent and suitable to many callings—the Rhodesian Ridgeback.

Grooming Procedure

To groom the Rhodesian Ridgeback show dog or pet, the requirements are quite simple:

1. A good bath followed by vigorous brushing with a bristle brush. Ears should be cleaned and nails clipped closely for a neat foot.
2. For show—A) The muzzle may be cleaned of whiskers by clippers or scissors. Eyebrows and side whiskers should be included.
   B) Excessive hair on pads should be trimmed to prevent slipping.
   C) For a heavy winter coat, thinning shears may be used on the neck for a slimmer look. Also trim back of thighs and around the flank area.

The Ridgeback is a very natural dog so his basic good looks should come naturally too.

Courtesy, Rhodesian Ridgeback Club of The United States
by Sandra Fike

The Whippet

Standard Regarding Coat

Coat and Color—Close, smooth and firm in texture. A coarse, or woolly coat should be penalized. Color immaterial.

Breed Note

Even to the most uninitiated eye, the Whippet's close physical connection to the Greyhound is obvious. And, like the Greyhound, the Whippet is a highly successful racing dog.

Northern England, particularly Lancashire and Yorkshire, was the Whippet's birthplace. There he was used to pursue rabbits and in a variety of racing styles to provide sport for the working-class breeders who developed him.

Today's Whippet is an elegant, clean, quiet companion and a show dog that is easy to work with because of his sleek coat, small size and amenable temperament that allows him to be channeled by his trainer.

Sadly, most people looking for a pleasant pet never consider the Whippet. This is a real mystery as the breed has so much to offer the person looking for an ideal, personal companion.

Grooming Procedure

Although the Whippet has a smooth coat, there are several fine points in grooming for the show ring beyond the fundamentals. Trimming the whiskers on the muzzle, using blunt-nosed scissors is mandatory and clippers may be used to remove any heavy growth of hair under the neck. The hair on the underside of the tail may be clipped but not the top. The sides of the tail may also be clipped or trimmed with scissors.

Smoothhaired Working Dogs

The Boxer

Standard Regarding Coat

Coat—Short, shiny, smooth, tight to body.

Breed Note

The Boxer is a Mastiff-type breed of German origin. He has a strong, compact build and can move very quickly. He is easily trained and can be an excellent watchdog or bodyguard. He competes with the German Shepherd in his capabilities as a guide dog for the blind or as a police dog.

The Boxer has a sweet and gentle nature, patient with children and equally adaptable to life in city or country.

Grooming Procedure

The Boxer is a typical representative of the smooth-haired breeds, who in general require little grooming. Brushing is done with a rubber curry comb. Although called a comb, it is shaped more like a brush and it is made of rubber with teeth cut into the edges. Its main function is to pull out the loose hairs and enhance the natural sheen of the coat.

For that show look, trim the whiskers, long hair on the ears, the underbelly, tail and back thigh seams. The trimming may be done with clippers or scissors. Regular bathing is not necessary. Nails are trimmed and ears are cleaned regularly.

Courtesy, The American Boxer Club

The Bullmastiff

Standard Regarding Coat

Coat—Short and dense, giving good weather protection.

Breed Note

The Bullmastiff is a cross between the Bulldog and the Mastiff and is obviously a big, powerful dog. He was developed in England as a weapon in the war against poachers.

His greatest success was as a watchdog and woe betide any burglar who intruded on his master's property. He is very easy to train and has become a good family pet. He is an aggressive dog and requires a firm hand to keep him under control.

Grooming Procedure

The Bullmastiff differs little in his grooming requirements from other smoothhaired breeds. They rarely need bathing, usually not more than once or twice a year. It is important to note, however, that there is some incidence of skin problems in the breed (Pyoderma, allergic dermatitis, loss of hair due to thyroid imbalance) and any evidence of a skin and/or coat problem should be referred to a veterinarian. Strong shampoos and rinses should not be used (unless there is a parasite problem) since these may well cause an allergic reaction.

As with other drop-eared breeds, it is important to keep a Bullmastiff's ears clean since the lack of air circulation does lead to more incidence of ear infection than with erect-eared dogs. Some Bullmastiff ears tend to "fly" during the teething period and, if these are not taped, they will not return to the correct position. Groomers should not tape the ears but, rather, should refer the owner back to the dog's breeder or our organization for proper instructions since if this procedure is not properly done, it can result in serious ear problems.

Since the breed does seem to be particularly prone to pyoderma, keeping the dog's face clean, particularly after eating, is a wise ounce of prevention. Wipe the dog's face with medicated soap and warm water after he eats. The feet, particularly the area between the toes, should be kept clean and dry since there is an occasional tendency in this breed for interdigital cysts to develop.

Entropion is occasionally a problem in Bullmastiffs. Special note should be made of any eye discharge or irritation and prompt referral to a veterinarian should be made.

The only grooming done for the show ring other than brushing (using a rubber curry comb) is trimming the nails and clipping the dog's whiskers.

Courtesy, The American Bullmastiff Association by Tami Raider

The Smooth Collie

Standard Regarding Coat

The Smooth Variety of Collie is judged by the same Standard as the Rough Variety, except that the references to the quantity and the distribution of coat are not applicable to the Smooth Variety, which has a short, hard, dense, flat coat of good texture, with an abundance of undercoat.

Breed Note

Traditionally, the Smooth Collie was the drover's dog while the vastly more familiar Rough Collie was the guardian of the flocks on farm and at pasture. And, while the Rough Variety was closely associated with the Scottish Highlands, the Smooth was more familiar in Northumberland and other places in the North of England.

Today the Smooth differs from the Rough only in the coat. He has all of the splendid virtues normally associated with the breed and a smart, sleek look into the bargain.

Grooming Procedure

The Smooth Collie is very simple to groom. Your Smooth should be bathed several days before the show unless he looks as though he may shed his coat. (A Smooth may be shown in or out of coat, but looks miserable while he is shedding.) If a bath is not necessary or advisable, a good dry cleaner should be used. The nails, which should be trimmed regularly, should be given a final shortening at this time.

On the evening before a show, wash the feet and legs again and dampen any other white areas. Towel them off and apply powdered chalk. This is then brushed in and allowed to remain overnight.

After arriving at the show, trim the whiskers and eyebrows. If the feet have become soiled, they should be rechalked. The chalk should then be brushed out thoroughly, along with any other powder that has remained in the coat. All that remains then is the final rubdown. For this purpose, use any of the following that suits your preference; a hound glove, turkish towel, bristle or wire brush. I find the wire brush most effective. For the final touches, comb everything as flat as possible with a metal comb. The most effective one is made in Belgium and can be obtained at most shows from one of the booths selling grooming supplies.

If you are interested in having your Smooth look extra smart, the following trimming should be done. You may want to follow all of the steps or only a few, but they do put a finished look to the dog.

1. Trim the hair at the base of and on the inside of the ear.
2. Trim around and in between the pads on the foot. Also trim the long hairs that hang out over the nails.
3. Even the underline, preferably with thinning shears, to remove all straggly hairs.
4. The flank area should also be trimmed to give a nice, rounded line.

Most important, any of this trimming, feet excepted, should be done at least five to seven days before the show to allow it to look natural, which is its object. Never trim the hair too short, but only enough to give the dog a nice, smooth appearance.

Courtesy, Collie Club of America
by Tom Kilcullen

The Doberman Pinscher

Standard Regarding Coat

Coat—Smoothhaired, short, hard, thick and close lying. Invisible gray undercoat on neck permissible.

Breed Note

The Doberman Pinscher is named after the man who developed the breed, Herr Louis Dobermann. The "Dobe" is one of the most beautiful and intelligent of all the breeds. Originally bred to be very aggressive, he has been toned down through subsequent, careful breeding. Nevertheless, like the German Shepherd, the Dobe is a guard dog par excellence and during the World War II was the official dog of the United States Marines. He is universally famous as a defender of life and property, and also makes an excellent companion and show dog.

Grooming Procedure

Grooming the Doberman should begin from puppyhood on. Even the still-nursing pup should have its nails trimmed in order not to scratch its mother.

With the electric clipper, clean the outside edge of the ear. Cutting against the grain of the hair, come down

to clean up the outside edge, slanting the clipper toward the inner side of the ear. Trim out the excess hair on the base of the ear and remove all hair from the inner ear, tip to bottom. Trim cleavage at the base of the ear (where the hair grows in opposite directions shows the line to trim). Do NOT blow into the ear to get the excess hair out but remove with a finger.

Trim the cowlick on the throat (from base of ear down) only with thinning shears—never regular scissors or electric clippers. Regular scissors may cut out hair in large pieces leaving the dog too bare in spots. Always push up against the hair. Trim a little bit on forechest and upper arm with thinning shears. A "cowlick" on the back or anywhere else, may be thinned as needed. Any "cowlick" tends to break symmetry, so minimize them as much as possible.

Trim whiskers and eyebrows with curved scissors. Curved scissors are best for cutting whiskers as there is no big cutting edge to take off extra hair on the muzzle. The dog has a way of "pulling his whiskers in" so that when you are all finished and congratulating yourself on a job well done, they reappear looking like a week's growth. To prevent this, put your finger under the lip of the dog just under the whisker to cut close. Open the mouth to get the hairs on the bottom lip.

Doberman Pinscher Trimming Chart

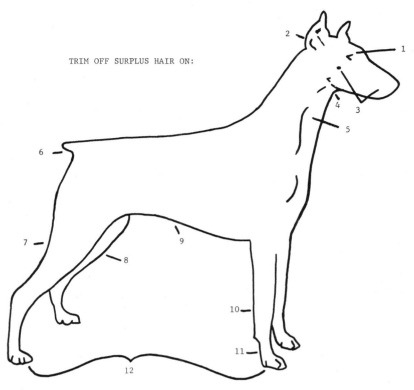

TRIM OFF SURPLUS HAIR ON:

1. Eyebrows (curved scissors)
2. Ears (clipper)
3. Whiskers (curved scissors)
4. Throat (thinning shears)
5. Neck (thinning shears)
6. Tail (scissor)
7. Shanks (thinning shears)
8. Stifle (scissors)
9. Belly (clipper)
10. Forelegs (scissors)
11. Rear of pastern (clipper)
12. Nails (nail clipper and file)

Next comes the loin and here you must be very careful to always keep the cutting edge of the clippers parallel with the top of the dog's back, tilted toward the stomach rather than out. Take off excess hairs on the stomach around the nipple.

To make the foot look tighter, remove excess hair from between the toes on the bottom of all four feet. Don't dig in with the clippers in the web between the toes. On the front feet remove all of the hair from the pad to the top pad on the pastern. Do not go above the pad. Roll the clipper a bit to bevel the outside on the pastern trim for a smooth, sleek look.

Next go to the sides of the leg. Smooth with hand and get all stray, long hairs. On the rear, trim along the back outside of the leg from tail down. Trim excess hair from around the tip and on each side of the tail.

Never trim any hair under the front "arm pit" above the elbow. As the hair grows back, it may prove irritating and possibly cause the dog appear out at the shoulders and unfavorably affect his gait.

When you have finished trimming, tilt the dog's head to the side to remove loose hair from the ears. Now is a good time to clean the ears with alcohol.

Remember—Curved scissors on eyebrows and whiskers; clippers on ears, loin, and rear of pastern; and thinning shears on all other parts. When you become an expert you can use the electric clippers on all parts except the whiskers. Go lightly—take a few hairs at a time so as not to trim too closely and DO practice *before* you plan to enter a show, so that if you do take off a few too many hairs there will be time for them to grow out again.

When you are showing your Doberman, make a final check for any loose hair that should be trimmed. Just prior to going into the ring, give a final rub-down with a Show Coat pad going with the grain of the hair, then go over the coat with a towel. Now is the time to put a drop of lanolin on any calloused elbow which has turned white. This will darken it but be SURE to work it in well then remove all excess so that there is no trace of lanolin left on the dog. Put a drop of Visine into each eye to clean out the dust from the trip.

Most important—take your time, be patient and make grooming time a special time for you and your Doberman. They love that towel or brush and the extra undivided attention. It does take a bit of preparation and work to have your Doberman perfectly groomed but whether he takes home the blue or not, you will have the pleasure of knowing your Doberman looks his beautiful best.

Courtesy, The Doberman Pinscher Club of America

The Great Dane

Standard Regarding Coat

Coat—Very short and thick, smooth, and glossy. **Faults**—Excessively long hair (stand-off coat); dull hair.

Breed Note

Great Dane is somewhat of a misnomer since this breed was developed in Germany and at one time was called the *Dogue Allemand* or German Mastiff. He is one of the giants of the canine world, standing 32 inches at the withers with an imposing, majestic appearance.

The Great Dane is a powerful dog and notably graceful considering his size. Today his greatest usefulness is as a guard dog, and here his size alone commands respect. He is an amiable family companion, eager to please and easy to train. The Great Dane is a wonderful choice for a spacious home.

Grooming Procedure

Attention to the fundamentals of grooming is all that is necessary for the grooming of pet Great Danes. The only fine points that distinguish grooming the Great Dane for the show ring are:

1. Trimming of the whiskers on the muzzle and the lower jaw.
2. Trimming hair off edges of ears.
3. Trimming wisps of hair and ragged edges on tip of tail, legs, belly line and backs of legs.
4. White chalk can be used to clean Harlequins but must be brushed out before the dog enters the ring.

The Mastiff

Standard Regarding Coat

Coat—Outer coat moderately coarse. Undercoat, dense, short and close lying.

Breed Note

The Mastiff is one of the world's oldest known breeds that is still among us. Synonymous with England, the Mastiff was bred as a giant protection dog as well as a participant in blood sports involving other dogs, wild animals and even human opponents.

Despite his history as a canine gladiator and his fierce appearance, the Mastiff is a kind, gentle companion to those he knows and is always ready to stand between them and whatever threatens.

Grooming Procedure

The Mastiff is a smooth-coated dog and does not require much grooming at all. Most grooming consists of brushing and curry combing, keeping nails short and ears cleaned. A show dog will have its long, coarse face feelers removed and the hair evened behind the thighs for clean angulation.

Courtesy, Mastiff Club of America
by Jacqueline Guy

The Rottweiler

Standard Regarding Coat

Coat—Hair should be short, coarse and flat. The undercoat which is absolutely required on neck and thighs should not show through outer coat. The hair should be a little longer on the back of front and hind legs and on tail.

Breed Note

The Rottweiler was developed in the city of Rottweil on Germany's Neckar River. Here he came into use as a cattle drover and peerless guard dog as were the ancient Roman drovers' dogs he sprang from.

When driving cattle with dogs became illegal in Germany, the breed was in real danger of disappearing. It was then that his other laudable qualities became recognized and the breed not only lived on but achieved new, unprecedented popularity. Today the Rottweiler is universally regarded as an excellent police, military and personal protection dog. He is keenly intelligent and competes with great success in obedience and *Schutzhund,* or protection dog trials. Happily, like any other good bodyguard, the Rottweiler can easily distinguish between friend and foe and makes a wonderful family companion.

Grooming Procedure

The Rottweiler is shown *without trimming*. Whiskers may be clipped off close to the face at the discretion of the owner. The brush used for the coat is the rubber curry comb.

Courtesy, American Rottweiler Club
by Sharon Conrow

Smoothhaired Terriers

The American Staffordshire Terrier

Standard Regarding Coat

Coat—Short, close, stiff to the touch, and glossy.

Breed Note

Originally developed in England from a cross of the old fighting Bulldog and an unspecified terrier ancestor, the American Staffordshire Terrier developed along distinctly different lines from his near relative, the Staffordshire Bull Terrier. The "Amstaff" is much higher on leg than the latter breed and also carries more weight. While no one can argue away the breed's original purpose, it is also a fact that this dog makes a first-class companion and guard. He is a real "people" dog. His aggressive posture toward other dogs does not carry over to his human family. In fact, he is very trainable and obliging.

Grooming Procedure

By following the instructions given in the Fundamentals of Dog Grooming (Part I) of this book, you can have almost all the required grooming for an Amstaff down pat. The breed's smooth, sleek coat is very easy to look after. Regular grooming sessions with a hound glove will keep the coat and skin in top shape.

If shows are on the schedule, the owner should trim the coarse whiskers on the muzzle and over the eyes. Also the long hairs on the backs of front and hind legs and on the sides of the neck can be tidied with either fine thinning shears or an electric clipper fitted with a #10 or #15 blade.

Many Amstaffs carry white markings to a greater or lesser degree. For a show dog, the white areas should be rubbed with chalk. The chalk should be well worked in and then removed. A drop of brilliantine rubbed into the colored portions of the coat will also enhance the dog's appearance.

The Bull Terrier

Standard Regarding Coat

Coat—Should be short, flat, harsh to the touch and with a fine gloss. The dog's skin should fit tightly.

Breed Note

The dog we know as the Bull Terrier has the distinct knack for arousing strong feelings in people. Most people who come in contact with the breed, however, superficially, either love them or hate them. There seems to be no middle ground.

The breed's extremely distinctive appearance is one factor contributing to the foregoing observation. The look is his alone with an egg-shaped head, Roman nose and tiny eyes all contributing. And you either like it or you don't. It's that simple.

The Bull Terrier was bred for fighting and was very fashionable in English sporting circles during the latter half of the 19th Century. Today the breed lacks none of its early fire, but is considerably easier-going than its pit-fighting ancestors. In fact the Bull Terrier is one of the most loving canine companions one could hope for. He is faithful, eager to please and naturally protective—the perfect single dog for a family.

Grooming Procedure

There is no grooming required on a Bull Terrier. If one is showing the dog in conformation it is desirable to clip the whiskers on the face and above the eyes. Other areas of tidying-up are strictly optional—the inside hair at the base of the ear, the tail can be neatened, the hair at the rear of the thigh smoothed.

Courtesy, The Bull Terrier Club of America
by Drue King

The Smooth Fox Terrier

Standard Regarding Coat

Coat—Should be smooth, flat, but hard, dense and abundant. The belly and under side of the thighs should not be bare.

Breed Note

Of the two varieties of the "Gentleman Terrier," the Smooth is reckoned the older. Indeed crossings with Smooth Fox Terriers were used in an effort to give the Wire added elegance and refinement. That this objective was successfully achieved is proved by the stylish Wires of today.

The Smooth Fox Terrier is familiar in virtually every part of the world and was used as the symbol of RCA records. This famous trade mark shows a Smooth (albeit a coarse one) sitting in front of an old-fashioned gramophone and listening to "his master's voice."

The Smooth Fox Terrier epitomizes all the best attributes of the terrier tribe. Bright and lively, he is very loyal to home and family and is the fearless foe of all vermin.

Grooming Procedure

It might surprise many people to know that the Smooth Fox Terrier requires judicious trimming despite the basic nature of his coat. At one time it was commonplace for matings between Smooths and Wires to occur. Today's legacy of those now-clandestine matings is a Smooth with a longish, rather harsh coat. Sometimes we even come across a Smooth with a wavy coat!

In the ring the Smooth should be sleek all over and so it becomes necessary to do some very careful stripping to get rid of rough fringes and to get the coat to lie down hard and close to the skin. To do this right requires considerable practice and experimentation with various kinds of knives and techniques. This is one place where it's good to ask questions, so if you can reach a proficient handler or Smooth breeder, try to find out how best to turn out a Smooth.

The Manchester Terrier

Standard Regarding Coat

Coat—Smooth, short, thick, dense, close, glossy, not soft.

Breed Note

The Manchester Terrier is a product of Northern England and was used for rat killing and rabbit coursing. When the breed won the right to be exhibited in English shows, he was named for the industrial metropolis in which he was so popular.

Although he has lost much of his early popularity, the Manchester Terrier still offers many positive attributes to endear him to even the most fastidious housekeeper. To his claim as one of the easiest keepers, the Manchester also adds his attractive appearance and very charming personality.

Grooming Procedure

Brushing is the most important grooming procedure with the Manchester Terrier. A natural bristle brush is the tool of choice, and with regular brushing the need for frequent bathing is eliminated.

Brush in the direction of the grain, the way in which the hair is growing. It is essential that the Manchester be brushed daily. Two purposes are served thereby; the hair is kept free of dirt, burrs and foreign objects and the natural oils that make his coat shiny and beautiful are stimulated.

The Manchester Terrier is bred in two sizes, Toy and Standard, and the minimal grooming required for both is identical.

Courtesy, The American Manchester Terrier Club by Elsie Puleo

The Staffordshire Bull Terrier

Standard Regarding Coat

Coat—Smooth, short and close to the skin, not to be trimmed or dewhiskered.

Breed Note

The Staffordshire Bull Terrier resulted from a cross of the Bulldog and an unknown terrier ancestor. His proverbial courage kept interest going in the breed after the abolition of blood sports in England and in due course the Staffordshire did find its way to the show bench and respectability.

He shares with other breeds from a fighting background an interesting paradox in being a sweet, loving family dog despite his formidable reputation as a powerful and determined combatant.

Grooming Procedure

In mentioning the coat, the Standard for the Staffordshire Bull Terrier specifically forbids any kind of trimming or coat removal.

Condition is built from within and consists of bursting good health evident in hard muscle tone, no excess lumber anywhere and a pliant skin together with a shining, healthy coat.

The grooming tool of choice is a good-quality hound glove. After being worked on with the hound glove the coat should be rubbed down with a piece of dry chamois leather.

Smoothhaired Toy Dogs

The Chihuahua

Standard Regarding Coat

Coat—In the *Smooth,* the coat should be soft texture, close and glossy. (Heavier coats with undercoats permissible.) Coat placed well over body with ruff on neck, and more scanty on head and ears. In *Long Coats,* the coat should be a soft texture, either flat or slightly curly, with undercoat preferred. Ears fringed (heavily fringed ears may be tipped slightly, never down), feathering on feet and legs, and pants on hind legs. Large ruff on neck desired and preferred. Tail full and long (as a plume).

Breed Note

The Chihuahua has been known in Mexico for centuries. He was important in the ceremonial life of both Toltec and Aztec peoples and is still a popular pet in his native land and around the world.

The Chihuahua is the smallest of all dogs. The average weight of an adult Chihuahua is about three pounds. He looks very tiny and fragile but he is, in fact, quite hardy and courageous. He is known to be a one-person dog and can be ferocious in defending that person. The distinguishing features of a Chihuahua are small size, large ears, prominent eyes and a long tail.

Grooming Procedure

Check teeth to see if they need to be cleaned and do so if necessary.

Check the anal glands and, if necessary, express their contents. Follow by washing the area with a little soap and water.

Bathe the dog in warm water so as not to shock or chill him. Begin with the face and thoroughly wash him, using a cloth. Care should be taken that the soap should not get into his eyes.

Ears—The interior of the ear canals should be gently cleansed. Special attention should be given to drying the ears inside and out. As ear infections can arise from moist ear canals, make sure the ears are dried before washing the rest of the dog. Following the bath, the dog must be completely dried. A hair dryer is preferred for this.

Nails—The Chihuahua's nails should be moderately long, according to the breed Standard.

Weekly combing and brushing will keep a Chihuahua's coat healthy.

For the show ring cut the hairs on the muzzle with a curved scissor and, for Long Coats, trim around the feet and between the pads.

Courtesy, Chihuahua Club of Metropolitan New York by Shirley Thomas

The Italian Greyhound

Standard Regarding Coat

Coat—Skin fine and supple, hair short, glossy like satin and soft to the touch.

Breed Note

Toy breeds, for the most part, are the deliberate breeding down from larger canine forms and in the Italian Greyhound we can easily note the similarity to the larger sighthound breeds. The similarity is not merely physical, for, as with the larger Greyhound, this ancient Toy is fastidious, affectionate and sensitive.

A product of the Mediterranean, the Italian Greyhound became a popular pet in Renaissance Italy and was depicted by many famous artists of the period.

Today the Italian Greyhound enjoys the loyal patronage of fanciers that appreciate his positive combination of beauty, engaging temperament and ease of care.

Grooming Procedure

The Italian Greyhound requires the same care as does any other small, smooth dog. Although his coat needs little grooming, his nails should be periodically trimmed and his teeth cleaned. He has an inherent dislike of cold and rain; when being walked on a leash in winter, he will be happier wearing a coat or sweater.

In addition, if there is long hair on the underside of the tail or between the toes, or in the ears, it should be trimmed to give the smoothest possible appearance. Occasional brushing with a natural bristle brush will curb dandruff.

Courtesy, Italian Greyhound Club of America
by Lillian S. Barber

The Toy Manchester Terrier

Standard Regarding Coat

Coat—Smooth, short, thick, dense, close and glossy; not soft.

Breed Note

The Toy Manchester Terrier is descended from the Manchester Terrier, both deriving their names from the city of Manchester, England. The Toy was developed as a result of selective breeding, where the smallest members of a litter were mated until the present Toy size resulted. At one time there was interbreeding between Standards and Toys but after 1959 they were regarded as a single breed with two varieties. Besides the difference in size, the only other difference in the two varieties concerns ears. In the Standard size the ears may be cropped; in Toys, cropping disqualifies.

Grooming Procedure

Grooming the Toy Manchester Terrier consists of the fundamentals and is identical to that of the Standard Manchester Terrier.

The Miniature Pinscher

Standard Regarding Coat

Coat—Smooth, hard and short, straight and lustrous, closely adhering to and uniformly covering the body. **Faults**—Thin, too long, dull; upstanding; curly; dry; area of various thickness or bald spots.

Breed Note

The Miniature Pinscher is the German development of the toy terrier and has been known in Germany and other European countries for centuries. There are old illustrations showing the breed as a ratter and he still retains his keenness as a watchdog. He seems unaware of his own small size in protecting home and family.

The breed has done well in the show ring where judges appreciate his stylish, high-stepping action and his alert demeanor. He makes an admirable, clean pet for any size home and is suitable to the family with older children.

Grooming Procedure

A Miniature Pinscher's grooming requirements are negligible and for the housepet, brushing several times a week will keep the coat and skin in good condition.

For the show ring it is also advisable to trim the coarse feelers from the muzzle, above the eyes and face moles. Any long hair such as is found on the sides of the neck, and up the backs of front and hind legs should be trimmed or thinned as needed to give the desired, sleek appearance.

Particular attention should be paid to the feet and in this connection the nails should be shortened regularly to achieve a tight, compact foot. Nothing looks worse than a Miniature Pinscher whose nails have been neglected. Such a dog will show thin feet with ugly, outspread toes—an avoidable blemish.

The Pug

Standard Regarding Coat

Coat—Fine, smooth, soft, short and glossy, neither hard nor woolly.

Breed Note

The largest of the Toy breeds, the Pug orginally developed in the Orient and was introduced to the West by the merchant ships of the Dutch East India Company. The Pug became the rage in Holland and was adopted as the official dog of the House of Orange. Royal patronage in other countries also helped put the breed in the limelight and keep him there.

The Pug is primarily kept as a pet and companion, and he makes an admirable one. He is a sturdy little dog that can adapt well to any environment. He is fun-loving, anxious to please and gets on well with grown-ups and children alike. His short, sleek coat is easy to look after and he is a characteristically clean housepet.

Grooming Procedure

The Pug's over-nose wrinkle should be kept clean. About once a week draw the wrinkle smooth by lifting it up off your Pug's nose. Examine the skin to be sure it is free of any redness or rash. If it is in good condition, wipe it off with a cotton ball slightly moistened with baby oil, then put a dab of Vaseline on your finger and work it into the top of your pug's nose to prevent dryness and chapping. If you should discover a rash, your veterinarian can give you medication which will clear it up. We have found *Panolog* helpful—this must be obtained from your veterinarian.

The Pug's ears should also be checked weekly. If they are dirty wipe them out with a cotton ball slightly moistened with baby oil. If there is an accumulation of wax down deep in the ear canal, put one drop of hydrogen peroxide into the ear canal and *gently,* from the outside, massage the ear down at the base. Leave the peroxide in for approximately fifteen minutes. This will soften the wax and help to move it up to where you can remove it with a cotton swab. If there is any sign of rash or if the above method does not remove the wax from the ear you should consult your veterinarian.

Regular grooming is a matter of habit for both dog and owner. Start by combing and brushing your dog on a table. Proper care of the coat will insure that glands (which secrete oil) will keep the coat shiny. A Pug should be groomed at least once a week. A bristle brush or hound glove is the grooming tool of choice for a Pug's coat.

For the show ring it is necessary to do a certain amount of trimming on the Pug. With a curved scissor cut the hairs around the muzzle, under the chin, and above the eyes. Also the hairs on the moles. Also trim all the straggly hairs on his hindquarters with a straight scissor.

Courtesy, Pug Dog Club Of Greater New York by Shirley Thomas

Smoothhaired Non-Sporting Dogs

The Boston Terrier

Standard Regarding Coat

Coat—Short, smooth, bright and fine in texture.
Coat Faults—Long or coarse; lacking luster.

Breed Note

The Boston Terrier is one of the few native American breeds. Developed in and around Boston, Massachusetts, he was the result of crossings between the Bulldog and an English Terrier. Selective breeding seems to have favored more of the terrier side than the Bulldog. He is intelligent, lively and so gentle that he has earned the title of "American Gentleman". But he can fight when called upon. He is an ideal pet for any size home.

Grooming Procedure

One reason for the Boston Terrier's enormous, long-term popularity is his short coat and its great ease of care. Regular attention with a natural bristle brush will keep the coat lustrous and the skin healthy and pliant. For the pet Boston, the grooming fundamentals will be entirely sufficient.

When show dogs are considered there are several additional procedures. But all of them are simple, straightforward and easily executed in a short time.

The coarse whiskers on the muzzle and eyebrows should be removed with scissors, cutting them as short as possible. Also check moles on the cheeks and under-jaw for feelers. Most dogs have them and they, too, should be snipped off close to the skin.

Any hairs that detract from the Boston's sleek appearance should be removed. Such hairs will usually be found up the backs of front and rear legs and alongside the neck. Fine thinning shears are best here.

Chalk, talc or other whitener rubbed into the coat's white parts and then worked out will give a good finish. For the colored sections, a drop of brilliantine on the palms applied to the coat and worked in will set the dog off beautifully.

Fine thinning shears can be used where one desires to smooth out any overly-heavy patches of hair. The watchword in trimming a Boston is to make the dog look as though he had never been trimmed at all.

The Bulldog

Standard Regarding Coat

Coat—The coat should be straight, short, flat, close, of fine texture, smooth and glossy. (No fringe, feather or curl.)

Breed Note

Centuries ago the Bulldog was the butcher's dog that helped to control and subdue livestock. The old English sport of bullbaiting was the breed's reason for being and it forged the Bulldog's character in many respects. While, today, we may look upon bullbaiting and other blood sports with appropriate disgust, we should remember that the Bulldog's courage is a direct result of the centuries during which bullbaiting was a legitimate public diversion.

Similarly, the Bulldog's appearance was forged by the demands of bullbaiting. His massive, underslung lower jaw and pushed-back nostrils enabled him to hold tight to the bull's nose and breathe normally the whole while. Other components of the Bulldog's structure were also influenced by bullbaiting.

Blood sports were outlawed in England in 1835 and since then the Bulldog has been developed into one of the sweetest-tempered breeds in all dogdom. Ugly? Yes, one would have to admit that the Bulldog fits the word, but it's ugliness with a specific historic validity and also undeniable charm.

Grooming Procedure

The Bulldog's smooth coat can be looked after easily by following the directions in Fundamentals of Grooming (Part I) of this book. Special attention is required in the area of flews and face wrinkles. These should be checked periodically to make sure there is no rash or soreness present. Any developing skin condition should be brought to the attention of a veterinarian.

The French Bulldog

Standard Regarding Coat

Coat—Moderately fine, brilliant, short and smooth.

Breed Note

The French Bulldog originated in France during the latter half of the 19th Century. He is probably the result of crossing Toy Bulldogs with a variety of other breeds to fix the desired characteristics and enjoyed tremendous popularity around the turn of the century. The French called him *l'enfant préféré* which means "favorite child."

He has "bat ears," wrinkled skin and a short muzzle. He is small (about 25 pounds), strong, compact and vigorous. He is an alert watchdog and an engaging companion.

Grooming Procedure

It was American fanciers who first recognized this bat-eared, short-faced small dog as a separate and distinct breed. They set up the breed Standard and organized this first-ever club for the breed.

One of the delights of owning a French Bulldog is the ease with which it can be kept "ready for any occasion." The short, thick, shiny hair is easily kept clean with a rubber curry comb. It requires no trimming. Toenails should be kept short—a filing once a week or at least about twice a month keeps them the right length. The ears should be checked regularly and kept clean since they are erect and can collect dust and foreign matter. Any white hair should be kept sparkling white.

The Frenchy's whiskers can be left natural although most exhibitors trim them for shows, as many judges seem to prefer.

Courtesy, The French Bull Dog Club of America
by Helen Hover

The Dalmatian

Standard Regarding Coat

Coat—Should be short, hard, dense, and fine, sleek and glossy in appearance, but neither woolly nor silky.

Breed Note

Many nationalities have been claimed for the Dalmatian, but there is no hard proof that ties him to one specific country or location. He takes his name from the Yugoslavian province of Dalmatia, but was known in many places throughout his centuries-long existence as a distinct breed.

The Dalmatian's tremendous natural affinity for horses has provided the breed a unique long-term livelihood. At one time a stylish carriage dog, Dalmatians would be seen running in pairs under the front axle of a smart rig. Later the Dal followed the horse into the firehouse so that he became an integral part of the fire fighter's life. And later, when fire fighting equipment became motorized, the Dalmatian stayed on after the horses were put to pasture. Even today many fire companies keep a Dalmatian as a mascot, watchdog and companion.

A handsome dog as well as a highly trainable one, the Dalmatian is highly regarded among all breeds today and has distinguished himself as a companion, an obedience dog and an elegant show dog.

Grooming Procedure

One of the joys of a smoothcoated breed is the ease of grooming. In Dalmatians, maintenance grooming is the key. A concensus of opinion regarding grooming is as follows:

1. Good nutrition with an emphasis on oils and saturated fats for a bright, shiny coat.
2. Adequate exercise for the development of good muscle tone.
3. Regular brushing with a rubber curry comb or hound glove.
4. Bathe as necessary with a mild shampoo and a non-toxic bluing. Because the Dalmatian is pink-skinned and lacks overall protective pigment, the skin reacts frequently to harsh shampoos, shampoos with additives and detergents. Non-toxic bluing whitens the coat without irritating the skin.
5. Nail clipping becomes difficult when nails are black. A pen-light may be used to locate the quick before cutting. Short, even nails help to keep the feet tight and encourage natural trotting ability.
6. Clipping excess facial hairs and whiskers gives the face a clean, chiselled appearance.

Maintenance of the following should be with the advice of a veterinarian:

1. Tooth tartar may be manually scraped from teeth. The dog's diet should include biscuits to help reduce the production of tartar.

2. The ears may become irritated due to other dogs licking them or due to infection. Clean out with Q-tips. Apply small amount of veterinarian-approved antibiotic ointment.
3. Anal gland expression may be needed when dog does not produce bulky stool.
4. Ear-tip bleeding and tail-tip bleeding produced by excessive head shaking and tail wagging (a Dal characteristic) are difficult to heal. We recommend *Karaya* powder applied after wound is washed. This powder helps to heal the wound and provide protection against future injury. Daily application for two to three weeks has healed tails that were cracked for months.

Courtesy, The Dalmatian Club of Greater New York
by Catherine Newsome

Part V

Health, Welfare and Fine Points

IT IS NOT POSSIBLE, NOR IS IT within the scope of this book, to go into a detailed explanation of everything which may effect the health and welfare of a dog, but these matters do concern us insofar as they affect the grooming of the dog.

There is a direct relationship between good health and good grooming. For example, a healthy dog will have clear eyes, a lustrous coat, and stand and walk with a certain pride. You cannot camouflage a sickly, listless dog with good grooming. The healthy dog, on the other hand, will have all of its attractive qualities enhanced through good grooming.

When something is wrong with a dog and beyond your ability as a professional groomer to handle, you must make it clear to the customer that you are not a veterinarian. Never attempt to substitute for a veterinarian. If a dog is brought to you with an ear infection, skin infection, growths, convulsions, or any ailment which looks suspicious or contagious, you should notify the owner immediately, suggesting the need to visit a veterinarian.

There are some matters, however, such as nutrition, exercise, internal and external parasites, which are not strictly a veterinarian's province and which the groomer can handle. If the groomer can help when questions on these subjects arise, it will make for a better relationship with the customer.

Brush Burns

One problem with wire slicker brushes is the possibility of their inflicting "brush burns" on the dog. While the slicker brush, especially the Universal, is excellent for badly matted, long coats, a danger lies in the fact that the brush may be used in sensitive areas where brush burns will occur.

These brush burns usually occur where the hair is relatively sparse (face, thighs, armpits) and the danger of second-degree burns is a serious possibility. The dog would then be in real pain, and it may be some time before the irritation ceases.

While some relief can be obtained through the application of a soothing skin ointment, the best cure lies in prevention. Be extra careful in brushing sparse coated, sensitive areas. The old adage still applies—an ounce of prevention is worth a pound of cure.

Clipper Burns and Rashes

Clipper burns on the dog are a major source of complaint by patrons of grooming shops. A clipper burn can only be the result of allowing the clipper blades to become so hot that the dog suffers a second-degree burn. There is absolutely no excuse for this happening, and no reason why any groomer should not take the elementary precaution to avoid clipper burns, especially since they are so simple to prevent.

When you start clipping, you will note that the clipper blades get progressively hotter. There are a number of ways to handle this matter with extended running time. If you have extra clippers, just substitute a fresh one for the hot one. If you have an extra blade, just detach the one you are using, and put on the extra one. Or you can apply Oster Kool Lube Spray, which instantly cools the blade. But keep tapping the blade to see if it is getting hot. If you proceed in this fashion, you will never have a case of clipper burn.

A clipper rash may result from a hot blade on dirty skin, or on a very sensitive skin. Again, prevention simply involves keeping your blades cool. Just as a precaution, it is wise to have handy one of the many ointments on the market especially made for burns. Dull blades may also account for clipper burns, so keep your blades sharpened.

Scissor Cuts or Nicks

While a scissor cut could be one of the most harmful things that might happen in grooming a dog, there is no reason why the problem need ever arise if you are careful and concentrate on your work. Scissors must be sharp if you are to do a good finishing job. By the same token, you can cut the dog's skin if you are not careful. The one time not to allow any distraction at all is when you are scissoring.

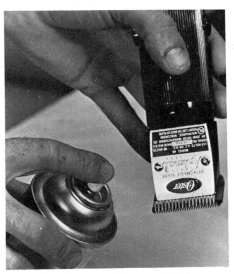

Aerosol lubricants cool clippers while in use.

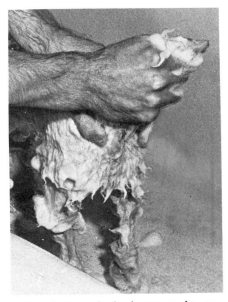

If a dog's anal glands are to be expressed, this is best done during the bath.

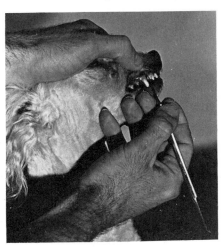

Use a dental scaler to remove accumulated tartar.

It is amazing how most dogs sense your need for care and will stand still while you are scissoring. But like everything else, take your time in the beginning until you gain confidence in the use of the scissors. Sometimes even professional groomers will become careless and nick a dog. You should have on hand at all times a medication to stop bleeding. Effective coagulants are usually sold by veterinary supply houses. Ask your local pharmacist or veterinarian for advice. For profuse bleeding, use the coagulant and apply an ice pack directly to the cut. And get to a veterinarian as soon as you can, since the wound may require suturing if it is serious enough.

Anal Glands

Whether or not to express the anal sacs as a standard part of grooming procedures is a matter of debate among many professional groomers. We feel that, *if and when necessary,* this is best left to the veterinarian. We have two compelling reasons. One, the treatment is only necessary when the anal sacs are clogged or impacted, and there should be no reason to do it otherwise. Two, if the anal sacs are incorrectly expressed, it can result in an infection of the anal glands.

However, every groomer should know how to express anal sacs when the need arises. So, if you do decide the clean the anal glands, do it when you bathe the dog. In this way the foul-smelling discharge can be easily disposed of and you will not be losing time. The anal sacs are two quite small sacs situated on either side of the anus. To express the sacs, first hold up the tail while covering the anal opening with cotton, a gauze pad or a paper towel. Grasp the two sacs, and press together in an upward motion. A liquid will squirt out. Make sure the entire anal area is thoroughly cleaned with soap and water afterward.

Teeth Cleaning

This is another procedure which may safely be left to the veterinarian. It does not properly fall within the province of dog grooming, any more than a beautician is supposed to be a dental hygienist. Most people do not expect the groomer to clean the dog's teeth, and most groomers do not offer this as a part of the grooming service. However, this instruction is included for those who want to develop the skill.

Certainly, a dog's teeth may need cleaning today more than ever before. Years ago there was hardly any need for special attention to a dog's teeth because the food dogs ate kept their teeth strong and clean. Today, however, most pet dogs are fed soft, commercial foods.

Chewing hard biscuits or a dense knuckle bone will keep the dog's teeth clean and shining by retarding the formation of tartar. Many dogs seem to relish chewing hard nylon bones which accomplish the same purpose.

In cleaning a dog's teeth, use a dental scaler and proceed very carefully to scrape away whatever food is lodged between the teeth and whatever tartar has been formed. Always draw the scaler away from the gums. Go very slowly at first, until you gain experience. When you are finished scaling, use a cleansing agent to polish the teeth. A child's toothbrush and tooth powder are good for this purpose.

Fleas and Ticks

Fleas are probably the most common parasite problem in dogs. They not only cause irritation and scratching, but also are hosts for tapeworm. Fleas carry tapeworm ova and the dog becomes infested when he ingests some fleas. From the grooming standpoint, this is disastrous because flea and tapeworm infestation destroy the coat. The coat loses its luster and the hair becomes thin, dry and scurfy.

Since it is fairly easy to get rid of fleas, the sensible dog owner will not wait but will get rid of the parasites at once. If it isn't done at home with one of the many preparations now available, the owner will bring the dog to the groomer for a *flea bath*. Today many excellent flea shampoos will effectively kill fleas while the dog is being bathed. Also, a good insecticide should be sprayed over the dog's sleeping quarters.

The latest flea preventatives available are flea collars and flea tags. These are intended for various periods to protect dogs against fleas. There is no doubt that the chemicals in these products will keep fleas away, but veterinarians have reported side effects on some dogs. The safest course is to consult your veterinarian.

More difficult to handle than fleas are ticks. Tick problems are becoming almost as common as flea complaints. At one time ticks seemed to cause trouble only in rural areas. Now they appear to be equally well established in urban environments. Ticks originate in rural areas, mostly flourishing in cow or sheep pastures or swampy, wooded areas. It may be that the avalanche of ticks in the cities is a result of more people getting out to the country all the time, naturally taking their dogs with them, and bringing them back tick-infested. Parks and vacant lots are often tick breeding areas, and dogs can become easily infested just by walking through tall grass in such places.

Many dog owners will bring their dogs to the groomer for a "tick bath." The groomer should first examine the dog thoroughly. There may be just a few ticks present, in which case a "tick dip" may not be necessary. A few ticks can be pulled out with tweezers or forceps, but be sure you get the tick's head out (it is buried in the skin). Applying the heated head of a match or a drop of alcohol to an individual tick will make it release its hold, allowing removal and destruction.

If the dog has more than just a few ticks, give it a tick dip immediately, before doing anything else. In the

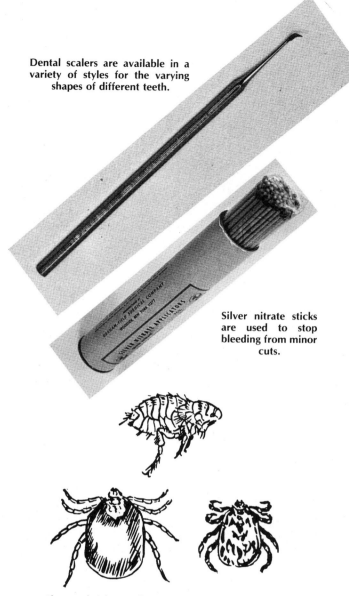

Dental scalers are available in a variety of styles for the varying shapes of different teeth.

Silver nitrate sticks are used to stop bleeding from minor cuts.

Fleas and ticks are the most common external parasites in dogs. Groomers must be well versed in how to deal with these stubborn pests.

Every dog being groomed should be thoroughly examined for external parasites before any work is begun. If fleas or ticks are found, the dog should be dipped immediately.

Using a safety chain in the bathtub will insure that the dog will not leap out and escape or cause itself injury.

Use a separate cage for each dog being groomed. Even a mild-mannered dog can bite when removed from a familiar environment and caged with another dog in a grooming shop.

past, only veterinarians could do this adequately, but now there are some good tick shampoos on the market. If the tick infestation is very bad, the safest course is to refer the owner to a veterinarian.

SAFETY AND SANITATION

It is to your interest to insure that dogs in your care are completely safe at all times, and if you are properly trained for this, it will make a definite impression on your customers. You must be aware of and alert to all the risks inherent in being responsible for others' dogs and anticipate every possible precaution for their safety.

The same applies to the measures you take for proper sanitation. Customers will appreciate the cleanliness of your shop and reward you with their loyalty. The evidence of scrupulous hygiene, odor control and generally inviting atmosphere are some of the things that spell the difference between the trained and untrained groomer, the professional and the non-professional.

Safety Measures

For baths, an excellent safety measure to insure that the dog never jumps out of the tub, is a safety chain or grooming loop which is put around the dog's neck and drawn taut with a snaplock.

Each dog should go into a separate cage. The only exception can be compatible dogs from the same household. Strange dogs put into the same cage may quarrel and hurt each other. It is doubly important that each dog have a separate cage if a bitch in season is in your shop to be groomed. Possibly you may wind up with an unwelcome pregnancy but more likely, her presence might instigate fighting among males that have access to each other. While on this point of a bitch in season, it would be better to groom the bitch when no males are present. If this is not possible, make sure that the bitch is completely isolated. It is also an elementary precaution, when grooming a bitch in season, to place an old towel or cloth on your table.

When a dog is put in a cage, always double check to see that the latch is securely locked. Dogs have been known to open doors that have not been bolted down. In the twinkling of an eye, a dog can open a door, jump to the floor, and be out the door. A further precaution in this respect, to prevent dogs from ever running out, is a barrier at or before the grooming room door. Either the door itself must be closed at all times, or a special barrier should be erected. There is no excuse for a dog ever escaping from a shop.

When you put a dog on a table, don't go away and leave him alone. Even if the dog is in a post loop, do not turn your back on him. *Never* leave a dog unattended.

Do not take anything for granted. The safest course to follow, when you might be away from the dog for an extended period, is to put the dog back in the cage.

Safety Measures for You

It is equally important that you, the groomer, are protected against any dog which may be sick or vicious, and it is wise to take proper precautions. A sick dog is easily detected, even to the unpracticed eye. The symptoms may be running eyes and nose, body sores, infected, bad smelling ears or foul breath. A wise, elementary precaution in such cases is to notify the owners and refer them to their veterinarian.

A more difficult problem arises with dogs inclined to snap or bite. This is not always obvious and the problem is complicated by owners who neglect to mention the problem. As a routine precaution, ask every new customer if the dog is inclined to snap. Some customers will tell the truth, and some will not. Always approach new dogs carefully. Spend a minute or two getting acquainted. A dog intent on snapping will almost always give unmistakable notice of that intent.

Most dogs will not try to bite the groomer. But exposure to dog bites is always a possibility. So, if in spite of all precautions, you do get bitten, wash the cuts immediately with soap and water. Then see your doctor at once. Also get in touch with the dog's owner to make sure that the dog has had his rabies shot.

As a part of your overall program of safety, you should form a rapport with a veterinarian in whom you have confidence, whom you can use when you need any advice or for any emergency.

Sanitation Measures

Special attention should be paid to cleaning cages and floors. Cages should be made of galvanized metal, stainless steel, or fiberglass. The galvanized metal cages are the least expensive and quite adequate. Wooden cages are the cheapest, but they are completely unsatisfactory because they can easily harbor bacteria or parasites, and the wood is subject to warping. When you buy your cages, be sure to look for two things: One, the cage doors should be easy for you to open and close (but impossible for the dog to open). Two, the cages should be equipped with pans on the bottom which can be taken out for easy cleaning.

The cleaning itself should be done with a good germicide. First clean the pans and the bottom of the cage. Then spray the rest of the cage. Do this at the end of each day. The floors should be vacuumed every day, and at least once a week should get a special cleaning with the same germicide used for cages. And, like a barber shop or beauty salon, hair should be removed from the floor after each dog is groomed. The rubber mats on the

Germicides and deodorant cleaners are essential in a grooming establishment to curb bacteria and to provide a wholesome environment.

268

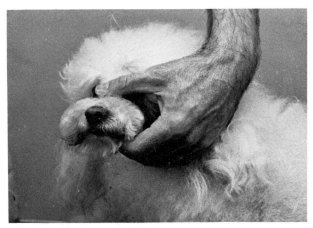

Some Poodles and other dogs with hairy faces look well with moustaches. If the owner wants a moustache on his pet, the groomer must honor that wish.

The bite on the left is a *level* bite and not usually considered faulty. The overshot (center) and undershot (right) mouths can be effectively minimized by fashioning a moustache on the dog's muzzle.

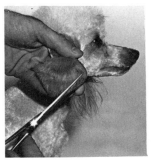

Forming diamond tassels on ears

Forming rectangular tassels on ears

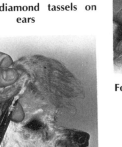

Whenever ears are clippered, the edges should be scissored to remove any raggedness.

table tops need cleaning at least once a week, preferably oftener. Get a hard scrub brush (not plastic or nylon) and again with the same germicide, give the rubber matting a good cleaning.

The bathtub, which should be cleaned every day, should also get special attention at least once a week. A good scouring powder should be used, and the tub should come out sparkling. The customers will be impressed, and you, too, will feel better using a clean tub. (Stainless steel tubs, while more expensive, require less maintenance.)

Tools require periodic cleaning (follow instructions for care and maintenance that come with your clippers). Blades and scissors should be frequently sterilized in alcohol. Keep *all* your tools clean and properly stored after the day's work. Your care will be rewarded by better service and longer life from all your tools.

FINE POINTS

There are many skills that distinguish a good groomer from a mediocre one. The styling of a moustache or beard, or tasselled ears in Poodles, coat care, effectively cleaning the genital area and making a beautiful ribbon bow are all sophisticated examples of the groomer's art. These are some of the fine points of dog grooming.

Moustaches

Many owners of Poodles and other hairy-faced dogs consider a moustache and/or beard very cute and will feel strongly about having one on their pet. Woe betide the groomer who takes off the moustache by mistake! Of course, if a customer is uncertain about the pet having a moustache, you can advise him based on your observation of the dog's facial conformation. For example, if a dog has any kind of bad bite, a moustache will help hide such blemishes. The dog's sex does not enter into consideration as far as a moustache is concerned. Some dogs, male or female, look cute with a moustache. Sometimes the only way to tell if a moustache will work is by trying. If it doesn't look right on a given dog, a moustache can always come off. But you can't put it back on. Once a moustache has been requested, the most attractive style for the individual dog must be picked out.

Moustaches (with or without whiskers)

The moustache with whiskers is the most popular. You will recall when you first started clipping the face in the Basic Poodle clip, your first stroke was from the ear to the corner of the eye. This remains the same. Your second stroke, however, should stop halfway down the cheek, to the mouth. Do not clip around the mouth. All succeeding strokes should be in porportion to the second stroke. The whiskers on the under jaw are clipped in proportion to those on top.

The finished shape (as with all finished work) is formed with the scissors. The moustache should be uniform in size and shape. A little artistic flair is called for here.

It may be said in general that when a moustache is called for, the beard underneath gives it a more rounded, pleasant effect.

Tasselled Ears

Although we prefer the full, long-flowing ear feathering on the Poodle, there are Poodle owners who prefer tasselled ears, which means that the top part of the ear flap is clipped, and the remaining ear feathering is styled in a tassel. There are several types of ear tassels, but the one which probably looks best is called the Rectangle Tassel.

This is the simplest tassel to make. Using the #7 blade, clip down the ear flap, always starting from the top and clipping down with the grain, about a quarter or halfway, and leave a straight line across. That's it. If you like a closer, clipped look, use the #10 blade.

With tasselled ears, always clip with the grain, and don't try to clip the outer edges of the ear leather. This is done with the scissors to remove any ragged ends.

Ribbons and Bows

Bows are extra work for the groomer, but there are times when some Poodle owners want them. Moreover, bows lend a purely decorative touch to the finished pet dog. Some groomers go overboard and put too many bows on a dog, and some (we suspect) try to cover up a poor job with bows.

To make a bow:

1. Cut off about a yard of ribbon. The ribbon should be ⅜" wide.
2. From this yard cut another piece about 5" long. Splice this in half lengthwise.
3. Cut the remainder of the yard in half. This material should give you enough for two ribbons or bows.
4. Wrap one of the long pieces around two fingers. Slip the folded ribbon off your fingers and double it over.
5. With a utility scissors, snip off a piece at the corners in a "V" shape, but not a sharp V, for you will lose any thread of support. There should be a piece of ribbon left at the centerfold to hold it all together.
6. Take one of the spliced pieces (5") and tie the ribbon at the centerfold securely.
7. Then separate each fold by gently pulling out and twisting each fold out from the center. Do both sides. When all the folds are pulled out and twisted, the bow is completed. All that remains is to fasten the bow to a tuft of hair, using the ends of the center splice to tie the knot. You can now cut off any excess ribbon that remains.

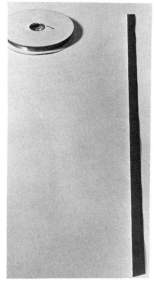

To fashion a bow, start with one yard of ribbon.

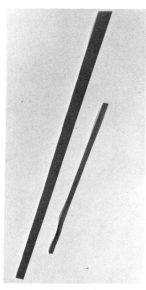

Cut a 5" length from the yard and splice it in half.

Splice the remainder of your ribbon in half.

Wrap a long piece of ribbon around two fingers.

Take off and double ribbon over.

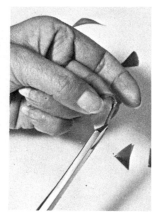

Now snip to form into a wide "V" shape.

After forming the "V" there should be a centerfold to hold the piece of ribbon together.

Tie the ribbon securely at the centerfold with one of the smaller pieces you cut earlier.

Pull out and twist all the folds to make the bow.

The completed bow ready to be worn.

If you are using one bow on the dog, the best place for it is just behind the ear, at the point of separation between the ear and the topknot. Never place the bow in the center of the topknot, for it will flatten it out and ruin it. If another bow is desired, it can be placed on the opposite side of the dog, in the rump area. One bow is good. Two bows are more than enough. More than two is too much.

The Genital Area

The abdomen is clipped with a #10 blade with the grain, to the navel.

With a long-haired male, the penis should be clipped clean (still with the #10 blade) as soon as the stomach has been completed. Gently clip down, always with the grain holding the sheath down if necessary. Do not clip too close. At the same time you can clip shaggy hair on the scrotum as closely as possible always clipping down and away, never toward or into the testicles.

With bitches, there is no need to be concerned about the nipples when going over the underside. Just let the clippers glide over them, clipping lightly (without pressure) with the grain.

CORRECTING FAULTS BY GROOMING

No dog is perfect—all have faults and some are more obvious than others. With Poodles, for example, overshot or undershot bites, long bodies, short legs,

The bow in place, enhancing the wearer's new trim.

"turned in" or "turned out" feet, incorrectly docked or undocked tails are esthetically unpleasing. Every breed though, can turn up a faulty specimen and it is often possible to render faults less glaring by little tricks in trimming and grooming. The following helpful hints concern camouflaging obvious faults.

Undershot or Overshot Jaw

The best camouflage for the undershot or overshot jaw, where possible, is simply a moustache, preferably the full moustache with whiskers. This should tone down any fault around the mouth.

Correction at Ankle

One of the most common mistakes in Poodle grooming is to clip too high up at the pastern or ankle, so that the dog looks like he is growing out of his pantaloons. As pointed out in the section on the Basic clip, the guideline for correct clipping at the ankle is the top of the paw. The "incorrect," too-low position in the accompanying illustration may be in order for a dog with short legs, where the overlapping of the paw will make the leg look longer. By the same token, the "incorrect" too high position may be right for the dog with very long legs.

Malformed Legs

In the case of malformed legs, the best camouflage is a full coated leg. Leave as much coat as possible so that bowlegs or bandy-legs, will appear straighter. Obviously, if you trimmed the legs close, following their own contour, faults would become more obvious. Of course, camouflage is not really possible with the smooth breeds.

Not So Heavenly Bodies

Obesity can be "corrected" by very close trimming just as underweight can be hidden by leaving on more coat. Ideally, correct weight is achieved and maintained by the right amount of a balanced ration. This is more a matter for the concientious owner than the skillful groomer. A long body likewise should be trimmed closely front and rear. The too-short body requires leaving more coat.

Tails

Many tails are never "docked" properly. The accompanying diagram shows how to "correct" improperly docked tails.

The professional groomer must learn how to improvise in order to "correct" faults. For example, a dark stain under the eyes caused by tearing can be camou-

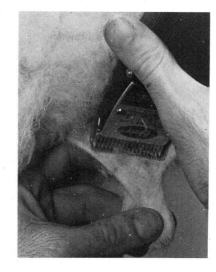

Clip very gently on the male dog's sheath and only in the direction of coat growth.

If the clipper is gently guided over the bitch's nipples, it will not damage them.

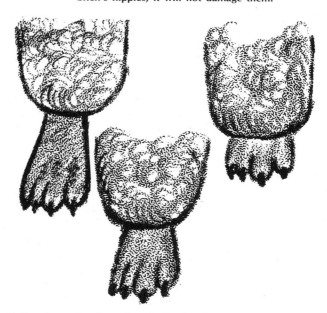

In the above drawings the clipping has been carried too high above the paw at left, is the correct height in the center and too low at the right.

When a Poodle's tail is the proper length, (left) fashioning the pompon poses no special problems. With a long tail (center) and short tail (right), the pom must be placed to compensate for surgical errors.

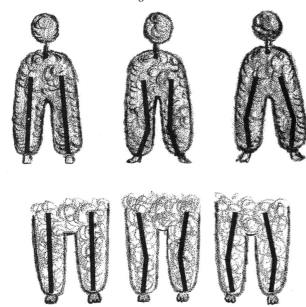

Poodles and other deep-coated breeds offer the possibility of covering such blemishes they may have by clever trimming as may be required by individual conformation.

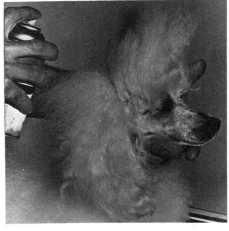

It is advisable to spray the show coat with a conditioner before brushing it.

flagged by applying a white, cosmetic lining stick. On white terrier breeds the use of specially prepared white chalk worked into the coat will make for a sparkling white look.

THE SHOW COAT

Developing a good coat takes time and infinite patience, even with an individual from a family of good-coated dogs. Not only is it painstaking work but the groomer must learn the skills of a beautician-cosmetologist. You will have to know something about oil treatment, coat wrapping, chalking, coat conditioners, shampoos, creme rinses and numerous other refinements. This is dog "hairdressing" in earnest. If you are not geared for such work, forget about show grooming longhaired breeds.

If a dog's sire or dam had a thin, sparse coat, it would be highly unusual for the dog to be beautifully coated. The magnificently coated animals seen at dog shows inherited their crowning glory from good-coated ancestors. Great show coats are born, but then they are lovingly developed. A show dog's coat must be treated and prepared from *puppyhood on*. There is no question, however, that a good coat will be better with proper treatment and a poor coat will be improved with proper care.

Brushing the Show Coat

Brushing a show dog's coat is of paramount importance. It must become a regular routine, carried out at least two or three times a week, preferably daily.

This regular brushing will prevent formation of mats or snarls and help stimulate the natural oils that promote a healthy skin and a lustrous coat. A show coat is brushed in layers, one layer being held back while another layer is being brushed from the skin out. The pin brush or a natural bristle brush are the only safe brushes to use on a show coat, as they will not split, break or pull out live hairs. Only the dead hairs will be removed.

The pin brush requires a slightly different technique than the wire slicker brush used on pet coats. A sweeping motion, following the lay of the hair, one layer at a time, is called for. Avoid twisting the wrist as this will break the hair ends.

Bathing the Show Coat

If the show coat is kept in oil at all times (except when being shown), the dog should be bathed regularly every two weeks. The oil cannot be left in too long or the pores will become clogged. The oil must be completely removed in bathing. Only the best shampoo will do, as a cheap shampoo can destroy all your work by

273

leaving a dry, lusterless, and even scummy coat. The best shampoo, on the other hand, will help to bring out the luster and texture which is so desirable. The bathing technique remains the same as for the pet but you must be even more careful and thorough.

Part the hair down the back and work the shampoo into the coat, kneading it in with your hands. However, you must be careful not to tangle the coat at this point. Unless a harsh texture is desired, it is a good idea to use a creme rinse after shampooing. This helps prevent matting. Follow the standard procedure of blow-drying the show coat after the bath.

Oil Treatment

Oiling the show coat is not for the purpose of growing hair (it is doubtful if it has this benefit), but rather to prevent the coat from matting up and the hairs from splitting and breaking.

Spray on an oil-base coat conditioner and brush it into all parts of the coat. The topknot and ear furnishings will require extra special care (on some breeds) which we will deal with a little later on. There are a number of oil-based coat conditioners on the market which are good for this purpose.

In order to get full value out of this oil treatment, it must be applied as close to the skin as possible. The only way to do this is by picking up one layer of hair at a time, area by area, spraying and brushing in the coat conditioner. Many show dogs are trained to lie on their sides to be groomed. If the dog you are to groom is trained accordingly, so much the better. It will make it easier all around. The oil can remain in the coat for a day or two, provided the dog is kept in a confined area, where he will not brush up against furniture or walls. If this is not possible, keep the dog confined for several hours and then bathe him.

By the time the dog is a year old, the coat should have attained all or most of its full growth, and it should have matured into its typical adult texture. After this stage is reached, regular oil treatments are even more important than during puppyhood, since the adult coat can become more easily broken.

Topknot and Ears

In some breeds, the topknot and ears require special care because the hair on these parts seems to be most easily broken and split. The ear feathering also has a tendency to become coated with dirt and food. The best way to prevent matting of the topknot and ears is to turn to the rather tedious alternative of putting these furnishings up in "wrappers." The material used for wrapping the hair can be any kind of flexible plastic paper, tissue or similar material. Remember that only the hair is wrapped, not the ear leather.

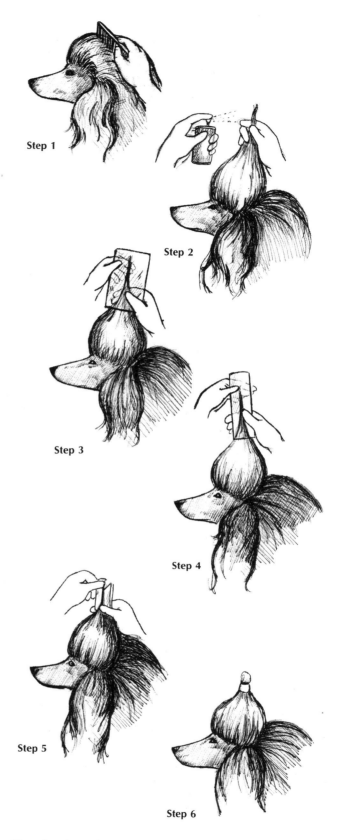

Step 1

Step 2

Step 3

Step 4

Step 5

Step 6

Wrapping the topknot and ear feathers are essential operations for show Poodles and certain other longhaired breeds. The specific instructions for the above diagrams are included on the facing page.

1. Comb the topknot until it stands straight up. Then spray on the coat conditioner.
2. Holding the front part of the crown, wrap a piece of cotton around the base. Spray some oil on the cotton before wrapping.
3. Twist a piece of wrapping material around the cotton.
4. Double the wrapper over. Then double it again.
5. Twist latex band around wrapper.
6. Follow the same basic procedure for the ears, except that you have to be especially careful that the latex band is not fastened around the ear *leather*, as this would stop circulation.

This routine with the topknot and ears should be repeated at least twice a week. Before putting the wrappers up again, brush and comb out the hair you've wrapped, spray on coat conditioner, then re-wrap.

Positions

Learning to use both hands will prove very helpful in assuring the proper positions in grooming dogs. It is true that most of us are not ambidextrous, and most of us are naturally right-handed, but given a chance, it will prove less difficult than imagined to learn the use of the left hand, primarily in clipping.

Practically every one of our students reacts unfavorably to learning how to clip with the "other" hand, but in practically no case has this not been overcome, and by the end of the course the use of both hands is being done automatically.

The advantage of learning how to clip with both hands is best illustrated in trying to clip the right side of the face or the left rear paw of the dog. If the "wrong" hand is used, the awkward position you must assume will be very uncomfortable.

While learning the use of both hands is most desirable, it is by no means mandatory. One can be an excellent groomer without being ambidextrous. It is very rare, for example, that one can learn to scissor with both hands, for scissoring requires a great deal more care and precision than clipping.

The professional groomer should learn as quickly as possible the appropriate times for sitting positions while grooming. Obviously, standing most of the day while grooming will be tiring. In many grooming procedures, you can sit comfortably; for example, while brushing and combing or while blow-drying and working on certain areas in clipping and scissoring. So stand when you have to, and sit when you can. At the end of the day you'll be far less tired.

Controlling the Dog

Every professional groomer is sooner or later confronted with a dog that is not happy about what is happening to him and demonstrates a complete willingness to put teeth into his side of the argument.

With most such dogs, grooming results are never likely to be completely satisfactory. True, the dog can be muzzled and his body trimmed effectively. But what happens when the head must be groomed? Everyone who grooms dogs owes him or herself an obligation in basic safety.

In the overwhelming majority of cases, a dog that actively resists grooming is grossly spoiled by its owner. The process begins in puppyhood when a person buys the dog and is loath to brush and comb the new pet for fear of hurting it. When the owner does try to groom the dog, natural resistance from the puppy soon discourages any attempt to use a brush or comb. Eventually, as the dog grows larger, stronger and better-coordinated, it is more than equal to any grooming attempt. In the case of longhaired dogs, that grooming becomes more sorely needed as time goes on. Many times, with such dogs, owners are as weak-willed as their, by this time, smelly, dirty, matted unkempt dogs are resolute. It's a vicious cycle.

The professional groomer to the rescue—and the groomer is the solution in many instances. Many dogs will respond to an authority figure outside the home and offer little or no resistance in a shop. They are different animals outside their own surroundings.

Also, remember this, most pet owners—when they do try to groom their dogs—will attempt it on the floor, or perhaps on a rickety card table or even a counter with a slippery surface. Everyone experienced in the handling of animals knows that best results come from grooming on a sturdy table with safe footing for the dog, but the pet owner is often ignorant of these facts. Instead of grooming the dog effectively and enjoying the experience, he or she often succeeds only in frightening the dog and getting a backache. So the dog can't always be blamed for putting up a fuss when he knows grooming's on the agenda.

Everyone who grooms dogs professionally must have tables that are specifically designed to accomodate the dogs properly. These can range from sturdy grooming tables, either homemade or store bought, to professional tables with hydraulic lifts in the bases and revolving tops. Regardless of how basic or sophisticated your tables, they should always be equipped with skid-proof surfaces. A slippery table top will unstring any dog, and a frightened dog is a potentially dangerous dog.

Your grooming tables should also be fitted with posts and loops to prevent a dog from sailing off the table as you work on it. These are available in many styles and sizes all for the same purpose. Most tables will come with their own specific models. Other models can be used on any table. But even in a post and loop, the dog should *never* be left unattended on the table. Dogs have been known to try a "swan-dive" while under such restraint. Some have been injured—others have not been that lucky.

It would be wonderful if every dog that comes to the groomer is accustomed to regular attention and behaves perfectly at all times. Of course, this will never happen, so what the groomer must do is learn to exercise authority over the dogs in his care. Groomers and others involved with pet animals must develop effective control measures while avoiding the need for rough handling. Obedience training is not the groomer's responsibility. Control is his obligation to himself, his clients and all the dogs he grooms.

ANATOMY AND THE DOG GROOMER

In a very real sense, success in grooming dogs is not possible unless one acquires a working knowledge of canine anatomy. Like anyone else whose livelihood involves handling animals, dog groomers can greatly upgrade their work by knowing how the parts of a dog relate to each other and how, in beautifying each part, they can beautify the entire dog.

Being familiar with canine anatomy will enable a groomer to deal much more effectively with structural faults. By knowing what these faults are, he can better cover them than the groomer who just trims hair without regard to each animal's individual differences.

In many cases, one must consider the moving dog to best trim the standing dog. A dog can look picture-perfect standing on the grooming table. But the same dog can look terrible off the table and moving about. He can show shortcomings in structure he doesn't even have. For example, a groomer can leave too much hair on a dog's elbows, resulting in the dog looking "out at elbow" when it moves. It's as possible to create a fault that does not exist as it is to cover up one that does.

The beginning groomer may ask where does he go and what does he do to acquire this desirable knowledge. The learning process in this case is two-sided. The student must research the subject in books, and many exist that the layman can understand. He can also familiarize himself with anatomy by minutely examining and evaluating the living dogs brought to him to be groomed.

It is truly amazing how much one can get out of handling a living dog after reading a good book on structure and movement. One of the best is *The Dog in Action* by McDowell Lyon (Howell Book House).

This book was originally published in 1950, but is still recognized throughout the dog world as one of the finest books available on the subject for lay persons. Many other books can also help in this connection and you should read and observe anatomy at every possible opportunity.

If you as a groomer, are not familiar with the parts

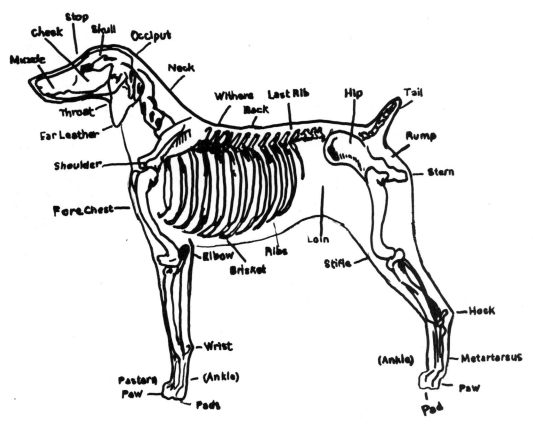

Skeletal and external anatomy of the dog.

of a dog, how will you be able to set a pattern on a Poodle, trim rear angulation onto a straight-stifled Bichon Frise or enhance the ear placement of an English Springer Spaniel? It would be like grooming blindfolded and that renders good grooming impossible.

It simply boils down to the fact that a groomer who has some degree of familiarity with how dogs are built and how they function is probably more capable than one who does not have this knowledge. So whether you groom professionally, part time, work on show dogs or just want to keep your own dog presentable, being familiar with structure and movement and how they relate to each other will help you produce better looking results.

Dog Shows and the Professional Groomer

Many who groom dogs for others started with their own dogs first, getting them ready for dog shows. Others got interested in shows from hearing show-oriented fellow groomers discuss this important part of the modern world of dogs. Whether a groomer starts as a show person or a show person starts as a groomer is less important than understanding something about dog shows and their value to those who groom professionally, semi-professionally or only for themselves.

The first-time visitor to an average all-breed show is frequently stunned by the sophisticated extent of grooming techniques, the range of grooming tools and preparations and the seemingly endless patience of the dogs being prepared to appear before the judge. It is truly an amazing revelation and for most a very enjoyable experience. For the serious groomer a trip to a dog show allows him to study, first-hand, the art of the professional handler. And this can be a real help to upgrading and perfecting his own ability.

If you, as a groomer, haven't any background in dog showing, going to one of the hundreds of annual all-breed events held all over the USA and Canada can be tremendously educational. There you will see breeds almost never encountered elsewhere and you'll see them trimmed, groomed and conditioned to the nth degree of perfection.

At this point you should understand something about show dogs and their relationship to their owners and handlers. A dog can be shown by an amateur (usually the owner or breeder) or a professional handler. Dog showing is one of the few sports where amateur and professional compete against each other on equal terms. A skilled owner-handler can compete successfully against any and all top pros. The owner handler needs a very fine dog perfectly conditioned in order to prevail over professional rivals. In the history of dog shows there have been many famous dog-owner teams in many breeds that have swept the boards and at some of the best shows in the land.

On the other hand there are the professional handlers. A professional handler earns his livelihood by showing dogs owned by others. The handler takes the

Working Group judging at the Westminster Kennel Club dog show. Dog shows offer all persons interested in dog grooming excellent opportunities to learn and observe numerous sophisticated grooming techniques.

Many consider outdoor dog shows the most enjoyable of all. People tend to be more relaxed at most outdoor venues and more willing to discuss their dogs and answer questions.

dog from his owner and keeps it in his own kennel. Here the handler trains the dog and conditions it for a show career. Some dogs live with their handlers for years and don't even know their real owners. Not infrequently, when such a dog is retired from the ring, the owner will leave it with the handler as a special pet.

The two main differences between a groomer and a professional handler working on a dog is that 1) the dog lives with the handler and is constantly under the handler's supervision and 2) the groomer is only responsible for making dogs in his care presentable when they are brought to him (often not frequently enough) while the handler must groom and condition the dog constantly to be able to win in competition regularly.

By visiting dog shows, groomers become more familiar with show grooming. Taking that knowledge back to their shops, they can translate show ring presentation to the pet idiom, thereby combining the best of both worlds.

The groomer visiting a show should be tactful about approaching handlers. It is much better to wait with questions until after a breed has been judged and all the exhibitors are back at their crates. Competition can be rough on the nerves and some dog people can over-react when approached with basic questions just before entering the ring. So wait with those questions until after the judging when exhibitors are generally happy to speak about their dogs.

If you have never been to a dog show and would like to go, check *Dog World* magazine (available at most large newsstands). This magazine features a listing of upcoming shows. An inquiry to your local newspaper, kennel club or the American Kennel Club, 51 Madison Avenue, New York, N.Y. 10010, will also result in the information you want.

The whole subject of dog shows is quite a lengthy one and is more thoroughly covered in numerous specialized books on the subject. Any groomer considering getting into the show scene is best advised to visit the shows, ask questions and do some independent study. It is likely to prove well worth one's while.

PUPPY SELLING AND THE PROFESSIONAL GROOMER

It sometimes happens that a professional groomer is approached for help by someone looking for a puppy of a specific breed. In such cases, probably the best course of action is the referral.

Learn who in your area is breeding what breeds. You can do this by checking with local veterinarians and the telephone directory, of course. But also, it would be wise to develop sources through local all-breed dog clubs. Most communities have dog clubs for the purpose of holding shows and sponsoring other dog-oriented activity. Many area breeders belong to the local club and so establishing club contact is a good way to meet the people who have puppies to sell.

If you are asked about a puppy and you know of a breeder in the area, it is a simple matter to provide a recommendation. Many breeders are glad to pay a commission for a referral that leads to a sale. As you can see, the referral route can be good for your business by itself and can lead to new clients for grooming too.

As there are 125 recognized dog breeds in the United States at this writing and several others presently with Miscellaneous status, it would be virtually impossible to maintain a referral file of local breeders in all breeds. When you get a request for a breed that is not represented by breeders in your area, the classified ads in *Dog World* are a good source for finding the desired puppy. Of course, there would probably be less chance of a commission resulting from a long-distance referral. On the other hand, there is more likelihood of your getting to do the grooming, since the breeder is not immediately available to the puppy buyer for subsequent help in grooming the dog.

The referral system gives the groomer the opportunity of extending his capacity for service to dog owners and would-be dog owners without the need for keeping and looking after varying numbers of young puppies.

The foregoing remarks concern the groomer in a shop who wants to concentrate on grooming dogs rather than merchandising them. For the person who is breeding and grooms dogs, things are a bit different. Such individuals can also refer inquiries for other breeds, limiting their own grooming to the dogs they sell or to dogs of their own and/or similar breeds. This is entirely an individual decision and every groomer must make his or her own determination.

Groomers connected to shops that do sell puppies are in an entirely different category and are governed by shop or franchise policy.

It is not within the scope of this book to provide guidelines on puppy selling or to advise on what to look for in buying a puppy. That must remain to be worked out in other books and between buyers and sellers. The point here is that puppy referrals are frequently the most satisfactory means of satisfying your customers' needs and, at the same time, boosting your image with local dog breeders. Use the service wisely and you will reap appropriate dividends in many ways.

MIXED BREEDS

Not every dog that is owned, loved and cared for by an individual or a family is purebred. Millions of dogs all over the country cannot claim an illustrious family tree or champion ancestry. But these dogs also guard the

Before and after for this mixed-breed pet shows how attractive it can be made in the hands of an imaginative dog groomer.

Every dog has appeal, and when grooming a mixed breed, the groomer should try to call attention to the individual dog's strongest physical assets.

279

home, play with the children, and gladden the hearts of the entire family.

In recent years stage, movies and TV have all provided their own doggy superstars and three top ones are mixed breeds. The successful play ''Annie'' featured ''Sandy'' as the young heroine's faithful companion while ''the Benjie'' movies packed theaters nationwide and ''Boomer'' became an overnight TV celebrity.

In addition to the spotlight shining on dogs of multiple breed ancestry, certain crossbreeds have found acceptance with many pet owners. Notable among these are the ''Cock-a-Poo'' (Cocker Spaniel × Poodle) and the Peke-a-Poo (Pekingese × Poodle). There is a brisk demand for these and other crossbreds.

Mixed breeds occur in any shape, any size and any color. They can also carry any kind of canine coat. This can range from the smooth, thin coat of a Boston Terrier to the long, dense covering of an Old English Sheepdog. And the coated ones can be trimmed and groomed just like purebred dogs. In fact, mixed breed dogs are visiting shops in greater numbers and more frequently than ever before. They are being seen regularly in grooming contests as well.

It is exactly because the mixed breed dog can occur in such infinite variety, that the groomer must apply flair to grooming such a dog, approaching the work with art and imagination.

The first thing to determine is what pure breed an individual dog most closely resembles. Having done so, trim the dog to accentuate this resemblance. Always trim and groom to flatter the dog as much as possible.

GROOMING AIDS

Pet Ladder

The pet ladder is simply a stepladder especially designed for big dogs, which may be too heavy to be lifted into the tub for bathing. With a little persuasion, the big dog will walk right up the ladder and into the tub. The same ladder may also be used to get the big dog up on the grooming table.

Grooming Tray

A much-needed aid in a grooming shop is a storage area for the various tools which should be within the groomer's constant reach. The pegboard setup referred to in Part VI is fine for such items as brushes, conditioners, medications, etc., but the clippers/blades/scissors setup should be at your fingertips. This is what the grooming tray permits.

It is mounted under the grooming table and swings in and out at will with the touch of a finger. No modern, sophisticated groomer should be without one.

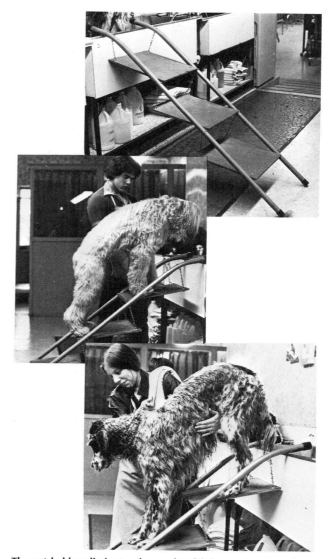

The pet ladder eliminates the need to lift larger dogs in and out of tubs or on and off grooming tables—a labor saving refinement in a busy grooming shop.

The grooming tray attaches to the underside of the table and keeps important tools at the groomer's fingertips.

280

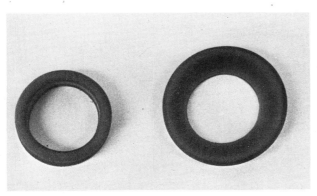

Scissor guards are intended for use by groomers with very small fingers.

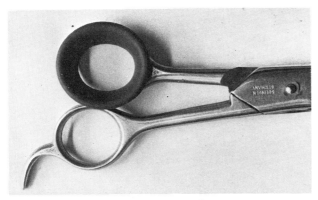

The scissor guard in place.

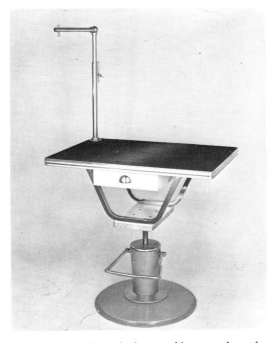

The hydraulic table is the last word in convenience for the dog groomer. It can adjust to the height of any dog and can swivel to show either side of the dog being groomed without the groomer making one extra step.

Scissor Guards

These guards are meant for groomers whose fingers may be too small to fit into the shanks of the scissors. The scissor guards usually provide for a perfect fit.

Hydraulic Table

A hydraulic table lowers and raises so that all sizes of dogs can be accommodated and the table can be adjusted to a perfect height. The top also revolves so that at no time is it necessary to move the dog.

The hydraulic table does cost considerably more han the regulation table. But the difference in cost should oe justified for a busy groomer or for those with back problems.

Boarding

If you have a kennel operation or you are primarily a breeder with boarding facilities, there is no question about the value of boarding for you, for this would be an integral part of your business. However, if grooming is your exclusive activity, either in your own home or in your own shop, boarding may be a debatable additional service for you. There is no doubt that boarding is profitable but you should be fully aware of the tasks and responsibilities involved.

First, boarding is a seven-day operation. The dogs must be fed at least once a day and supplied daily with fresh water. The kennel beds must be laid with paper, either flat or shredded. Shredded paper is a must for puppies. The cages and kennel floors must be cleaned whenever necessary and thoroughly treated with a germicidal disinfectant every day.

Moreover, adequate boarding facilities must provide for regular exercise for the dogs and if the dogs are being boarded for long periods of time, the kennels should have runs where the dogs can exercise at will.

Perhaps the most important aspect of boarding is that the operator must live on or near the kennel quarters so that if there is any disturbance or danger, someone is at hand to attend to whatever is necessary.

CAT GROOMING

Cats and cat grooming are not the subjects of this book, but professional groomers may find their services in enough demand by cat owners to warrant some discussion here of general procedures. The fundamentals of cat grooming are essentially the same as for dogs. Refer to the chapter on fundamentals in Part I of this book for some idea of what is involved.

Cat grooming represents a constantly growing area of demand for the services of the professional groomer. The increasing popularity of Persian, Himalayan and other longhaired breeds has created a need that must be met by the modern groomer.

Perhaps the most important difference between cat grooming and dog grooming is handling and control, especially in the bathing process. Many cats hate getting wet and will fight in the bath. Paradoxically, cats clean themselves and are naturally immaculate animals. But cats which are unaccustomed to water may prove very difficult to handle, showing their displeasure by biting vigorously. The bite of a cat can be far more serious than a dog bite with correspondingly more serious consequences. This is one reason many dog groomers shy away from cat grooming.

Nevertheless, if one becomes experienced in handling cats it can prove to be a lucrative source of income.

For the troublesome cat here are a few hints in handling and control:

Since the main problem occurs during bathing, be extra careful while the cat is in the tub. Be aware that cats are extraordinarily quick so extra precautions are in order.

Cats should have something to hang on to so that they don't slip and slide. A wire mesh platform would be helpful at the bottom of the tub.

If it is necessary to tie something around the cat's neck while in the tub, a slipknot would be better than a snap lock.

Part VI

The Professional Groomer

CURRENT ESTIMATES VARY CONsiderably on the number of active professional groomers in the United States, ranging anywhere from 50,000 to 100,000. Considering all the work done in grooming shops, pet shops, kennels, with veterinarians, as well as out of private homes and hobby kennels, the 100,000 figure is probably more accurate.

Although the Poodle, which at one time accounted for a major share of the grooming business, has steadily declined in popularity during recent years, the rise in popularity of the Lhasa Apso, Shih Tzu, Bichon Frise and Old English Sheepdog, as well as the resurgence of the Cocker Spaniel, seems to have more than offset the loss of Poodle popularity. In fact, there are more dogs being groomed today than ever before.

Documented Increase

This increase in dogs groomed is reflected in the statistics on money spent in this country for grooming services. According to the authoritative pet trade magazine *Pets/Supplies/Marketing,* in the last year reported, there were sales of grooming services in the amount of $293,000,000 which was an increase of $20,000,000 over the previous year. In the last five-year period reported there was a 21% increase in grooming services.

The increasing interest in the grooming profession is also reflected in the number of students entering our school each year and the constantly increasing number of grooming shops opening up in every part of the country. In 1979 there were over 300 students graduated from our school, a 25% increase over the year before. At the end of 1980, there were over 400 graduates for the year, another 25% increase. The prospects for the future are even brighter. While this includes *all* graduates of a diversified curriculum (Dog Grooming, Obedience Training, Veterinary Office Assistants, Kennel Management) most of the increase is in the dog grooming department.

The professional groomer is a rather unique, as well as a relatively new, entry into the professional world. The dog grooming industry started really flourishing in the 1950s, coincident with the prosperity and rising standard of living in the country. The Poodle became the status symbol, and it seemed like everybody had to have a Poodle. As this prosperity leveled off, so did Poodle popularity, although the Poodle still remains America's favorite breed. But, as mentioned earlier, other breeds have taken up the slack.

Outside the family, the professional groomer is the one person closest to the pet, superseding the veterinarian. Certainly the professional groomer has the best rapport of any outsider with the family pet. The professional groomer will see the pet regularly on a monthly or bi-monthly basis, and in many instances will be the surrogate owner. The knowledgeable professional groomer will be asked for advice on matters of health, breeding, to board the dog occasionally, and to supply various dog products if he sells them. The extent to which the professional groomer fills these roles affects the relationship between groomer and pet owner. A close bond between the family and the pet often means a close bond between the family and the groomer.

In recent years, the grooming profession has come of age, with professional groomers and shops becoming integral factors in communities across the country. The pet-owning public has also become more aware of the need for grooming the family pet. This, in turn, creates the need for more professional groomers and further growth of the profession.

Another indication of the growing strength and professionalism of dog groomers, is the rise of regional grooming associations. No national association has yet been formed which claims the allegiance of most professional groomers in the United States. This is an area which remains to be explored and developed.

There is no doubt that a strong, national association of dog groomers would significantly enhance the profile of the profession.

The grooming profession would also benefit greatly from a nationally-recognized set of standards for the Poodle clips. In this way, a given clip would be called by the same name in every part of the country. Since the Poodle clips cause the most confusion, the problem would be resolved if uniformity were applied to the nomenclature and execution of these clips.

The illustrations in this book could serve as the basis

for this much-needed national uniformity. The authors have compiled sets of these charts which are available to the grooming profession. But no matter how this uniformity is achieved, the sooner it happens, the better.

Professionalism in Grooming

The dictionary definition of the word professional is "one skilled in a profession, craft, or art." Professionalism is defined as "The methods, manner, or spirit of a profession; also its practitioners."

Professional groomers certainly fit this definition well. Good ones are certainly skilled in the art of dog grooming, and certainly conduct themselves professionally. Dog groomers must undergo as much training and vocational education as human hair stylists. Canine beauty culture demands as much artistic skill as the human counterpart (some groomers contend even more).

The industry is so new that we are still defining what professionalism means to us. We can start out with some basic precepts of professionalism that would apply to dog groomers:

1. To strive for the highest standards in the quality of our grooming.
2. To guarantee that we will make the care and safety of our clients' pets our first priority.
3. To attain the ultimate in cleanliness, sanitation and hygiene.
4. To treat our pet owner clients with the respect and consideration they deserve.
5. To promote good public relations by collaborating and cooperating with all persons or organizations devoted to animal welfare, on a non-profit basis.
6. To see to it that the pets put in our care are always treated humanely and with love.
7. To devote ourselves to the humane treatment of all animals and to further the cause of all those devoted to animal welfare.

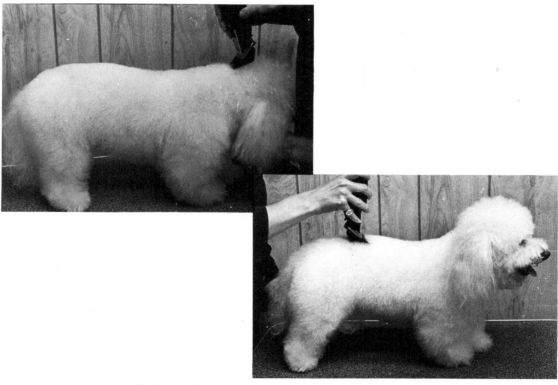

A groomer is judged by the work he does. Every dog is either a walking testimony to the groomer's skill or proof of his inability. Let the dogs you groom always be a mirror of your expertise in the field.

The Grooming Shop

THE OBJECTIVE OF MANY PRO-fessional groomers is to own their own shops. Usually, the relatively low investment cost makes this objective attractive, practical and realistic. Many home groomers start out in the basements of their homes and graduate to their own shops on Main streets in towns throughout the country. The average grooming shop, therefore, becomes virtually a "mom" or "pop" or a "mom and pop" operation.

Many new grooming shops have sprung up all over the country in recent years and the competition therefore has become more intense. With proper training and planning, the professional groomer can still establish and maintain a thriving business, regardless of new entries in the field competing for the same dogs.

Quality Training

The growing demand for quality grooming makes it imperative that the professional receive the best instruction available. This instruction should come from licensed, qualified instructors in state-approved locations with adequate space and facilities. Proper training is the most important part of the investment, for without it there is no business.

Good dog grooming instruction means training in grooming all breeds with access to dogs of as many breeds as possible. The school's facilities should be not only adequate and spacious but approved and licensed by the respective State Education Departments. An *accredited* school means that the school has been approved by the Accreditation Committee of the National Association of Trade and Technical Schools (NATTS), which sets even higher standards than the individual states. Above all, the school's reputation is most significant. If you are thinking of becoming a professional groomer and attending a school, consult first with your State Education Department, the Better Business Bureau and other consumer agencies. Then make a personal visit to the school.

Site Selection

Once the new groomer is fully trained, the next most important consideration in setting up a shop is choosing the best location. The best rule to follow in site selection is to go where the action is. Pet owners who regularly patronize grooming shops like locations in a good part of town, preferably one with plenty of traffic and good parking. If one can afford to start out first class, then the best location is the busiest shopping mall because that indeed is where the action is. If you find the rents too expensive, then the next best choice is to locate on a main thoroughfare leading to the mall, wherever there is visibility. Above all, don't hide your light under a bushel.

Another important factor to consider when deciding on a location is the element of competition. If there is a dog grooming shop already established in the area, you may not want to be too near it, especially if it has a good reputation. If it is not a top-flight shop, you should still weigh carefully if this is the decisive factor. The ideal situation, of course, is an area with little or no competition or obviously inferior competition. Not only would competition affect your choice of location but even your timing for opening a shop. If you get in on the ground floor in your area or wherever you decide to set up business, you are more likely to wind up with the lion's share of the business. This will be even truer if you are the best groomer around.

Incidentally, when you sign a lease, try having a clause included giving you the option to renew for a long term at the same rental, if possible. You may not always succeed, but you should still try. Try getting the best deal possible. If a good lawyer or business expert can help you, so much the better.

Zoning

Most state laws are very loose about zoning requirements for dog grooming shops. Usually you are safe in a commercial area or on a main street. If you groom at home you might have to cope with complaining neighbors. However, if you limit your grooming to your own dogs you have nothing to worry about. In all cases, check your local zoning laws.

The exterior design of a grooming shop is the face it shows to the world. This homey-looking shop uses its window to merchandise dog supplies and advertise puppies.

SHOP DESIGN, OPERATION AND MANAGEMENT

There are three major factors to consider in planning and opening a dog grooming shop: 1) shop set-up or design; 2) operating to achieve maximum production and 3) management, or the business end of the operation. These factors are interrelated, and in many cases overlap, but for the purposes of simplicity and clarity we have divided them into three categories where some clear distinctions can be made.

Interiors

Start with the proper perspective on decorating your shop because how you decorate will render your shop attractive or unattractive, inviting or uninviting. Flattering in-shop decor will contribute to the lightness and brightness of the environment and create a favorable impression on your customers. Light colors should dominate the decor since the shop should be as light as possible. Dark colors are a poor choice in a grooming shop. They tend to create a somber, "down" mood and also make an area appear smaller than it actually is. If you want to be very decorative, you can try combining such pastel shades as mist blue, rosebud, candy pink or any others you may like. You might even be bold enough to try something wild on the walls. If you are conservative and prefer safe, simple decorating ideas, stick to a color such as antique white or sky blue. Whatever your decorative impulses, try selecting only light colors. It's perfectly acceptable to try something colorful on the walls or hang up some attractive paintings.

The ideal decorative setup includes using materials that make frequent painting unnecessary. For example, wall paper is much easier to maintain and will last much longer than paint. Panelled walls will last longer than anything else, but your budget may be strained by this initial, additional expense. Tiled floors are most desirable, especially good tile. (Avoid rugs for obvious reasons.)

The sign above the door indicates that the shop can handle grooming for terriers as well as for Poodles.

Exterior Decor

The exterior decoration of your shop is just as important as the interior. When planning the color scheme, think of the outside as well as the inside. You may be more limited with the exterior, depending on the type of structure, but in any event, try something different to attract attention, without being offensive. One of the

In some communities, dog groomers may work in conjunction with a veterinarian. In its corner location, this small animal clinic gives conspicuous notice that grooming as well as veterinary service is available.

288

The reception area of this shop is sunny and uncluttered and encourages the client to be at ease.

This reception area is quite different from the one in the top photograph. The opulent decor is either a reflection of the groomer's taste or the perceptions of what his clients want in a grooming shop.

This reception area is both busy-looking and friendly in a casual kind of way. The good mix of photos and drawings on the wall occupy clients while they wait.

Another view of the reception area shown above which includes the grooming room.

most attractive exteriors we have seen featured painted red and white stripes.

Your window display is a part of your exterior decoration. A nicely lettered sign on the window with your shop name, should be given careful consideration. Perhaps a colorful, attractive canopy overhead might be added. The window display itself should not only have eye appeal, but it should be exciting to look at. That doggie in the window is always eye catching, especially a dog which has just been groomed to perfection. This is a perfect window display (with the owner's approval) as well as a testimonial to your skill. An early shop owned by the authors had a figure of a Poodle painted on the window (by Mrs. Stone) dressed in tophat and tails and appropriately enough, the shop was named *The Tailored Pet*.

Reception Room

A wall or partition separating the reception room from all work areas in the shop is most desirable. The reception room should be just that—a section where customers bring their dogs and wait in to pick up their dogs when they are finished. Of course, it should be the most attractive area in the shop. Furnish the area with some inviting chairs (colored fiber chairs can be inexpensive and attractive) and a coffee table or long reception table with some dog magazines and books on it. The customers should be able to relax here while waiting for their dogs. Another desirable (and profitable) piece of furniture is the accessory display cabinet. One or two cabinets depending on available space, tastefully displaying a variety of accessories is a feature of many shops. The kind, price range and selection you offer must be dictated by your customers' preferences. You can also enhance the reception room with paintings or photos of dogs and puppies, photos of your grooming work, and anything else you think customers will appreciate. If you show dogs, a display of ribbons, rosettes, trophies and win pictures is most impressive.

A price chart displayed prominently in the reception room is essential. This way no one can quarrel about price discrimination. Prices for dogs of different sizes should be clearly itemized, and extra charges for flea baths, tick baths, dematting coats and other extra services should should be posted very clearly.

For the convenience of Poodle owners, prominently display illustrated charts of the major clips. That way, all the customers have to do is point to the clip of their choice. This will eliminate confusion and forestall dissatisfaction. Illustrations of other popular breeds, correctly groomed, should also adorn the reception room walls.

Lastly, a ''Dutch'' door should separate your work area from the reception room. The Dutch door is a swinging door made in two parts. The bottom half can be locked with a sliding bolt while the top half remains open. A Dutch door keeps the customer out of your work area, but you can still communicate with each other. Customers should be confined to the reception room and definitely discouraged from entering the work area. Otherwise you can be sure your work will become completely disrupted. You can be very polite and even sociable, but don't fraternize and turn the shop into a social club.

Work Area

The work area should be as immaculate as the reception area. If you are normally systematic in your work habits, it will extend to your cleaning routine. Your work area will then be clean and neat at all times. A busy schedule is no excuse for untidiness. If you let your shop run down, you are doing something wrong. Usually those shops which permit unchecked fraternization use the excuse of being too busy to clean up.

In setting up your work area, have everything close at hand for maximum efficiency. You should not have to waste any time looking for tools or walking unnecessarily from one place to another. Incidentally, when putting up any partitions, always favor your work area as far as space is concerned. Your work area should be spacious enough to preclude that closed-in feeling. Plan ahead to keep an ample work area. This part of the shop will have a great bearing on the expansion of your business.

Grooming Table and Tool Pegboard

Your grooming table should be in the lightest part of the room, preferably near a window. A pegboard should be on the wall nearest your grooming table. It should hold almost all your tools so that all you have to do is reach over to pick up whatever you need. A shelf, to store spray cans and any items you can't hang from a pegboard is a practical addition to your work area. Your grooming table should be the center of the stage, so to speak, and a most desirable feature of such a table is a swinging tray underneath for additional storage of frequently-used tools and preparations.

Cages

Arrange your cages on a wall near your table. Your cages, like your other equipment, should be set up for maximum efficiency. If you want to start with the minimum, order a unit of four cages, and when your business starts to grow, order another unit of four, so that you will be able to accommodate at least eight dogs. Since the dogs do not always come in and go out at the same time, you will find that you can handle as many as ten dogs per day with the two cage units. Larger grooming shops can devote a separate room just for cages. A back room is usually ideal for this.

Most well-organized grooming shops separate the reception and work areas by means of a Dutch door. This keeps clients and visitors out of the groomers' way but still allows for necessary communication.

This airy, spacious work area is highly conducive to high productivity. The cleanliness of floor, cages and groomer's station are also obvious.

A well-organized bathing area includes a storage area for all shampoos and other bathing materials. In this particular case there is even a drying table adjacent to the tub with a floor dryer at the ready.

A well-equipped shop will have enough cages to meet its needs. Your bank of cages should be as close to your grooming area as is practical for your set up.

A comfortable stool such as this one can be a big help for those times you can groom sitting down.

Bathtub

When the tub is installed, the height of the groomer should be considered and should be waist-high for the operator's comfort. Storing bathing materials below the tub further utilizes your work area.

The rest of the work area should be organized with an eye to expansion. As the business grows, you may have to hire another groomer, or bather, or even more helpers. You may need three or more grooming tables.

Sit When You Can

A comfortable stool for the times one can sit while grooming gets many groomers through the day. The best stool for an individual groomer will suit his or her height and come equipped with a thick foam seat for real comfort. Such stools truly make the day far less tiring.

Electrical Power

You may have to compromise if you can't find a shop with everything you want. However one of the most important things your new shop must have is sufficient electrical power. The more power a shop has, the better. Electricity can be quite an expense in a grooming shop, where overhead lights, clippers, dryers, and in the hot weather, air conditioners are all essential. Daylight, of course, is the best light of all as well as the cheapest. But there is never enough daylight, especially on cloudy, rainy days and in winter, when night comes all too quickly. Many shops must have their lights on because

adequate advance planning was not made for electricity usage before these shops opened.

At the very least, make sure the shop has enough outlets in the right places and sufficient current to support the load. If all your electrical equipment and appliances were on at the same time, the total load might be 30 to 40 amps. If your power amperage is not equipped to handle this load or if you do not have separate lines for each major appliance, you will have a constant flow of short circuits. Call in a good electrician for advice, consultation and installation. If you do it right from the start, you will save yourself a lot of headaches and expense in the long run.

We stress the importance of adequate electrical power because it would be a shame if you had everything else going for you, and your operation becomes crippled because of inadequate electrical power or facilities. Sometimes this problem may be bad enough to slow down an operation or stop it completely. Adequate lighting in the work area is more important than anywhere else in the shop. If you have your own electrical fixtures installed, remember that fluorescent lighting is best. Have as many fixtures as you need and don't skimp in this area.

In summarizing the essentials for setting up a shop, the major elements are location, interior and exterior decoration, shop layout, including the reception room, the work area, and, if available, a back room for cages. Maximum efficiency can be obtained by the proper location of your grooming table and tools. The most essential items are adequate lighting and power for your other electrical needs. Attention to these details will help to make your shop attractive, comfortable and efficient.

Shop Operation

YOUR MANNER OF BUSINESS operation is as important as the shop design. A dog grooming shop should have a definite operating plan if it is to achieve maximum productivity and profitable return.

Productivity

The professional groomer should be able to groom as many dogs a day as possible, without sacrificing quality. Develop a practical system that enables you to groom just one more dog a day. That means five or six more dogs per week, at an average fee of $15.00 per dog, or a minimum of $75.00 extra weekly income. That translates to over $300.00 a month—usually enough to pay the rent!

In considering productivity, remember what was explained in the previous chapter under *Shop Design*. In planning your work area, try locating your grooming table near a window, with a pegboard setup on the nearest wall. Practically all your tools should be on that pegboard so that no time is wasted looking for tools. Whatever you take from the pegboard, shelf, or drawer should be put back immediately after use and always kept in the same place. Make this a habit from the start and you'll save valuable minutes amounting to many extra hours.

Another way to increase productivity is to develop an "assembly line" or "rotation" system. For example, if you start the day with six dogs to groom, what is the most productive way to handle them? Of course, you could simply do one dog at a time from start to finish. But you would soon discover that this was the least productive approach. Here is a highly productive step-by-step system for efficient, quality, volume grooming.

1. The best method, used in the most successful shops, is "rough clipping" all the dogs first. In this system grooming fundamentals are done first, and the pattern (if any) is set on all the dogs requiring it before anything else is done. All dogs are now rough clipped.
2. Assuming you operate on a first come, first served basis, brush and comb the first dog to arrive. After this, bathe the dog and put him in a cage to damp dry. The drying process should take from five to 10 minutes.
3. While the first dog is drying, brush and bathe the second dog. By the time the second dog is bathed and put in the cage, the first dog will be ready for blow-drying. When you finish blow-drying the first dog, the second will be ready for the same process. When the second dog is finished you can turn your attention to the other dogs.
4. Repeat the rotation with the next pair and then the last, so that all six dogs are blow-dried hopefully by noon. What now remains is to finish grooming with the necessary techniques (depending on breed) of shaping and blending, finishing off every dog with scissors. Start the trimming rotating with the first dog that came in and which ordinarily should be the first dog going out.
5. Now completely finish one dog at a time. If the first dog is a Poodle going into a Sporting clip, do your shaping and blending and finish off with scissors. Then systematically, finish each dog in the order in which it came in. The only exception to this procedure is if a particular customer is promised a certain priority.

The foregoing system is most productive for the groomer working alone. Does the system change if there is one or more helpers? To be sure, it does. It you have one or two helpers or assistant groomers, you can go on a "production line." There would have to be some modification of the system you use when working alone. For example, if one assistant does the fundamentals, you rough clip all six dogs, one after the other. Let your helper concentrate on the fundamentals, and you'll find this system usually works out pretty well. If you can do four to six dogs alone, with a helper and using this system, you will find you can do as many as eight to ten dogs per day or even more.

A happy predicament might arise if you are fortunate enough to have a fast-working helper who has all the rough work done before you finish half your dogs. If your helper has nothing else to do he or she can keep busy by:

1. Making sure that the floors, tables and cages are clean.
2. Answering the phone and making appointments.
3. Waiting on customers who may come in off the street.
4. Selling accessories when necessary.
5. Training your help. If your helper has been doing the brushing, bathing and blow-drying, it would be a good

idea to teach him or her to execute the Basic Poodle clip and techniques for Yorkshires, Lhasas and other breeds popular in your area.

If your shop turns out more than ten dogs a day, there will be less time available for your helper to spend with other tasks. Naturally some days are busier than others, and you must plan your time accordingly. Traditionally, the busiest day in the week is Saturday and the slowest is Monday. Some shops operate only five days a week—from Tuesday through Saturday. Shops that close on Mondays find they can do the same amount of business in five days as in six. If your business grows to the point where it spills over into six days, you will have to adjust your schedule accordingly. We are not mapping out a blueprint, just a guide. Conditions may vary from shop to shop.

Work Area and Work Slip

A major problem which arises in grooming shops from time to time is the confusion caused by a lack of coordination between the "front office" and the work area. Here's a classic example. Two black, female Miniature Poodles are both in a shop to be groomed on the same day. Both are going into the Sporting clip. A friend of the owner of one dog is sent to pick up the dog at the end of the day. Are you sure you are giving the right dog to the right person?

One way to avoid any traumatic consequences is through the use of the "work slip". This is an identification which accompanies the dog through the day. The information on this work slip is taken from the master card made out for each dog and which remains in the permanent file. Only the basic information for the dog's grooming is put on the work slip. Part of this information is the customer's name, the dog's name and the grooming instructions. The work slip is put on the cage in which the dog is placed at the beginning of the day, the slip accompanies the dog to the grooming table when the work commences, and should be on the cage when grooming is finished. Mistakes in identification are virtually impossible if this procedure is followed.

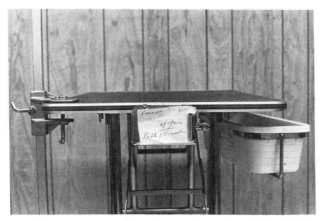

A work slip assures that the right procedures will be followed with each dog and that the right dog goes home with the right owner at the end of the day.

Shop Management

SOME MAY ARGUE THAT THE cost of investment is the most important factor in the perspective of owning a dog grooming shop and therefore should be given first consideration. We would not take issue with this opinion. But we are not necessarily considering all of the factors that might go into making a decision in the order of their importance. We are just putting all the factors together in a systematic, organized form.

Cost of Investment

What are the costs involved? Following is a list of the major elements in setting up a shop together with approximate costs:

1. Rent and Security Deposits		$ 800
2. Alterations and Renovation		1,500
3. Tools and Equipment		1,250
4. Furniture and Fixtures		750
5. Legal and Accounting Fees		500
6. Insurance		350
7. Advertising and Promotion		850
8. Pet Supplies		500
9. Cash Reserve		1500
	Total	$8,000

From this total figure, let's now consider the individual costs of each item.

Rent—What you pay to rent a shop will vary according to the specific location you work in. The rent for a shop in a major metropolitan center will be greater than for one in a rural area with a relatively small, scattered population. So let's consider an average rent of about $300.00 per month. Since the landlord usually demands at least one month's security, the cost of the initial rent and security comes to $600.00. In addition, there are deposits required for utilities (telephone and electricity) which may cost $200.00, hence a total of $800.00 for your initial rent and security deposits.

Alteration and Renovation—Here again there can be considerable variation depending on the shop's condition when rented and how much work must be put into

it. With luck, one may find a location requiring very little to get going. Conversely, one may find the perfect spot, but it might need considerable work before opening day. So, again, a theoretical average sum is needed. From our experience, $1,500.00 for alteration and renovation is realistic at the time of this writing. This tab comes down considerably if you can do some of the work yourself.

Tools and Equipment—Your basic assortment of clippers, blades, scissors, shampoos, brushes, combs and other tools and cosmetics costs about $250.00. Heavy equipment—dryers, cages and tables fitted with post loops, cost about $1,000.00 for a total of $1,250.00 In this category, cages are the most expensive item.

Furniture and Fixtures—This item is primarily for the reception area and will cost about $750.00 for a desk and chair, showcase and settee.

Legal and Accounting Fees—A lawyer or astute businessman who knows how to negotiate a lease on the most favorable terms, is a virtual necessity. If you choose a lawyer, his or her services can cost about $300.00. That investment, however, will be well worth the protection and security it brings.

After a good lawyer, you need a good accountant. Today, with close scrutiny by government into the income declared by every self-employed individual, the accountant is the one to set up your books and advise you on how to keep your records. The accountant's services should cost about $200.00, so we have a total of $500.00 for both the lawyer and accountant.

Insurance—This is another "must-have" item. The most common form of insurance coverage is for fire, public liability and property damage, plate glass and possibly contents. The cost for this insurance coverage should be approximately $350.00 per year.

Advertising and Promotion—Before opening your doors, you will want to stimulate some business coming your way as quickly as possible. Some ways this can be done are through the Yellow Pages, newspapers, direct mail, and flyers. Sometimes you can get some free publicity on radio or even television. Notwithstanding, about $350.00 will start you off with some advertising and promotion. Signs are a necessity on your windows. You might want a large sign overhead to give the greatest possible visibility and exposure. These signs can be expensive, so estimate the cost at $500.00. Your advertising and promotion including your signs, will therefore total about $850.00

Pet Supplies—An additional source of income, pet supplies make a busy grooming shop into a miniature pet shop as well. Of course, the amount of pet supplies a shop will carry can vary considerably. For our purposes of discussion, allot $500.00 for the cost of pet supplies.

Reserve—This $1,500 can be called escrow money to be held in reserve for any emergency or in case it takes a little longer than expected before reaching the break-even point. Hopefully you will not have to touch this reserve money, so your actual investment cost may be only $6,500 rather than the $8,000 already calculated. If the proper planning and preparation went into the venture, this would help insure that the reserve money could be saved.

Return on Investment

An investment of $8,000.00 is a relatively small one. A good rule in measuring your potential success in the venture is: if you can make your investment back in two years, you have done well. If you can make it back in one year, you have done very well. Let's estimate the volume of business we must do in order to get our investment back in one or two years.

Monthly Expenses

First you must know what your *monthly* expenses are. Following is a hypothetical chart itemizing these monthly expenses:

1. Rent		$300.00
2. Telephone		75.00
3. Electricity		75.00
4. Advertising		50.00
5. Insurance		30.00
6. Supplies		40.00
7. Miscellaneous		30.00
	Total	$600.00

With a total of $600 for monthly expenses, you now have a yardstick. You know how much business to do to break even and, beyond, to make a profit. Since this calculation is based on a self-employed, one-person or mom and pop operation, salary is not included.

Monthly Income

If your average fee for grooming a dog is $15.00, simple arithmetic will tell the whole story. If you groom two dogs a day or ten dogs a week, this totals approximately 40 dogs a month or $600.00

You now know your break-even point is two dogs per day.

Let us further assume that, as an average groomer, you can groom six dogs a day, which brings in $90.00 a day or $450.00 a week for $1,800 a month. You augment this grooming income by selling pet supplies for $100.00 a week. You make a 40% markup or a $40 a week profit on your sale of supplies, for a monthly profit of $160.

Your monthly profit and loss statement would then look like this:

Monthly Income		
Grooming	$1,800	
Pet Sales Profit	160	
Total		$1,960
Monthly Expense		600
Profit		$1,360

Using the above figures, the shop makes a monthly profit of $1,360.00, or the equivalent of $340.00 a week. It is really academic whether you call this income profit or salary. What is meaningful is that it adds up to $17,860.00 annual income.

While $17,860.00 a year will not make a person rich, it does represent a handsome return on an investment of $8,000.00 or less. What makes this investment even more attractive is that it is calculated on a one-person operating basis. There is, however, no reason to limit the operation to one person grooming six dogs a day. Hiring a helper or assistant for doing the fundamentals should enable the groomer/owner to groom ten to 12 dogs per day, thereby increasing shop income considerably.

This projection must be taken in the context of hard work and time. Success does not come easily or overnight. But it will come—with the added virtues of persistence, perseverance, motivation and dedication. These may sound like old-fashioned cliches, but they remain the key to success. Another good maxim to follow is—whatever you do, strive to be the best around.

RECORD KEEPING

Appointment Book

A dog "beauty" parlor should be operated very much like a human beauty parlor. One essential requirement for this type of operation is the appointment book. Many businesses and professions rely on a regular appointment schedule, and dog grooming is one of them. The appointment book is one of the most important records you can have for maintaining an efficient operation.

There are many different kinds of appointment books, but the one we have found best is called *Week At A Glance*. In this book, each week is laid out in day-by-day columns, and each day is broken down hour by hour. For example, if you made an appointment for a customer on a particular day at a particular hour, there would be a column in the appointment book where you could record this. If a customer called you on a Tuesday to make an appointment for a Friday at 9:AM, you would simply make the notation in the appointment book in the appropriate column. Make the notation *immediately* in the appointment book so that there is no possibility of forgetting. Do not rely on your memory because many things can happen in the course of the day to make you forget.

Customers should be educated and encouraged to call in advance for appointments. This may take a little time to develop, but eventually your clients will get the idea. Appointment only grooming will provide you multiple benefits in many ways. You would know almost exactly how many customers you could expect on any given day and plan your time accordingly. It will also help you avoid underbooking one day and overbooking the next. A busy-looking shop always impresses and reassures a customer. Sometimes you can influence a customer to come in a day earlier or later to suit your schedule.

There are a number of complicating factors in perfecting an ideal schedule for any operation. Customers may call up (sometimes at the last minute) to cancel an appointment. Customers may come in off the street, asking you to take their dogs immediately. Common sense, so essential in any service business, comes to the rescue. The wise groomer anticipates at least one cancellation on any given day, or one customer may simply not show up. Under those circumstances booking one ''extra'' dog on that day works well for all concerned. As for those who may come in unexpectedly, you must use your discretion. Several questions should occur to you. How busy are you that day? Are you already overbooked? If not, what shape is the dog in? Is the dog badly matted? If this is a new dog for you, does it appear easy to groom? Is it a small dog and accustomed to grooming? If you have any doubts on this score, the acid test is to try clipping the dog's front paw (if it is a Poodle, or the pads for any other breed). Any new customer should have no reason to object to this. If the dog does not put up a real struggle on the front paw, you know you have a dog amenable to grooming.

On the subject of appointments, you will probably find that many people want to make Saturday appointments. If you allowed this without any control, you might find yourself swamped on Saturday and almost idle on Tuesday. Can you control or influence this in any way? There is one successful way to avoid Saturday overbooking. Inform customers that Saturday is very busy and with weekday appointments, they would get better service. While you may not persuade too many customers to change, those that do, will help you operate more efficiently.

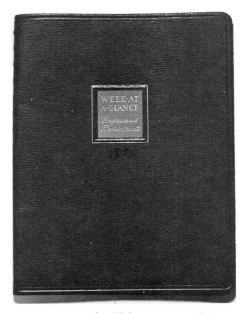

Every groomer should keep an appointment book, develop the habit of making appropriate notations immediately and keeping the book current.

Your appointment book should tell you immediately how busy a week you can expect to have.

Every groomer gets people bringing in new dogs without making an appointment. Before grooming a new dog in these circumstances, ascertain whether the dog is amenable to the grooming routine.

A grooming shop should keep master cards for every dog that comes in. The front of the card gives a complete essential description of each dog with telephone numbers in the event of an emergency.

Date	Amt.	Date	Amt.	Date	Amt.	Date	Amt.

The back of the master card serves as a record of appointments and prices paid for services rendered.

The number of appointments a groomer books should never exceed the number of dogs he can turn out well. The bottom line is the professional pride you can take in the look of every dog you groom.

A final word on appointments—a survey of a number of shops indicated the ways in which appointments were handled ran the gamut from no appointments at all (first come, first served daily), to shops with very firm scheduling policies. Shops in between used appointment systems but were very flexible in operation.

Some successfully-run shops limited the number of dogs handled each day, and these had to come in regularly every four to six weeks. These well-established shops could also charge higher rates because of their good reputations. This goal of any professional dog groomer will take some time to reach, but is the obvious goal for the determined newcomer.

For the shop just starting out, the middle course of a definite appointment system but with some flexibility is best. The worst system of all is not keeping any appointment record and taking anyone any time. Shops operating in this slipshod manner usually do not even have a list of customers, thereby considerably lowering the value of their businesses. This brings up an additional reason for good record keeping, with appointment books and the customer list. If you ever sell your business, well-kept records and a good-sized list would make a considerable difference in the selling price.

Master List

As important as the appointment book is the master card, or the *list* as it is called in the trade. This list is a valuable commodity to be safeguarded and kept under control at all times. It is not only an indispensable record of each and every pet and pet owner, but is also your "good will" with considerable, potential market value. Technically, it is called a "master list."

Note the front and back of the card in this illustration. The front provides for the dog's vital statistics, including any special instructions or comments (type of clip, disposition, special instructions). There is a line providing for two telephone numbers. The first is for the home telephone, the second for the customer's business phone. In case of any emergency, you should be able to contact the customer at home or office. There doesn't even have to be an emergency, just a need for more information. Many owners only have a home phone number, but many others have both. Get as much information on each customer as possible. Many groomers neglect getting the number(s) and then regret it.

The back of the card is simply a chronological listing of the dates the dog came in and the prices charged. When you turn to the back of the card, you should be able to tell at a glance how often the dog has been groomed. This will also tell a great deal about the dog and the owner.

Each dog and owner should be listed on a separate card, even if the owner has more than one dog. One dog may be quite different from another, even if they are from the same litter. They might have different temperaments and different grooming and handling requirements. Don't try to save a card. It may seem like more effort, but it is always preferable to use a separate card for each dog.

This list of customers on your record cards should be kept in a file box and listed alphabetically, last name first. It is desirable to have a 4″ × 6″ file box and an A to Z guide card for each letter of the alphabet. This will help you to find the card quickly. When a regular customer calls for an appointment, get the customer's card out and determine if there are any special questions you might want to ask or if the customer has any special instructions. If it's a new customer phoning for the first time, just take down the essential information on a pad, then transfer it to the master card with all the other detailed information when the customer brings the dog in for the first grooming.

Pickup and Delivery

Pickup and delivery of dogs is an important matter of policy for any groomer. Many shops have a pickup and delivery service that is essential to their profit picture. In the beginning especially, when you are anxious for business, you might want to advertise this service. Some shops offer pickup and delivery free, as an accommodation, but this is unusual and should be done only under exceptional circumstances (no problems concerning time or help). Most shops charge from $2.00 to $2.50 each way for transportation, but with the volatile state of fuel prices, the prices for the service are very subject to change. Customers who want the convenience will not usually find a reasonable fee objectionable. Some shops do not offer pickup and delivery, feeling it more a nuisance than it's worth. Each shop must determine its own policy based on its needs and those of the clientele.

Make sure you understand the risks for you in pickup and delivery. The most important item will be carrying adequate auto insurance. You *must* be covered in the event of accident or other mishap while you are transporting clients' dogs.

If you decide in favor of pickup and delivery, the ideal vehicle for this is a station wagon or van, equipped with travel cages. Advertisements by manufacturers and distributors of cages appear regularly in trade and hobbyist magazines. However, not every beginning groomer can afford the ideal way. The only other approach is using your own car, and here more care is required. Do not transport more than one or two uncrated dogs at a time in an ordinary passenger car. So if you have a larger number of dogs to pick up, you will have to make several trips.

Pickup and delivery service involves extra work and responsibility, and some shop owners choose not to be burdened with it. If you feel enough customers will come to your shop, you too may not want to offer the service. We can only pose the question and point out the pros and cons. We can suggest, if in doubt, try it and see what happens. You can always drop it if you want to or have to.

Pet Supplies

As with pickup and delivery, each grooming shop operator must decide whether the shop will offer supplies and accessories and to what extent. In many shops, these items have proven unprofitable from the standpoint of time—time which could be more profitably used in a very busy shop in grooming dogs.

Some ambitious groomers with dressmaking or knitting skills have made their own lines of dog coats and sweaters, developing their skills into a profitable sideline.

The sales volume of your accessories department will greatly depend on the time you want to put into it and the selling expertise you develop. If you wait for customers to ask for something, you'll sell very little.

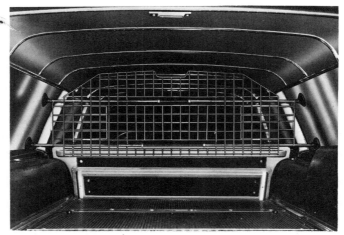

A station wagon barrier is a worthwhile investment if you offer pickup and delivery to your clients. You should also have portable traveling crates in your vehicle for the dogs' safety—and yours!

Sometimes all it takes to make a sale is to ask the customer if there is anything he or she needs for the dog—a brush, comb or some other item. If your approach is a little aggressive, you will sell a lot more. Just remember, if you can make $75.00 weekly profit on sales of merchandise, a good part of your overhead will be paid for.

Insurance

Adequate insurance coverage is necessary for any dog grooming operation. Three major types of insurance, which cover practically any possible contingency, are applicable to a dog grooming business. *Property Damage and Public Liability* protects you in case anyone is ever injured on your premises. *Fire* or *Fire and Theft* is self-explanatory, and finally, carrying *Plate Glass* insurance is prudent. The front glass of your shop is usually vulnerable to the most damage, and if you ever have a cracked or broken glass in a large window, cost of repairs could easily exceed your premiums.

Insurance costs for a groomer's needs are so nominal, it would be foolish not to have them. Under the subtitle of *Monthly Expenses* we estimated the cost of insurance at $25 per month. In other words, for $300 a year you don't have to worry about injuries, losses from fire or theft and any damage to your plate glass windows.

Advertising and Promotion

When you first open your shop and are most concerned with establishing and building up the business, telling the world you're there can accelerate the growth of your clientele. Contact local veterinarians and any boarding kennels for prospective leads. Obviously, you won't approach them if they also do grooming. Assemble a list of dog owners, with breeds requiring professional grooming and send out a mailing. Try some advertising in the local papers and see what kind of business comes in from that source. Putting an ad in the Yellow Pages of the phone directory is one of the best means of advertising.

Some initiative and imagination is called for on your part. There are various ways of getting good publicity and promotion, sometimes free of charge. Think of something novel to attract the attention of local media and don't ever be bashful about seeking publicity. Another free form of advertising is your exterior signs. You can have an expensive electric neon sign or a lettered sign, but whatever you do, let it be big and bold. Let it be seen, with the shop telephone number outstanding. Do something to capture attention on the outside. If the local zoning ordinances permit, an outside canopy with the shop name on both sides is a surefire way of getting attention.

A dog in the window is another way to draw a crowd. But the window must afford the dog good security. When you finish grooming the first dog of the day, put him in the window if he looks really good and you have the owner's permission to do so. The willing owner will be thrilled, too, that you thought enough of the dog to display him.

Another effective means of promoting a new shop is to leaflet the area. Have flyers with announcements put under the doors of homes and apartments in the area.

The most effective advertising of all, of course, is the satisfied customer. Never forget this. If each of your customers returns regularly, you've got it made. The repeat business is the successful business. If you treat the dogs and customers right, they will remain loyal for the lifetime of the dog and successive dogs. Satisfied customers recommend you to others, further increasing your business. You may struggle along for the first few months, and it may seem like pulling teeth to get new customers. Then, suddenly, or so it may seem, there will be a chain reaction, and you will be doing a thriving business. Just remember that the first impression you make is often the lasting one.

Grooming Fees

Your schedule of fees should be prominently displayed where everyone can see them as they enter your shop. There should be no price discrimination, up or down. No one should be able to say that you charged more or less to someone else. Save yourself an unnecessary headache by charging the same fees to one and all. The following is a *suggested* list of grooming fees (base year 1980).

Job	Price
Toy Dogs	$15.00 & up
Small Dogs	15.00 & up
Medium-size Dogs	20.00 & up
Large Dogs	25.00 & up
Giant Dogs	35.00 & up
Brush and Bath	10.00 & up (depending on size of dog)
Removing Mats	10.00 & up (depending on size of dog)
Medicated Bath	10.00 & up (depending on size of dog)
Flea and Tick Dip	12.00 & up (depending on size of dog)

Some of the above prices include the word "up" as prices to these services must vary according to the size and condition of each dog. For example, if the dog's coat is very badly matted, then $10.00 extra would be reasonable. The $10.00 fee for brush and bath only must be considered reasonable for Toys and small breeds, but for larger dogs, an additional fee would be fair. An Afghan, for example, requires only a brush and bath, and *no* trimming. However a $15 to $20 fee is in line, as this is a large, heavy-coated dog and takes a long time to brush, bathe and dry.

Remember to prominently display your fees, preferably on a bulletin board or by other attention-getting means. Fees will, of course, vary from region to region and change with the greater economy. Find out what your competition is charging and be guided accordingly.

The name of a shop should be short, easily remembered and suggest pleasant associations. That name, together with the quality grooming the shop becomes known for will open the way for it to achieve success as a viable business venture.

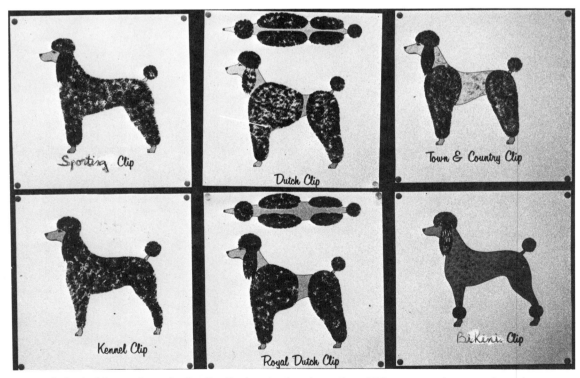

Sporting Clip

Dutch Clip

Town & Country Clip

Kennel Clip

Royal Dutch Clip

Bikini Clip

A chart of the most popular Poodle clips is not only a decorative addition to reception room decor, it is essential to assist Poodle owners in selecting the clips they want for their pets. Many people do not know the clips by name, so owner and groomer must depend on visual selection rather than nomenclature.

Naming the Shop

Your shop's name should be as carefully planned as that of a baby. The name will be your trademark, and what your reputation will be built on. The name should be short, appealing and to the point. Some of the most effective names of the shops we know are called "Sophisticated Dog," "Pampered Dog," "Glamor Manor," "Poodle Boutique," "Salon de Chien," "K-9 Villa," and "Pet Haven." Note that the names are short and sweet and easy to remember. There are hundreds of similar names from which to choose. Some owners prefer to call the shop after themselves, such as "Gloria's Dog Grooming," "Harry's Dog Salon" or "Marion's Dog Beauty". While there is nothing wrong with this, and it has a certain warmth and intimacy, be aware that it may not have the value of a regular trade name. If the shop ever changed hands, the name of the former owner would become a liability, not an asset.

Clip Charts

Charts of the different styles for Poodles and other breeds should be framed and prominently displayed on the reception room wall. All the dog owner need do is indicate a choice, and there is no confusion as to what is wanted. It would be wise to have these diagrams blown up as large as your space allows and nicely framed, individually and collectively.

Supplement these diagrams with photographs of dogs you have groomed, preferably including the satisfied owner. Give the biggest display to as many breeds as possible so customers know you can groom all breeds.

Accessories

The more grooming you do, the more you will do with accessories. A dog owner will often be motivated to buy accessories when he is satisfied with the services rendered. While certain accessories are essential, each individual shop owner must decide how much to carry and how deeply to get involved. Brushes, combs, collars, leashes, shampoos, rinses and perfumes form a basic stock. If you want to go further, consider such profitable items as coat conditioners, coat dressings, eye and ear preparations and vitamins. We can only suggest you might want to feel your way with accessories, and then decide what to carry based on the amount of time spent, turnover and profit.

Bookkeeping or Finances

Good management means doing your bookkeeping in a neat, orderly way. Your bookkeeping can be kept to a very simple minimum, but it must be organized properly if you are going to know what kind of business you are doing. In this regard, the first thing you must do is open a business checking account at your local bank, so that you will be able to make your deposits and withdrawals by check. This automatically provides you with a record of your income and expenses.

Also, a simple set of books should be set up so that you will know what kind of business you are doing from week to week and month to month. All that is basically needed is an Accounts Receivable and an Accounts Payable. In addition a good accountant is always desirable.

Conclusion

YOU MUST CONSTANTLY STRIVE to improve your work. Never be completely satisfied, for there is always room for improvement. Don't become over-confident, and never allow yourself to fall into sloppy work habits.

Quality grooming includes your best efforts at every step of the grooming way, but equally important is the evidence that the dog has received the best care and attention, so that you, or the owner, are satisfied with the results. There must be no clipper burns, no nicks, cuts or injuries, and no mistakes in grooming the dog. People are just as happy that their pet dogs have been well treated as that they are well groomed. In essence, quality grooming means living up to professional standards. These standards are high, but if they are followed, the chances for your success in grooming dogs will be infinitely better.

As we have indicated, not everyone can be a superb groomer, but almost anyone with a liking for dogs can be a *good* groomer, and that is sufficient. If the desire is strong enough and one wishes to make a livelihood from dog grooming, then all it takes is a little extra time, patience and perseverance. Everyone develops and progresses at different tempos. Some people are very talented and artistic or may have a natural flair for dog grooming. For these fortunate few, everything comes easier and faster. But the average student-novice will become pretty good after six months. You should reach your peak in about a year. After that you will level off, and you can only strive to become better in small increments as time goes by.

Naturally you are all thumbs at first. You must learn the fundamentals of dog grooming and the specifics of grooming your own breed (all breeds, if you are interested in being a professional). Additionally, you must absorb all the fine points and tricks of the trade. How to use the tools properly, how to manipulate the clippers, scissors, thinning shears and nail trimmers. As you gain experience, your confidence will increase and before long, you will automatically do things that just a short time before you thought were so difficult. Eventually you will earn the title of *professional groomer*.

For those who might become discouraged, we can only say we have known students who were sure that they could never become groomers but went on to become some of the best. Today they are skilled, professional dog groomers with successful businesses.

When we caution the average student to move carefully before making any substantial investment, we should also mention that many of our former students went into business very quickly and did very well. You must be the best judge of your own development. As in everything else, common sense must prevail.

Your preparatory period should consist of closely studying this book, always using it as a reference work and doing as much practice work as possible, before thinking of going into business. Practice on dogs owned by friends, relatives, neighbors and anyone else whose dog you can work on. Don't charge any fee until you feel your work justifies it.

While on this point of gaining as much experience as possible, you might also think of working for an established shop before branching out on your own. It may not be easy for a beginning groomer to break into a shop. Some owners are always suspicious of potential competition; others may just be reluctant to hire a raw beginner. Training in a good school may be the best investment of all.

Home Groomer

We think it important to repeat here that one of the best ways to get started in this business is by grooming at home. Start out grooming in your basement, garage or a spare room. To this you can add grooming in the customers' homes. Many of our former students started out this way. Once you have built up a foundation, you can start your own shop with a ready-made following.

In Closing

This book has been conceived and written for professional dog groomers and for those amateurs who want to groom on a professional level. This includes individual pet owners who want to groom their dogs with professional quality. It has also been designed for those who want to work as dog groomers in a commercial shop, or who just want to groom in their spare time in order to have some extra income. We also hope it has added to the knowledge of those who already groom professionally.

To all our readers who want to groom dogs for one reason or another, we say, do the best job of grooming of which you are capable. And to all of our readers/students/professionals, past, present and future, we wish you the very best of grooming!

BIBLIOGRAPHY

ALL OWNERS of pure-bred dogs will benefit themselves and their dogs by enriching their knowledge of breeds and of canine care, training, breeding, psychology and other important aspects of dog management. The following list of books covers further reading recommended by judges, veterinarians, breeders, trainers and other authorities. Books may be obtained at the finer book stores and pet shops, or through Howell Book House Inc., publishers, New York.

Breed Books

AFGHAN HOUND, Complete	Miller & Gilbert
AIREDALE, New Complete	Edwards
AKITA, Complete	Linderman & Funk
ALASKAN MALAMUTE, Complete	Riddle & Seeley
BASSET HOUND, Complete	Braun
BEAGLE, New Complete	Noted Authorities
BLOODHOUND, Complete	Brey & Reed
BOXER, Complete	Denlinger
BRITTANY SPANIEL, Complete	Riddle
BULLDOG, New Complete	Hanes
BULL TERRIER, New Complete	Eberhard
CAIRN TERRIER, Complete	Marvin
CHESAPEAKE BAY RETRIEVER, Complete	Cherry
CHIHUAHUA, Complete	Noted Authorities
COCKER SPANIEL, New	Kraeuchi
COLLIE, New	Official Publication of the Collie Club of America
DACHSHUND, The New	Meistrell
DALMATIAN, The	Treen
DOBERMAN PINSCHER, New	Walker
ENGLISH SETTER, New Complete	Tuck, Howell & Graef
ENGLISH SPRINGER SPANIEL, New	Goodall & Gasow
FOX TERRIER, New Complete	Silvernail
GERMAN SHEPHERD DOG, New Complete	Bennett
GERMAN SHORTHAIRED POINTER, New	Maxwell
GOLDEN RETRIEVER, New Complete	Fischer
GORDON SETTER, Complete	Look
GREAT DANE, New Complete	Noted Authorities
GREAT DANE, The—Dogdom's Apollo	Draper
GREAT PYRENEES, Complete	Strang & Giffin
IRISH SETTER, New Complete	Eldredge & Vanacore
IRISH WOLFHOUND, Complete	Starbuck
KEESHOND, Complete	Peterson
LABRADOR RETRIEVER, Complete	Warwick
LHASA APSO, Complete	Herbel
MINIATURE SCHNAUZER, Complete	Eskrigge
NEWFOUNDLAND, New Complete	Chern
NORWEGIAN ELKHOUND, New Complete	Wallo
OLD ENGLISH SHEEPDOG, Complete	Mandeville
PEKINGESE, Quigley Book of	Quigley
PEMBROKE WELSH CORGI, Complete	Sargent & Harper
POODLE, New Complete	Hopkins & Irick
POODLE CLIPPING AND GROOMING BOOK, Complete	Kalstone
ROTTWEILER, Complete	Freeman
SAMOYED, Complete	Ward
SCHIPPERKE, Official Book of	Root, Martin, Kent
SCOTTISH TERRIER, New Complete	Marvin
SHETLAND SHEEPDOG, The New	Riddle
SHIH TZU, Joy of Owning	Seranne
SHIH TZU, The (English)	Dadds
SIBERIAN HUSKY, Complete	Demidoff
TERRIERS, The Book of All	Marvin
WEST HIGHLAND WHITE TERRIER, Complete	Marvin
WHIPPET, Complete	Pegram
YORKSHIRE TERRIER, Complete	Gordon & Bennett

Breeding

ART OF BREEDING BETTER DOGS, New	Onstott
BREEDING YOUR OWN SHOW DOG	Seranne
HOW TO BREED DOGS	Whitney
HOW PUPPIES ARE BORN	Prine
INHERITANCE OF COAT COLOR IN DOGS	Little

Care and Training

DOG OBEDIENCE, Complete Book of	Saunders
NOVICE, OPEN AND UTILITY COURSES	Saunders
DOG CARE AND TRAINING FOR BOYS AND GIRLS	Saunders
DOG NUTRITION, Collins Guide to	Collins
DOG TRAINING FOR KIDS	Benjamin
DOG TRAINING, Koehler Method of	Koehler
DOG TRAINING Made Easy	Tucker
GO FIND! Training Your Dog to Track	Davis
GUARD DOG TRAINING, Koehler Method of	Koehler
OPEN OBEDIENCE FOR RING, HOME AND FIELD, Koehler Method of	Koehler
STONE GUIDE TO DOG GROOMING FOR ALL BREEDS	Stone
SUCCESSFUL DOG TRAINING, The Pearsall Guide to	Pearsall
TOY DOGS, Kalstone Guide to Grooming All	Kalstone
TRAINING THE RETRIEVER	Kersley
TRAINING YOUR DOG—Step by Step Manual	Volhard & Fisher
TRAINING YOUR DOG TO WIN OBEDIENCE TITLES	Morsell
TRAIN YOUR OWN GUN DOG, How to	Goodall
UTILITY DOG TRAINING, Koehler Method of	Koehler
VETERINARY HANDBOOK, Dog Owner's Home	Carlson & Giffin

General

AKC'S WORLD OF THE PURE-BRED DOG	American Kennel Club
CANINE TERMINOLOGY	Spira
COMPLETE DOG BOOK, The	Official Publication of American Kennel Club
DOG IN ACTION, The	Lyon
DOG BEHAVIOR, New Knowledge of	Pfaffenberger
DOG JUDGE'S HANDBOOK	Tietjen
DOG JUDGING, Nicholas Guide to	Nicholas
DOG PEOPLE ARE CRAZY	Riddle
DOG PSYCHOLOGY	Whitney
DOGSTEPS, Illustrated Gait at a Glance	Elliott
DOG TRICKS	Haggerty & Benjamin
ENCYCLOPEDIA OF DOGS, International	Dangerfield, Howell & Riddle
FROM RICHES TO BITCHES	Shattuck
IN STITCHES OVER BITCHES	Shattuck
JUNIOR SHOWMANSHIP HANDBOOK	Brown & Mason
MY TIMES WITH DOGS	Fletcher
OUR PUPPY'S BABY BOOK (blue or pink)	
SUCCESSFUL DOG SHOWING, Forsyth Guide to	Forsyth
TRIM, GROOM & SHOW YOUR DOG, How to	Saunders
WHY DOES YOUR DOG DO THAT?	Bergman
WILD DOGS in Life and Legend	Riddle
WORLD OF SLED DOGS, From Siberia to Sport Racing	Coppinger